D0450928

Advance Praise for

DOING DEMOCRACY

Doing Democracy is the practical guide to movement building for which I've long been searching. Clearly written, useful, wise, informative, and well-grounded in experience, it is essential reading for every activist who wants to achieve real change and for every citizen who wants to know how democracy really works.

— DAVID C. KORTEN, author of *When Corporations Rule the World*

Bill Moyer has mined the gold from forty years of experience with social movements of many kinds to make a powerful picture of what can go wrong and what works best. This is not only fine strategic counsel from one of our wise elders, it is also good social science, and gives activists the kind of sharp insight they need to win with their good causes. Once you see his picture of how movements unfold over time, you will never think the same again about what makes for good strategies.

— PAUL H. RAY, Ph.D. co-author of *The Cultural Creatives: How 50 Million People are Changing the World*

I'm indebted to Bill Moyer for his practice theory of the four roles of activism. I have used Bill Moyer's MAP practice theory and its four roles of activism for many years — in lectures, workshops and consulting — because of its relevance to contemporary strategies for social change. I'm delighted that his work has now been situated within broader theories of social movements. *Doing Democracy* has made his work even more accessible for university teaching.

— DR. LYN CARSON, Lecturer in Applied Politics, University of Sydney; author (with Brian Martin) of *Random Selection in Politics*

An indispensable guide to the process of transforming subjects into citizens, spectators into participants, plutocracy into democracy.

— WALDEN BELLO, Director of the NGO Focus on the Global South, Bangkok, and Professor of Political Economics at the University of the Philippines

Doing Democracy is a treasured handbook for movement building — a book every organizer should read and share! Its clear, historical, theoretical, practical, and visionary blueprint for movement building will inspire you and serve as a guide for strategic action.

— LINDA STOUT, founder of Spirit In Action, and author of *Bridging the Class Divide: And Other Lessons for Grassroots Organizing*

One of the barriers to successful social movements is the lack of models for how they work which leads to a sense of hopelessness. By providing such a model, *Doing Democracy* will be an invaluable resource to the movement for economic justice. By helping us to understand the stages social movements move through, we can become strategically sharper. Through putting our work in this larger context, we can gain greater perspective and hope, allowing us to sustain ourselves for the long haul.

— FELICE YESKEL and CHUCK COLLINS, founding co-directors of United for a Fair Economy, and authors of *Economic Apartheid in America*

No one has done the work of analyzing the stages of nonviolent struggle better than Bill Moyer. Groups engaged in social change efforts would be foolish to ignore this resource. Reading this book could make the difference for your group between success and failure.

— WALTER WINK, Professor of Biblical Interpretation, Author of *The Powers That Be*

Bill Moyer did the activist world a huge service when he decided to put his organizing/analyzing experience to paper. His eight stages of social movements is absolutely essential reading for anyone actually fighting to win. This brilliant analysis — and much more — is now in book form. It could not arrive at a better time, just as corporate globalization is faltering. We need to fight smart and this book makes us smart. Buy it and read it.

— MURRAY DOBBIN, a Canadian activist for 30 years, is the author of *The Myth of the Good Corporate Citizen: Democracy Under the Rule of Big Business*

This book has long been needed in the formal study of social movements. It is a must for those who are activists and scholars in the field of social change.

— BERNARD LaFAYETTE, JR., Director,
Center for Nonviolence and Peace Studies, University of Rhode Island

This book goes a long way towards closing the gap between movement theorists and movement activists. Most significantly, it provides a series of benchmarks by which activists can plot their achievements along the way in trying to reach long-term goals; as such, it is a useful and needed anti-depressant for those in the trenches — without the biochemical side effects.

— TROY DUSTER, Professor of Sociology, New York University

Bill Moyer's contribution to understanding how social movements progress through many stages is so important. He points out that many movements think they have failed, when in fact they have actually succeeded and are just entering a different phase. There is an art to understanding social movements and Bill Moyer has captured it in *Doing Democracy.*

— MAUDE BARLOW, Volunteer Chair, Council of Canadians

The Movement Action Plan is a powerful tool for movement strategizing, and this book is the comprehensive discussion of the MAP that I always lacked. Whether it was the anti-nuclear movement in Germany, or the conscientious objectors' movement in Turkey, checking the MAP always led to new insights. A MAP book with less focus on the US and more focus on other countries still needs to be written.

— ANDREAS SPECK, nonviolent activist and staff at
War Resisters' International

OK, you support environmental protection, corporate accountability, and social justice. Now what? Bill Moyer's long-awaited book offers remarkable insight and encouragement for concerned citizens who are itching to take the leap into effective social action. Sage advice from a deeply reflective practitioner of the democratic arts of "people power." This book has provided my students with more "Aha" moments per page than any other text.

— STEVE CHASE, Director, Environmental Advocacy and Organizing Program,
Antioch New England Graduate School

This book makes a valuable contribution to social movement analysis and strategy. The authors engage both activists and academics in an informative, creative dialogue about theoretical issues in the crucial area of nonviolent movement strategy formation. Having used MAP in peace studies education since its first publication, I am certain *Doing Democracy* will also encourage students to discuss, question, apply, and criticize the model. In the process they will be further empowered to act for positive social change.

— DALE BRYAN, Director, Institute in Social Movements and Strategic Nonviolence, Tufts University

If every activist could read this book, victory would be certain. No book combines such strong scholarship, practical know-how, and common sense to inform and empower activists for change. *Doing Democracy* will be required reading for any course I teach on nonviolence and social movements.

— STEPHEN ZUNES, Associate Professor of Politics and Chair of Peace & Justice Studies, University of San Francisco

To have in book form, at last, Bill Moyer's important and enlivening work on social activism is good news indeed! This man's perspective on the key issues of our time has informed and inspired my life for almost 30 years. Now his social movement action plan comes to us complete with case studies, including the movement against corporate rule, which I will immediately use in my own teaching and organizing.

— JOANNA MACY, eco-philosopher, Buddhist scholar, deep ecology activist/teacher, and author of many books, most recently, *Widening Circles: A Memoir*

This book tells us what the power-holders never will: how grassroots movements can succeed against what seems to be overwhelming opposition. Especially relevant to anti-globalization, animal rights, ecology, anti-prison, and human rights activists.

— GEORGE LAKEY, TrainingforChange.org

doing
DEMOCRACY

The MAP
Model
for
Organizing
Social
Movements

Bill Moyer
with JoAnn McAllister,
Mary Lou Finley, and
Steve Soifer

NEW SOCIETY PUBLISHERS

Cataloguing in Publication Data:
A catalog record for this publication is available from the National Library of Canada.

Copyright © 2001 by Bill Moyer.
All rights reserved.

Cover design by Hélène Cyr. Cover photos - Top: Jean François Leblanc, Agence Stock. Middle: Ron Chapple. Bottom: PhotoDisc.

Printed in Canada. Fifth printing March 2007.

Published in Turkish as Demokrasi Yapmak: Toplumsal Orgutlemek Icin Map Modeli, translated by Acar Acar, published by ARI Yayinlari, 2004.

Paperback ISBN 13: 978-0-086571-418-2

Inquiries regarding requests to reprint all or part of *Doing Democracy* should be addressed to New Society Publishers at the address below.

To order directly from the publishers, please call toll-free (North America) 1-800-567-6772, or order online at www.newsociety.com

Any other inquiries can be directed by mail to:

New Society Publishers
P.O. Box 189,
Gabriola Island, BC V0R 1X0, Canada
250-247-9737

New Society Publishers aims to publish books for fundamental social change through non-violent action. We are committed to building an ecologically sustainable and just society not just through education, but through action. We are acting on our commitment to the world's remaining ancient forests by phasing out our paper supply from ancient forests worldwide. This book is one step towards ending global deforestation and climate change. It is printed on acid-free paper that is **100% old growth forest-free** (100% post-consumer recycled), processed chlorine free — supplied by New Leaf Paper — and printed with vegetable based, low VOC inks. For further information, or to browse our full list of books and purchase securely, visit our website at: www.newsociety.com

NEW SOCIETY PUBLISHERS   www.newsociety.com

TABLE OF CONTENTS

ACKNOWLEDGMENTS

CREATING THE Movement Action Plan (MAP) over these many years has not been a solitary process, so I want to thank all of the activists who have shared their struggles with me, appreciated my models and strategies, and given me feedback on using MAP. Creating a book is not a solitary task either, so I want to thank a number of people without whose support this book would not have been possible.

First, thanks to JoAnn McAllister who made the book happen. JoAnn has edited the entire book and provided many ideas and suggestions. She has also offered emotional support, humor, and strength in the ups and downs of the writing process for the last two years and has contributed to my thinking about social transformation during conversations over the last twelve years.

Thanks to my long-time friend Mary Lou Finley, who has been a participant with me in various social movements since the Chicago Movement in 1966 and who offered ideas, advice, and support in the evolution of my theories and methods of social activism. She is also the lead author of the academic theory chapter and the breast cancer movement case study.

Thanks to Steve Soifer for his persistent encouragement for me to write a MAP book, for his enthusiasm about MAP, and for using it in his social work classes. Steve conceived of the book's format of MAP theory, academic theories, and case studies. Steve is also a contributor to the academic theory chapter.

Thanks also to Nancy Gregory and Juliette Beck, who contributed case studies, to Murray Dobbin for background on the globalization movement, and to Tom Atlee for two of the charts in Chapter 3.

Thanks to Carol Perry for her companionship, support, and insights, including the title of the book, Doing Democracy.

I would like to thank the Quakers, particularly those in Philadelphia, Chicago, London, and San Francisco, especially Emily and Walter Longstreth, a couple in their 90s at the time, who introduced me to the spiritual, ethical, and action methods of peace and nonviolence that set me on my life-long journey. I also want to acknowledge the American Friends Service Committee, where I learned so much as a staff member in Chicago and Philadelphia and as a volunteer in San Francisco.

I want to thank those people connected to the Student Nonviolent Coordinating Committee, the Congress of Racial Equality, and the Southern Christian Leadership conference, particularly Martin Luther King Jr. for his moral, ethical, and courageous leadership; Bernard Lafayette, for his brilliant understanding of nonviolent movement organizing and for his friendship; and Jim Bevel for his creative and bold analysis and strategic thinking.

I want to give special appreciation to all the people in the Movement For A New Society and the Philadelphia Life Center during my 12 years living and working in that community, especially David Albert; Sandra Boston; Nancy Brigham; Sue Carol; Ginny Coover; Ellen Deacon; Vint Deming; Chuck Esser; Pamela Haines; Pete Hill; Bob Irwin; Dave Kairys for his brilliant legal support in our successful case against the Philadelphia Electric Company; George Lakey for his friendship and good thinking; Mary Link; Antje Mattheus; Mary McCaffrey; Marion McNaughton and Kate and Edmund; Jim Nunes-Schrag (deceased); Will Pipken; Betsy Raasch-Gilman; Dick Taylor for his support, friendship, and inspiration in getting me involved with the Quakers, Bryn Mawr graduate school, canoeing, ship blockades, and nonviolence; Phyllis Taylor; Erika Thorne; Lillian Willoughby; George Willoughby; Betsy Leondar-Wright; and Marty Zinn.

Thanks to Christopher Mogil who has given me encouragement, suggestions, and financial support over these years, and to Grady McGonagill for his counsel on organizing and financial support.

We would like to thank all those at New Society Publishers, especially Chris Plant, editor Audrey McClellan for her help with the manuscript, and Hélène Cyr for the cover design.

A warm thanks for the support of my two living communities: in San Francisco, Jan and Dave Hartsough for having me in their house for 16 years, and Kay Anderson and my community at Dharmananda Farm in Australia.

I have received lots of support and challenges that affect my daily life in personal growth, spirituality, and philosophy. Thanks to my Integral Transformative Practice community that meets weekly in Mill Valley, California, and to George Leonard and Michael Murphy who founded the practice, and Wendy Palmer's Aikido in everyday life training. I also have learned enormously from the writings of Ken Wilber, Don Beck and Chris Cowan's Spiral Dynamics, and Robert Kegan. A hug to the members of our weekly Ken Wilber study group in San Francisco: Christine Alford, Laura Dufort, Mark Ettlin, Fred Cook, Sean Hargens, Paul Hoffman, Mark Johnson, Eryn Kalish, Steve March, Bert Parlee, Clint Seiter, Norio Suzuki, and Karin Swann.

I also want to extend my appreciation to many people who have helped my work including Mary Beth Brangan, Carol Brouillet, Ken Butigan, Don Eichelberger, Penn Garvin, Roger Harried, Jim Heddle, Susan Holvenstot,

I also want to extend my appreciation to many people who have helped my work including Mary Beth Brangan, Carol Brouillet, Ken Butigan, Don Eichelberger, Penn Garvin, Roger Harried, Jim Heddle, Susan Holvenstot, Dorothea Kötter, Gil Lopez (deceased), Joanna Macy, Clare Morris, Sunny Miller, Linda Stout, Juliet Twoomey, Rich Watson, and the men working with the Marin Abused Women Services batterers program, especially Pete Van Dyke.

Finally, I thank my family, Edna and Jim Moyer Sr. (both deceased), Marion Moyer, Ron Moyer, Betsy Moyer, Jim Moyer (deceased), Jack Logue, and the rest of the Moyer clan for their love, humor, and support.

— Bill Moyer, San Francisco, CA
April, 2001

INTRODUCTION

Bill Moyer, JoAnn McAllister, Mary Lou Finley and Steven Soifer

T HROUGHOUT MUCH of human history, people have organized to change social conditions. Some collective efforts have had dramatic success, while others have failed miserably. Nonetheless, the advancement of human society has largely been achieved through citizen-based actions. In the United States, the recognition of basic human rights — the abolition of slavery, the right of labor to organize, child labor laws, the right for African Americans and women to vote — came about through the efforts of engaged citizens. In recent years, activists around the world have ousted dictators in Eastern Europe, the Philippines, and Haiti and ended apartheid in South Africa. Nonviolent *social movements,* based in *grassroots* "people power," are a means for ordinary people to act on their deepest values and successfully challenge unjust social conditions and policies, despite the determined resistance of entrenched private and public power.

This coming together of unrelated people to achieve common goals has long fascinated historians, theorists, and ordinary citizens. How do social movements work? How does a social condition become an issue to people? How do people get together to act? How do social movements form? What kinds of people join social movements? Are social movements effective, and how do they contribute to changing social norms and systems? These are all questions that people continue to ask. We think this book will answer some of them.

We believe the *Movement Action Plan* (MAP), developed by Bill Moyer as he worked in and with social movements over the last 40 years, clarifies the nature and dynamics of social movements and provides a framework for organizing and building them. We hope this book contributes to the effectiveness of social activism. We are eager, as well, to promote a dialogue among scholars and a dialogue between scholars and social movement activists by presenting a *model* of social movements that has grown out of activism itself.

WHAT IS A SOCIAL MOVEMENT?

Scholars and social critics have defined and described social movements in a variety of ways. For example, one sociologist describes a social movement as "a formally organized group that acts consciously and with some continuity to promote or resist change through collective action."[1] Other writers suggest that social movements may exist without an organizational structure per se, but characterize them as a "preference structure for social change consisting of a set of opinions, attitudes, and beliefs within a group."[2] MAP defines social movements as "collective actions in which the populace is alerted, educated, and mobilized, sometimes over years and decades, to challenge the ***powerholders*** and the whole society to redress social problems or grievances and restore critical social values."[3] This definition does not focus on one organization, but instead on "collective actions" carried out by a number of different organizations, all of which might be said to be part of the same movement. In the MAP definition, social movements go beyond the scope of changing governmental policies and structures to challenge all those who exercise ***power*** to maintain the status quo.

This definition of collective efforts describes engaged citizens as the core of the democratic process, hence the title "Doing Democracy." Through social movements, citizen activists put the spotlight on individuals, groups, institutions, and social systems that promote policies and practices they believe both cause the problem and violate revered social values. Then they challenge entrenched power and call on the whole society to solve the problem, repair the harm, and make changes that end the violation of those deeply held principles. In this description of the role of social movements, it is clear that there is, inevitably, a struggle for power. The central task of social movements is to win the hearts, minds, and support of the majority of the populace. Because it is the people who ultimately hold the power, they will either preserve the status quo or create change.

THE EVOLUTION OF SOCIAL MOVEMENTS

The record of organized, nonviolent, collective action goes far back in human history. For example, Gene Sharp describes how Roman plebeians in the fifth century BCE started a movement against their leaders in order to have their complaints addressed. Instead of staging a violent revolt, they withdrew from the city, refusing to work, and after a period of time the Roman leaders capitulated to their demands.[4] Over the centuries, collective direct action against oppressive nobles, invading forces, villainous tax collectors, or unscrupulous merchants has characterized political and social life. But most of these actions were immediate and targeted and did not continue over time. Social movements as we know them emerged in the West in the mid-18th century in Europe as a part of the general thrust toward democracy at that time. As political scientist Sidney Tarrow explained:

The societies that formed around consolidating states in the past two centuries provided more translocal connections; more rapid communications, denser association networks, and, especially, targets and arenas for groups that felt their interests were impaired ... The social movement was not an automatic outcome of modernization. It emerged from the long, tormented, and ultimately interactive process of state formation and citizenship and from the diffusion of these forms of interaction over time and across territory.[5]

During this period, people began to use mass meetings and *demonstrations* as they sought new ways to make their voices heard. The storming of the Bastille, which set the French Revolution in motion, and the Boston Tea Party, a protest against a new tax that catalyzed the American Revolution in 1773, were early direct actions that fostered liberation from oppressive power. In 19th-century America, the abolition, temperance, labor, and women's movements used many nonviolent *strategies*, such as marches and rallies, to raise issues and demand change.

Philosophers also began to theorize about social change methods and nonviolent social intervention in the 19th century. Thoreau's definitive work, "Civil Disobedience," was published in 1849 after his own act of *civil disobedience*: he went to jail for his refusal to pay taxes in protest of the Mexican American War. Tolstoy developed a *theory* of nonviolent movements and, somewhat later, Mohandas Gandhi began to elaborate a theory of nonviolent action.

Increasingly, nonviolent social movements have become a way for citizens to petition their governments or demand changes from other powerful institutions. In the 1930s, the organizing activities of the labor movement brought new tactical innovations, such as the sit-down strike, and a mass movement experience to many people. The civil rights movement from the 1940s through the 1960s was a watershed in the development of social movements in the United States and, to an important extent, throughout the world.

The modern era of social activism in the United States took off with the *lunch counter sit-in movement* that was carried out by southern college students beginning in February 1960. During the last half of the decade, another national social movement took off to address a second issue: ending the unjust Vietnam War. The war was viewed by many as an exception to normal U.S. foreign policy, which people believed promoted peace, prosperity, and democracy around the world. In the last three decades, the women's movement, which arose in the U.S. out of the civil rights and peace movements, has blossomed everywhere, with women in Africa and the Middle East also engaged in collective actions.

UNDERSTANDING SOCIAL MOVEMENTS

In Part II of this book, Mary Lou Finley and Steven Soifer discuss some of the different theories and models social scientists have developed to explain social movements. While there is much useful information in social movement theories, most do not help us understand the ebb and flow of living, breathing social movements as they grow and change over time. None of the theories provides a comprehensive overview of the issues that activists must deal with in organizing a social movement. With few exceptions, there is little focus on movement strategy,[6] the results of the movement's activities, or the impact of the movement on society – what academics call movement outcomes.

The gaps in the theory of social movements leave much to be desired from an activist perspective. The lack of focus on the agency of activists (i.e., their ability to act), on their means of activism, on movement dynamics, and on movement outcomes is of particular concern. Social activists are most interested in other questions: What strategies and *tactics* will give the movement the best chance of success? How can we respond to the actions of the powerholders opposing the movement? How can we frame the issues so that the largest number of people will be able to relate to them and come to support the movement point of view? How do movements typically change over time? What are possible outcomes for a movement's activities and how will we know if we are making progress?

MAP, which is both a theory of social movements and a guide for action, addresses many of these questions.[7] It both theorizes aspects of social movements that have received little attention from movement scholars and elaborates some perspectives already examined by others. The result is a comprehensive, action-based model for understanding social movements. Over the past decade, social activists around the world who have used MAP typically have had an "aha!" experience. That is, it makes intuitive sense to them and helps them grasp the complexities of what is going on, enabling them to more effectively organize the movement in which they are involved.

THE MOVEMENT ACTION PLAN (MAP): A NEW PARADIGM FOR SOCIAL MOVEMENTS

While doing training for Clamshell Alliance anti-nuclear activists following a major, well-publicized, successful, direct action event in the late 1970s, Bill Moyer found that they were disappointed, dejected, and feeling powerless. In order to convince these activists that they had actually accomplished a lot and that they were much closer to their goals than they realized, he presented his model to explain the different stages of movements as he understood them. During the training, Moyer noticed that the mood of most of the activists changed as they were able to identify and understand the *"take-off" stage* of their movement. As a result of this experience, the Movement Action Plan eventually came to include a series of strategic and theoretical tools.

One of the chief limitations of social movements has been the lack of strategic models and methods that help activists understand, plan, conduct, and evaluate their social movement. The absence of a practical model that describes and explains the normal path of successful social movements disempowers activists and limits the effectiveness of their movements. Without a guiding framework that explains the step-by-step process of social movement success, many activists are unable to set appropriate long- and short-term goals; confidently develop the most effective strategies, tactics, and programs; and avoid common movement pitfalls. In addition, without an understanding of this process, many activists develop irrational feelings of powerlessness and believe that their movement is failing. This often creates a self-fulfilling prophecy that prevents or limits their success. Consequently, many activists lose hope, become demoralized, burn out, drop out, play ineffective or even destructive roles, and make movements unappealing to the majority of the public. Far more socially concerned citizens are dissuaded from joining social movements than actually do become activists because social movements are not seen as effective, or because activists are perceived as outside of the mainstream.

The Movement Action Plan provides activists with the much-needed strategic analysis, model, and methods that address all those problems and empower both organizers and participants. It shows how successful social movements typically travel along similar long and complex roads, which usually take years or decades. MAP allows activists to –

- identify where, on the normal eight-stage road of movement success, their movement is at any specific time;
- create stage-appropriate strategies, tactics, and programs that enable them to advance their movement along to the next step on the road to success;
- identify and celebrate their movement's incremental progress and successes;
- play all *four roles of activism* effectively;
- overcome irrational feelings of powerlessness and failure; and
- engage ordinary citizens in the *grand strategy* of effective social movements — participatory democracy.

Since Moyer first published MAP as a newsprint broadside in 1987, it has been taught in dozens of universities, used by activists around the world, and translated into many languages including Chinese, German, Russian, Bosnian, Czech, and Polish. The English version of MAP has sold 36,000 copies, and over

20,000 citizen activists have attended MAP workshops and classes around the world.

WHY IS MAP IMPORTANT?

Social movements are needed now more than ever. While the modern era has brought unprecedented production, wealth, and consumption, it has also created social ills at crisis levels — poverty, hunger, war, oppression, and devastation to our environment. In most places these problems are bad and getting worse. Indeed, many activists and social theorists question whether life on the planet can be sustained without dramatic change.

Moreover, the existing powerholders and the established institutions and social systems are incapable of alleviating these planetary problems because the pursuit of their goals, policies, and programs creates and exacerbates them. For example, the dominant corporate and government elites tout the expansion and globalization of the world's capitalist "free market" economy as their highest priority because it increases their profits, control, and power. But it also increases unemployment, the gap between rich and poor, violence, ecological collapse, and unsustainability.

The good news is that social movements are more numerous and powerful than ever. Instead of being "something that happened in the 1960s," as the powerholders and mainstream media would have it, social movements doubled in size and number in the 1970s and have rapidly expanded since then.[8] For example, there are thousands of local anti-toxic waste groups in the United States, all but a few of which were created after the 60s.[9] The bad news is that not all movements have been successful. Many have failed and many of today's activists are prone to repeat the mistakes that have curtailed the effectiveness of past movements.

DOING DEMOCRACY

Doing Democracy consists of three parts. Part I presents Bill Moyer's Movement Action Plan. Chapter 1 introduces the MAP theory of social movements, especially the concepts of "people power" and participatory democracy. Chapter 2 presents the four primary roles that individuals and movements themselves play in social change. All four roles are necessary to successful social movements; their differences should be celebrated. However, there are effective and ineffective ways of playing each role, and this chapter describes these, paying special attention to the dangers of the *negative rebel* role and explaining how to overcome them. Finally, it discusses the need for activists to strive for personal and political maturity.

In Chapter 3 there is a detailed introduction to the eight-stage framework that is the core of MAP's analysis of social movement evolution. Analytical tools, such as the ability to distinguish societal myths and secrets, are applied to different social issues to show how these tools can be used to alert, educate, and mobilize the general public. Chapter 4 contains rebuttals to all those reasons activists offer for not believing in their social movement. It is a call for a new confidence in the potential of collective action and in the power of social movements to improve human society by promoting participatory democracy and engaging as many people as possible in the process of social change.

In Part II, Mary Lou Finley and Steven Soifer provide an overview of the different approaches to social movement theory within sociology, and identify MAP's contribution in this context.

Part III comprises five case studies that illustrate how MAP can be used to analyze earlier movements and applied to current ones. The study of the civil rights movement provides an excellent example of using MAP to analyze *sub-movements* within a larger movement. The study of the anti-nuclear energy movement highlights the various stages of MAP and the persistence of a social issue over decades, while the analysis of the struggle for gay and lesbian rights shows a movement in development. The study of the women's health movement focuses on breast cancer advocacy, illustrating the development of a sub-movement within the broader movement for women's rights. The case study of the anti-corporate globalization movement demonstrates the application of MAP to an international issue and movement.

The Conclusion, "Toward the Future," summarizes Bill Moyer's current thinking about the future of activism. He calls attention to the unsustainability of modern society, to the relationship between personal and social transformation, and to the important new ideas and skills that citizen activists need to bring to social change.

At the end of the book, the reader will find a glossary of specialized terms and abbreviations (these terms are highlighted in bold italics on their first appearance in the text), notes and bibliographic references, and contact numbers for the co-authors.

OUR HOPES AND GOALS FOR THIS BOOK

We hope that the Movement Action Plan will help activists become more effective agents of social change and make their movements more successful. Because it is grounded in the reality of social movement action, we believe that MAP not only provides tools of analysis and action, but also offers great hope to those working to improve their own and others' lives. By understanding the ebb and flow of social movements, activists can reflect on their activities and better understand where their movement is on the road to success, while deciding what strategies and actions will move it forward.

We hope that academicians from various social science disciplines will relate MAP to traditional theories and use this model to further refine their thinking about how social movements work. By understanding the practice of social movements, theorists and scholars can contribute additional insights into how societies change.

We also hope that concerned citizens will come to appreciate the breadth and depth of social activism and social movements. Since the media typically focus on public demonstrations, which represent only one role of activism and one aspect of social movements, the public has received an incomplete picture of social movements. Thus, people may not appreciate the positive contribution that social movements have made to our lives. We trust that an increase in understanding and appreciation will encourage more people to join movements to create a civil society in a safe, just, and sustainable world.

Part I

The Movement Action Plan

by Bill Moyer

1

The MAP Theory of Social Activism

SOCIAL MOVEMENTS are collective actions in which the populace is alerted, educated, and mobilized, sometimes over years and decades, to challenge the powerholders and the whole society to redress social problems or grievances and restore critical social values. Social movements are a powerful means for ordinary people to successfully create positive social change, particularly when the formal channels of democratic political participation are not working and obstinate powerful elites prevail.

In the United States today, there are hundreds of thousands of organizations and groups involving tens of millions of people who are working at the local, regional, national, and international levels to address critical societal issues. Many are engaged in social movements that are not only challenging powerholders and the social systems and institutions, but are also creating alternative solutions to problems, without waiting for official institutions to change.

PARTICIPATORY DEMOCRACY

Social movements promote participatory democracy. They raise expectations that people can and should be involved in the decision-making process in all aspects of public life. They convert festering social problems into social issues and put them on the political agenda. They provide a role for everyone who wants to participate in the public process of addressing critical social problems and engaging official powerholders in a response to grassroots citizen demands for change. In addition, by encouraging widespread participation in the social change process, over time social movements tend to develop more creative, democratic, and appropriate solutions.

Social movements are at the center of society. They are not exceptional or rare protest events on society's fringe, and their activists are not antisocial rebels. Quite the contrary, progressive nonviolent social movements are crucial to the ongoing process as society evolves and redefines itself. According to historian Alaine Touraine (1981), "Society is a system of actors in which people make their own societal history."[1] Through social movements, ordinary concerned people, not just the powerholders, play a leading part in the process. In the words of Martin Luther King Jr., social movements help to "fulfill the American Dream, not to destroy it."

Social movements must be based on widely held universal values. To place their social movement in the center of society, gain the support of the majority of the public, and advance society along the path of human development, movement activists must consciously stand for and articulate the culture's fundamental values, such as justice, democracy, civil and human rights, security, and freedom. They present a contrast to the vested interests that use public office and corporate institutions in ways that violate these principles. Social movements typically act in opposition to those conditions and practices that contravene society's universal values and principles, such as laws that prevent people from voting due to their race or gender, or regulations that permit corporations to control the world's political and economic systems.

Most citizens in democratic societies are steeped in their culture and believe in a range of universal values or principles. Movement activists, therefore, will be successful only to the extent that they can convince the great majority of people that the movement, not the elite powerholders, truly represents society's positive and widely held values and sensibilities. On the other hand, movements are self-destructive to the extent that they are defined as rebellious, on the fringes of society, and in opposition to the society's cherished core social values, symbols, rituals, beliefs, and principles.

Social movements, therefore, need to be totally nonviolent. The practice of strict nonviolence, following in the footsteps of Gandhi and King, provides social movements with the optimum opportunity for success because it is based on time-less universal human values and principles — love, compassion, cooperation, and caring. Nonviolence is less threatening to the majority of people and therefore helps them to be open to the movement's radical social message. In addition, non-violent methods allow almost everyone to participate in the movement: women, men, elders, youth, the frail, and even children, including those people who would be unable or unwilling to carry out militaristic and violent social action.

In this approach, the power of the people is engaged to apply maximum pressure on the various powerholders to change their views and policies. This method of exercising power is similar to what Gandhi described as *Satyagraha*.

He taught that the power of social movements is based on their ability to mobilize the populace in a moral struggle in which the people withdraw their consent to be governed by those in power, using methods such as noncooperation, defiance, disobedience, refusing benefits, and creating alternatives. This moral struggle requires total nonviolence in attitude and actions towards people and property. Consequently, nonviolent means are consistent with the ends sought by a good society; they are themselves the "ends in the making."

Finally, what makes nonviolence especially powerful is that it has the capacity not only to reduce the effectiveness of the powerholders' ultimate weapons of police and state violence, but it can also turn these powerholder strengths around to the movement's advantage, a process called moral jujitsu (see the description of Stage Four in Chapter 3).[2]

POWER

Enabling people to exercise their collective power is one of the ultimate goals of social movements. People power is important because throughout human history the distribution of power has been, and remains, unequal. Typically, an elite minority holds enormous political, economic, and social power. This *power élite* generally uses its influence to benefit itself at the expense of the general welfare and the majority of the population. The historian Arnold Toynbee concluded that the real struggle in the world was always between vested interests and social justice.[3] His analysis of the unequal distribution of power in the world obviously applies to our contemporary situation as much as it does to the past.[4]

Consequently, in an effort to promote democracy, justice, peace, general social welfare, and ecological sustainability, progressive social movements need to challenge the excessive power and influence of the elite minority. This inevitably leads to conflict with the political, economic, and corporate powerholders — whether they are presidents who run on an antiwar platform and then escalate a war, as U.S. President Lyndon Johnson did in 1964 when he sent more troops to Vietnam; contractors who want to increase the military budget and arms sales for their own profit; the American Medical Association opposing universal health care; or logging companies determined to destroy remaining old-growth forests.

At the core of the Movement Action Plan theory is a recognition of this differential distribution of political and economic power and an understanding of how power is used and achieved. Power is the ability to control, influence, or have authority over others. Today this includes power not only over what others do, but also over what people know and think. The word "power" comes from the French "poeir" and means, "to be able." Power is our capacity to manage the world around us and can be exercised through persuasion, persecution, different forms of coercion, or physical violence. Most of us believe that power is a "top down" dynamic and do not feel that we are very powerful. According to Gene Sharp, political power includes "the totality of means, influences and pressures — including authority, rewards and sanctions — available for use to achieve the objectives of the powerholder," including not only "the institutions of government and the state" but also "groups opposing either of them."[5]

Two views of power

Social movement activists need to be aware of two contrasting models of power — the **power élite** and **people power**. Each of these models leads to quite different and often contradictory movement beliefs, attitudes, strategies, constituencies, and activities.

In the *power élite model* (see Figure 1), society is organized in the form of a hierarchical pyramid, with powerful elites at the top and the relatively powerless mass populace at the bottom. The power elites, or powerholders, through their control of the state, institutions, laws, myths, traditions, and social norms, serve their own interests, usually to the disadvantage of the whole society. This model is represented by an upright triangle in which power flows from the elites at the top to the people at the bottom.

Figure 1: Power Elite Model

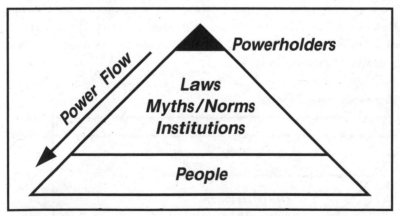

The power elite model is the traditional view of democracy. The founding fathers in the United States believed in this model of power; mainstream political and social theories still uphold this model;[6] and the public generally still believes in it. From this perspective, democracy is viewed as a struggle between competing societal elites, leaving the vote as the primary, if not the only, means by which the general population is expected to participate. Moreover, except for the right to buy or not buy goods, people are totally excluded from the economic system. It is worth noting that as a result of the founding fathers' power elite idea of democracy, during the first 20 years of U.S. history only propertied, rich, white men, who comprised less than 10 percent of the population, were allowed to vote in federal elections.

Since the majority of people are relatively powerless under the power elite model, social change can be achieved only by appealing to the elites at the top, seeking to get them to change their policies through normal political and institutional channels such as elections, lobbying, and litigation. In this model, the target of social activism is the powerholders and the method is persuasion — activists must try to convince existing powerholders to change their policies, laws, and programs or must elect new powerholders. *Professional opposition organizations* (POOs) generally conduct these efforts of the opposition in the halls of government and in corporate suites. On the other side, thousands of well-financed "special interest" groups, representing corporate and other elites, influence national, state, and local governments through elaborate campaign financing and constant lobbying.

The *people power model* (see Figure 2), on the other hand, holds that power ultimately resides in the mass populace. This model is represented by an inverse triangle, with the people at the top and the power elite at the bottom. This is an ideal that has not yet been attained as an ongoing political arrangement (though it has often been achieved during social activism), but even in societies with strong power elites, whether the United States or a military dictatorship, the powerholders' power is dependent on the cooperation, acquiescence, and tacit support of the great majority of common citizens.[7]

Figure 2: People Power Model

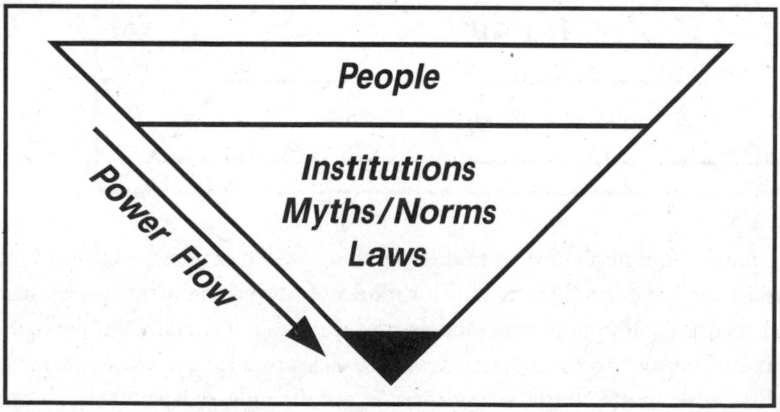

Nonviolent social movements are based on the people power model. Not only is placing power in the hands of the people their ultimate goal, but they are also dependent on the power of the people to create social change. The strategy in a social movement is to mobilize ever-larger numbers of ordinary citizens to assert their power and influence on the corporate and state institutions and also to create alternatives themselves.

POWERHOLDER STRATEGY

Most people living in Western political democracies believe in the ideal of "government by, for, and of the people." They believe that society should be based on a wide range of basic universal values, such as freedom, democracy, justice, and equality. Consequently, they believe that society's institutions and social systems should maintain these values and treat everyone equally. Indeed, in the United States, people become upset when they realize that their deeply held values and principles are being violated, especially by powerholder policies and practices.

Powerholders know that social conditions are ripe for change. They are aware that the private and public social system and institutions they head up often violate the people's cherished ideals. They know that these social systems and institutions unfairly distribute most of society's benefits to an elite minority at the top and most of the costs to the majority, especially those at the bottom. Consequently, they consciously try to keep their actual policies hidden from the public because they fear that a majority of the general public would rebel if it knew the reality. Power elites do this through a two-track system of *societal myths* vs. *societal secrets* and *official policies and practices* vs. *actual policies and practices.*

Societal myths vs. societal secrets

Societal myths are the slogans, beliefs, and values — such as, freedom, free market, democracy, and private enterprise — that the powerholders use to justify their self-serving policies and programs. In contrast, societal secrets are the exact opposite of the publicly proclaimed societal myths. They reflect the ideology that actually guides the powerholders as they carry out the power elite model in which most of the political and economic power and benefits go to the elite minority, while most of the disbenefits are borne by the environment and the majority of the people.

The founding fathers, for example, proclaimed the societal myth that the new nation was to be founded on the principle of democracy, but the societal secret was that democracy was only for a handful of rich white men. They realized that the slogan "Democracy for rich white men" would not go over very well with the 90 percent of the population that they called the "outdoors" people.

Official vs. actual policies and programs

The official policies and practices are those that the powerholders publicly pro-claim they are implementing. They are consistent with the high-sounding values of the societal myths. In stark contrast, the actual policies and practices are what the powerholders are really doing, which are consistent with the societal secrets. To use the voting rights example again, until the 1960s the societal myth was that the United States, including the South, was a democracy in which every adult had the right to vote. The societal secret, however, was that the southern powerhold-ers' ideology permitted only white adults to vote. The official policies and practices were that voter registration offices were open every day and available to anyone who wanted to register to vote. The actual policies and practices were that blacks were prevented from registering to vote through a variety of means: the reg-istrar's offices closed when blacks arrived, difficult tests were given to blacks but not to whites, and there were grandfather laws saying that you could only vote if your grandfather was registered.

Another example is the bi-annual "tax reform" laws passed by the U.S. Congress. The societal myth is that the powerholders want "tax reform," which would reduce taxes so that everyone gets a big tax break. The societal secret is that the powerholders believe in tax relief for the rich, but not for the people in the middle or near the bottom. The actual tax policies and practices since the early 1950s reduced the tax rates of the wealthy families 51 percent, while raising rates for middle-income families, a reality not publicized by the powerholders.[8]

SOCIAL MOVEMENT STRATEGY

Social movements involve a long-term struggle between the movement and the powerholders for the hearts, minds, and support of the majority of the popula-tion. Before social movements begin, most people are either unaware that a problem exists or don't believe that they can do anything about it. They believe the powerholders' societal myths and support the high-sounding official policies and practices, all of which seem to be consistent with the culture's deeply held values and beliefs. This was the situation before all of the social movements of the past 40 years. For example, before 1963, most Americans thought everyone could vote; before 1967, most thought the war in Vietnam was to preserve democracy for the people there; before 1976, most Americans thought that nuclear power was totally safe, necessary, and too cheap to meter; and before the anti-World Trade Organization (WTO) demonstrations in Seattle in 1999, most thought that corporate globalization was inevitable, provided good jobs for people in the Third World, and was sustainable.

The strategy of social movements, therefore, is to alert, educate, and win over an ever-increasing majority of the public. First, the public needs to be convinced that a critical social problem exists. Then it must be convinced that policies need to be changed. And then a majority of people must be mobilized into a force that eventually brings about an acceptable solution.

To carry out this strategy, social movements need to be firmly grounded in the values, symbols, beliefs, sensibilities, and traditions that are important to the general population. Only by proving to the public that the movement, not the powerholders, upholds these values and principles can the movement win over the citizenry and create a level of motivation that inspires people to challenge the powerholders and their policies. By the same token, movement activities and attitudes that violate society's values and sensibilities, such as acts of violence and rebellious machismo posturing, have the opposite effect — they turn off the mass population, including those people who are already involved, or would like be involved, in the movement.

To achieve the goal of winning over and involving the citizenry, social movements need to reframe the issue by exposing and proving to the public that the powerholders' actual policies and programs violate the societal myths. The best way to inspire the public to be actively involved in creating social change is to show continuously, over time, the gap between the powerholders' actual policies and programs and the culture's values and beliefs. Highlighting this gap is the most critical consciousness raising work and lies at the center of social movement strategy.

GRAND STRATEGY

The grand strategy is the broad framework that describes the overall process of movement success. It provides movement activists with a model they can use to create goals, strategies, tactics, and programs that are consistent with the movement's long-term goals. A shared understanding of the *grand strategy* provides activists in various organizations and sub-movements with a basic understanding of how each of their efforts can contribute to attaining the larger movement's ultimate goal.

Without a grand strategy, the disparate activists and groups involved in a movement do not have a common, consistent basis for planning, organizing, and evaluating their efforts and supporting each other. This leads to inefficiencies and unnecessary dissidence as groups go off in contradictory directions. Moreover, without a grand strategy there is no basis for challenging people and groups, including *agents provocateurs*, who either inadvertently or intentionally undercut the effectiveness of social movements.

   MAP's grand strategy is based on the people power model of nonviolent social movements. This process includes four strategic steps (see Figure 3):

1.   First, social movements must focus directly on the powerholders' policies and institutions to expose their societal secrets and challenge their actual policies and programs. This involves developing critical analyses, presentations, and publications and using all of the normal channels available to the public, including demonstrations, rallies, and marches that, when necessary, include civil disobedience. These are the activities of MAP Stages Two, Three, and Four.

2.   Second, the purpose of these activities is to put the public spotlight on the problem and on the powerholders' actual policies and practices in order to alert, educate, win over, involve, and inspire the general public to become involved in the movement. These activities are not intended to get the powerholders to change their policies and practices at this point.

3.   Third, social movements then mobilize the general public to put tremendous pressure on the powerholders and social institutions to change their policies and, at the same time, create a new peaceful culture and democratic political conditions. This is what happens during MAP Stages Six and Seven.

4.   Fourth, these activities attract additional members of the general public to become social activists and either join existing movement organizations and activities or create their own.

Figure 3: The Grand Strategy:
The Process of Creating Participatory Democracy

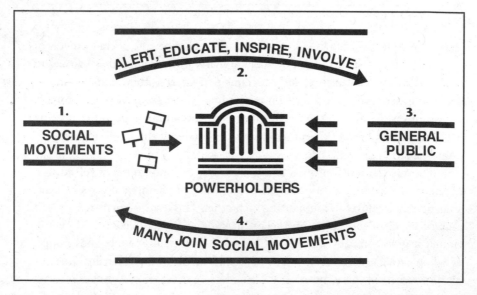

ASSUMPTIONS

The Movement Action Plan is based on the belief that nonviolent social movements are a powerful means for mobilizing people to become involved in a dynamic political process to address and resolve critical social problems. MAP has four underlying assumptions:

1. **A chief cause of social problems is the concentration of political and economic power in a few elite individuals and institutions that act in their own self-interest.** The political and economic powerholders act to benefit the privileged minority, while disbenefitting the majority and the general welfare to the detriment of the sustainability of the economy, environment, and natural resources.

2. **Participatory democracy is a key means for resolving today's awesome societal problems and for establishing a just and sustainable world for everyone.** The resolution of today's problems, therefore, requires an informed, empowered, and politicized population that assertively participates in the political and economic process to demand democracy, justice, security, equality, human welfare, peace, and environmental sustainability. Hence the basic theme of MAP is people power, a theme that is being sounded around the world.

3. **Political and economic power ultimately rest with the majority population; the powerholders in any society can only rule as long as they have the consent or acquiescence of the people.** The general population usually supports society's powerholders and institutions as long as they are perceived to be upholding the public trust by carrying out the interests and widely held beliefs and values of the whole society. All powerholders and governments, whether democratic or dictatorial, know this, which is why they spend vast amounts of time, effort, and money justifying their legitimacy to the citizenry

4. **The most important issue today is the struggle between the majority of citizens and the individual and institutional powerholders to determine whether society will be based on the power elite or people power model.** This struggle, between a belief in superiority and a belief in equality, is going on at all levels of life in the political, economic and social spheres of both democratic and totalitarian societies. It is also taking place in interpersonal relationships at work, in the community, or at home, and within social activism itself.

CONCLUSIONS

If a nonviolent social movement is to successfully address critical societal issues and create social change, it must be solidly based in participatory democracy, with a clear understanding of power — and of how to create people power that can withstand the onslaught of powerholder attack and counter-attack. The strategic requirements for social movements described by MAP run counter to the views held by some of today's activists. For instance, MAP makes it clear that social movements are not "happenings," where everyone is free to come and "do their own thing" – an obvious recipe for disaster. Quite the opposite. Organizing an effective social movement requires an understanding that social movements work as open-ended holistic systems with positive and negative feedback loops. What every component part of the movement does affects the entire movement, either negatively or positively, depending on how it fits into the overall strategic requirements for the movement.

The next two chapters will describe some of the main components: the four roles of activism and the eight stages of social movements. Then in Chapter 4 I will show how MAP can help activists believe in the power of their social movements and make them successful.

2

The Four Roles of Social Activism

WE ALL PLAY DIFFERENT ROLES IN LIFE. We are children to our parents and parents to our children. Sometimes we are conscious of the shift in roles and sometimes not. Activists need to become aware of the roles they and their organizations are playing in the larger social movement. **There are four different roles activists and social movements need to play in order to successfully create social change:** the *citizen, rebel, change agent,* and *reformer.* Each role has different purposes, styles, skills, and needs and can be played effectively or ineffectively.

Social movement activists need first to be seen by the public as responsible **citizens**. They must win the respect and, ultimately, the acceptance of the majority of ordinary citizens in order for their movements to succeed. Consequently, citizen activists need to say "Yes!" to those fundamental principles, values, and symbols of a good society that are also accepted by the general public. At the same time, activists must be **rebels** who say a loud "No!" and protest social conditions and institutional policies and practices that violate core societal values and principles. Activists need to be **change agents** who work to educate, organize, and involve the general public to actively oppose present policies and seek positive, constructive solutions. Finally, activists must also be **reformers** who work with the official political and judicial structures to incorporate solutions into new laws and the policies and practices of society's public and private institutions. Then they must work to get them accepted as the new conventional wisdom of mainstream society.

IMPORTANCE OF THE FOUR ROLES

Both individual activists and movement organizations need to understand that social movements require *all four* roles and that participants and their organizations can choose which ones to play depending on their own make-up and the needs of the movement. Moreover, they need to distinguish between effective and ineffective ways of playing these roles. This is especially important because many of the ineffective ways of performing these roles have been accepted as normal and acceptable social movement behavior. The Four Roles Model provides activists with a basis for choosing appropriate roles, evaluating their behavior, and holding themselves, as well as other activists and organizations, accountable for their actions.

Understanding a social movement's need to have all four roles played effectively can also help reduce antagonism and promote cooperation among different groups of activists and organizations. Rebels and reformers, for example, often dislike one another, each thinking that their own approach is the politically correct one and that those playing the other role undermine the success of the movement. However, when activists realize that the success of their movement requires all four roles, they can more easily accept, support and cooperate with each other.

PLAYING THE FOUR ROLES EFFECTIVELY

To play any of the four roles effectively, activists and their movements need to act in accordance with society's widely held democratic and human values. They must also behave in ways that are consistent with the long-term goals of the social movement and the vision of a good society. Besides following these guidelines, each role is different, defined by specific characteristics described in the following sections.

The citizen

Most Americans claim to be patriots, who firmly believe in the United States and its values, laws, and traditions. Although many people have become disenchanted with politicians, government bureaucracy, and the political and economic elite powerholders, they typically support the status quo on most key issues. Mistakenly, they often believe that the official institutions and powerholders are upholding society's values, principles, and laws. To gain a hearing from the majority of citizens, social movements need to be seen by the majority as the true promoters of society's basic values and beliefs. Most importantly, activists must remind the public that the source of legitimate power is the citizenry and not self-serving interest groups or institutional political and economic powerholders.

The key to movement success is ultimately winning over and involving the great majority of the public. In order to do this, social movement activists and organizations must be perceived by that majority as "good citizens" who are seeking the public good. The social movement needs to consciously place itself squarely in the center of society, not on its fringe. Keep in mind, however, that a chief strategy of the powerholders is to discredit the movement in the eyes of the public by portraying the movement as violent or anti-American. In the United States, powerholders have attempted to characterize activists as repugnant to Americans and the American way of life. Therefore, the more the movement is grounded in democratic values and national norms, the more likely it will be able to withstand these attacks and gain the influence and involvement of the general citizenry.

Activists must take advantage of the tendency for people to shut out information that contradicts what they already believe, while selectively admitting information that reinforces preexisting opinions and beliefs. (Psychologists call this "confirmatory bias.") Activists can use confirmatory bias to their advantage by highlighting their commitment to society's most cherished values. Social movements can also enlist the support and involvement of popular individuals and groups, such as entertainers, teachers, scientists, and religious groups, to help overcome the natural tendency of people to resist social change efforts and their new information and concepts.

Martin Luther King and Nelson Mandela are two of the most prominent models of the effective citizen. King and the 1960s black civil rights movement exemplified the citizen principle. While challenging racism across the United States, the movement focused on the American dream of equality and democracy. It did not condemn America, but called for the fulfillment of its vision. Rather than condemning white people, King, especially, challenged them to live up to their own highest standards. Nelson Mandela, after 27 years in jail under South African apartheid, had every right to condemn all South African whites as racists and call for the black majority to violently overthrow the oppressive white regime. Instead, he called upon everyone in the country — black, white, and colored — to work together nonviolently to create a nonracial, democratic society. Both Mandela and King placed their social activism in the center of society and grounded it in widely held humanistic values of democracy, freedom, equality, and justice to be achieved through active citizen-based democracy.

Over time, as activists fail to see immediate success, the potential increases for them to become frustrated and to act with hostility and violence. A strong commitment to positive social values and nonviolence discourages disgruntled activists from promoting attitudes and activities, including violence, that alienate the general public. Social movements can only achieve their long-term vision by incorporating it into their everyday practice.

In the citizen role, activists —

- advocate and demonstrate a widely held vision of the democratic good society;
- give the movement legitimacy in the eyes of ordinary citizens;
- enable the movement to withstand efforts by powerholders to discredit it; and
- reduce the potential for violent attitudes and actions within the movement.

The rebel

Rebels promote the democratic process, especially when a social problem is not publicly recognized and the normal channels of participatory democracy are not working adequately. They put critical social problems and moral violations in the public spotlight, often with dramatic and controversial actions, and keep them there. They educate ordinary citizens and involve them in dialogue. For example, mass marches, rallies, and civil disobedience launched widespread public discussion of civil rights and the Vietnam war in the 1960s, nuclear energy in the 1970s, nuclear weapons in the 1980s, and corporate-dominated economic globalization as the 21st century dawned. Such public dialogues are the first step to resolving a social problem in a democracy.

Rebels often use extra-parliamentary means, that is, methods outside of normal political channels, including nonviolent direct action and community education in the form of rallies, marches, leafleting, and petitions. Rebels literally use their bodies to stop the wheels and mechanisms of official institutions and powerholders. They block trains to prevent the transport of nuclear weapons, barricade doorways to keep officials from doing business, sit in trees to prevent logging, or protest corporate globalization with street demonstrations.

Rebels are usually the first to be recognized publicly as challenging the status quo. Nonviolent direct actions produce what Martin Luther King called "creative tension" by directing the public's focus to the gap between "what is and what should be." The rebel's work is sometimes dramatic, exciting, courageous, risky, and, occasionally, even dangerous. The rebel role requires courage, commitment, time, and a willingness to take risks, with the consequent danger of ridicule, sanctions, jail, loss of employment, burnout, disillusionment, and loss of life. As they confront the institutions of power, rebels are at the center of movement action and public attention, especially in the movement's "take-off" stage.

In the rebel role, activists –

- put issues on society's social agenda through dramatic, nonviolent actions;
- put issues on the political agenda;
- show how institutions and official powerholders violate public trust by causing and perpetuating critical social problems;
- force society to face its problems;
- represent society's democratic and moral vanguard; and
- promote democracy.

Change agent

The ultimate goal of a social movement is to create a healthy citizen-based democracy in which citizens are restored as the basic source of political legitimacy. Social movements accomplish this by alerting and educating the public about existing conditions and policies that violate widely held values. They must involve the whole society in the long-term process of social change, which includes changing current views and promoting alternatives. The true constituency of the change agent is the general public, particularly those people who are directly involved and affected by the social problem being addressed, but *not* the powerholders. In this process, activists work to redefine the problem to show how it affects every sector of society according to race, class, gender, location, social status, demographic, religion, etc., in order to involve everyone in the process of resolution.

Change agents play the key role when a movement has gained majority public opinion, just as rebels play the central role during a movement's take-off stage. In contrast to rebels, who put themselves in the public spotlight through direct action, change agents are less visible as they organize, enable, and nurture others to become actively involved in the democratic process. The change agent's goal, therefore, is to help create an open, public, democratic, and *dialectic* process in which all segments of society are engaged in resolving social problems. The change agent's role in building participatory democracy and creating new democratic structures is as important as winning on a specific issue.

This democratic organizing process requires activists to claim only that they have relative, not absolute truth. That is, the movement does not claim to have The Answer, only its own informed opinion. It provides a forum for *all* segments of the population to publicly discuss their own views on the issue. The process of democracy encourages all people to promote their own opinions in the public arena in order to achieve a resolution in which everyone's views and needs are considered.

Change agents not only help citizens redress the symptoms of a social problem, but they also promote the need to shift the *paradigm* or traditional viewpoint. That is, the movement must use the immediate symptoms of a specific social problem to educate and promote a change in the underlying worldview that causes the problem. For example, in addition to opposing nuclear energy, activists promoted the use of "soft energy," which included conservation and efficiency in energy use, as well as using energy sources that were renewable and less polluting (such as solar, wind, and water), as an alternative to the widely accepted "hard energy" path of inefficient and maximum consumption of energy from nonrenewable and polluting fossil fuels like gas and oil. Such shifts in perspective take time, so change agents must educate, motivate, and train citizen activists and help them organize for the long haul by providing a long-term perspective.

In the change agent role, activists –

- promote citizen-based democracy;
- support the involvement of large numbers of people in the process of addressing a specific social problem;
- redefine the problem to show how it affects every sector of society;
- promote a new social and political majority consensus favoring positive solutions,
- promote democratic principles and human values in an "open system" (that is, a system that is organized by citizens themselves, without being controlled by elite powerholders in the closed system of an oppressive hierarchy);[1]
- develop the majority movement;
- support the development of coalitions;
- counter the actions of the powerholders; and
- move society from *reform* to social change by promoting a *paradigm shift.*

The Reformer

It is not enough to convince and involve the majority of citizens to oppose specific social conditions and advocate alternatives. Reformers must then convert the acceptance of alternatives into new laws, policies, and practices of society's appropriate political, legal, social, and economic institutions. This requires parliamentary and legal strategies and actions, such as referenda, political campaigns, lawsuits, committee and commission hearings, and petitions, which make use of official judicial, legislative, political, and other institutional channels. In carrying out this role, social movement reformers often act as power brokers between the movement and the mainstream legal, political, economic, and legislative institutions and powerholders. One example of this role is the work of U.S. activists to ensure passage of legislation to re-authorize the Violence Against Women Act so that resources are available to carry out the policy changes achieved through social action. Another example is provided by the successful anti-nuclear energy movements in most Western European nations, which culminated in government declarations that no new nuclear energy reactors would be built.

This role is often played by the more establishment-oriented progressive people in large Professional Opposition Organizations (POOs), which have paid staff, boards of directors, large budgets, and powerful executive directors. The executive director and staff usually run their programs, while the grassroots members provide the mass political clout needed for the reforms to be enacted. In other words, reformers themselves have little innate power but are dependent on the power of the grassroots to create social change.

In the reformer role, activists –

- transmit movement analyses and goals to powerholder institutions and individuals;
- perform parliamentary and legal efforts — lobbying, referenda, lawsuits;
- work to create and expand new laws and policies;
- act as watchdogs to ensure the new laws and policies are actually funded and carried out;
- mobilize movement opposition to conservative backlash efforts; and
- nurture and support grassroots activists.

BARRIERS TO PLAYING THE FOUR ROLES EFFECTIVELY

Some activists have difficulty playing the four roles effectively. They may believe the roles are in conflict with each other because they fulfill different needs and require different styles, skills, and activities. The **citizen** says "yes" to society, while the **rebel** says "no," advocating protest against existing conditions and official institutional policies. In contrast to the rebel, the **change agent** says "yes," while advocating alternatives and supporting the broader public as people become active in bringing about change. The **reformer** also says "yes" and works with the public, grassroots activists, and the official institutions and powerholders to formalize the alternatives into new laws, policies, and structures. The reformer often compromises by advocating far less than what both rebels and change agents want.

Each role involves different political beliefs, attitudes, organizational arrangements, funding sources, organizing styles and methods, emotional qualities, personalities, and behaviors. Consequently, most activists and movement groups identify primarily with only one or two of the four roles. They may consider the roles that they play as the most important, while viewing those playing other roles as naive, politically incorrect, uninformed, ineffective, or, even worse, the enemy. Rebels, for example, often think that direct action is the only approach that makes sense against entrenched institutions and powerholders, especially since they believe that time is of the essence. Conversely, reformers may think that rebel actions, such as protest and resistance in the streets, are useless or undermine their own efforts. They fear that such activities alienate both the public and the powerholders and make it more difficult for them to work through the established institutions.

Activists need to recognize that successful social movements require all four roles to be played effectively and, to that end, should learn how to play all four roles. Dissension between those playing different roles heightens competition and reduces the movement's power and effectiveness. At the minimum, activists need to become allies with those playing other roles, since cooperation and mutual support will enhance the movement's likelihood of success.

Figure 1: Four Roles of Social Activism

CITIZEN

Effective

- Promotes positive American values, principles, and symbols, e.g., democracy, freedom, justice, nonviolence
- Normal citizen
- Grounded in the center of society
- Promotes active citizen-based society where citizens act with disinterest to assure the common good
- The active citizen is the source of legitimate political power
- Acts on "confirmatory bias" concept
- Examples: King and Mandela

Ineffective

- Naïve citizen: Believes the "official policies" and does not realize that the powerholders and institutions serve special elite interests at the expense of the majority and the common good

OR

- Super-patriot: Gives automatic obedience to powerholders and the country

REBEL

Effective

- Protest: Says "NO" to violations of positive, widely held human values
- Nonviolent direct action and attitude; demonstrations, rallies, and marches including civil disobedience
- Target: Powerholders and their institutions, e.g., government, corporations
- Puts issue and policies in public spotlight and on society's agenda
- Actions have strategy and tactics
- Empowered, exciting, courageous, risky, center of public attention
- Holds relative, not absolute, truth

Ineffective

- Authoritarian anti-authoritarian
- Anti-American, anti-authority, anti-organization structures and rules
- Self-identifies as militant radical, a lonely voice on society's fringe
- Any means necessary: Disruptive tactics and violence to property and people
- Tactics without realistic strategy
- Isolated from grassroots mass-base
- Victim behavior: Angry, dogmatic, aggressive, and powerless
- Ideological totalism: Holds absolute truth and moral, political superiority
- Strident, arrogant, egocentric; self needs before movement needs
- Irony of negative rebel: Negative rebel similar to agent provocateur

REFORMER

Effective

- Parliamentary: Uses official mainstream system and institutions — e.g., courts, legislature, city hall, corporations — to get the movement's goals, values, alternatives adopted into official laws, policies, and conventional wisdom
- Uses a variety of means: lobbying, lawsuits, referenda, rallies, candidates, etc.
- Professional Opposition Organizations (POOs) are the key movement agencies
- Watchdogs successes to assure enforcement, expand successes, and protect against backlash
- POOs nurture and support grassroots

Ineffective

- POOs: Dominator/patriarchal model of organizational structure and leadership
- Organizational maintenance over movement needs
- Dominator style undermines movement democracy and disempowers grassroots
- POO "Realistic Politics": Promotes minor reforms rather than social changes
- POO co-optation: Staff identify more with official powerholders than with movement grassroots

CHANGE AGENT

Effective

- Organizes People Power and the Engaged Citizenry, creating participatory democracy for the common good
- Educates and involves the majority of citizens and whole society on the issue
- Involves pre-existing mass-based grassroots organizations, networks, coalitions, and activists on the issue
- Promotes strategies and tactics for waging long-term social movement and Stage Six
- Creates and supports grassroots activism and organizations for the long term
- Puts issue on society's political agenda
- Counters new powerholder strategies
- Promotes alternatives
- Promotes a paradigm shift

Ineffective

- Too utopian: Promotes visions of perfectionist alternatives in isolation from practical political and social action
- Promotes only minor reforms
- Movement leadership and organizations based on patriarchy and control rather than participatory democracy
- Tunnel vision: Advocates single issue
- Ignores personal issues and needs of activists
- Unconnected to social and political social change and paradigm shift

Finally, the roles are related to specific Movement Action Plan stages (described in Chapter 3). While all the roles are needed in every stage delineated by MAP, one role is usually predominant in any particular stage. For example, the rebel role predominates in the take-off stage, while the change agent predominates in the majority public opinion stage. Change agents and reformers often get upset when their movement is in the take-off stage because of the dominance of rebels. They do not realize that at that particular stage the rebels are best suited for the job and that this is the normal developmental process of social movements.

PLAYING THE FOUR ROLES INEFFECTIVELY

Movement activists and organizations sometimes play the four roles in ways that violate the normal process of social movement success. Playing the roles ineffectively can greatly undermine a movement's effectiveness or even destroy it completely (see Figure 1).

Ineffective Citizen

Activists play the citizen role ineffectively by being naive, by believing the official party line and policies of the powerholders as if they were true. An ineffective citizen believes that powerholder leaders and institutions are acting in the best interests of the common good, rather than serving special elite interests at the expense of the rest of society. Many Americans, including most movement activists, have been socialized to uncritically believe in America and the "American Way of Life." They may accept the official story that the United States is always working for peace and democracy around the world against dictators, terrorists, communists, or "rogue states." They may fail to recognize that the United States supports ruthless dictators around the world, often opposing the efforts of oppressed people to establish their democratic rights. Many social movement activists, therefore, are only aware of the powerholders' harmful role in the particular issue that concerns them.

Ineffective rebel

Ineffective rebels often use strident rhetoric or aggressive actions and display defiant and anti-authoritarian attitudes against powerholder institutions and individuals. Their militant protest actions are usually driven by strong feelings of anger, hostility, and frustration. They advocate change by any means necessary, including disruption and destruction, regardless of how it affects others. Even when other activists have organized nonviolent social movement activities, many of these rebels characteristically engage in property vandalism and skirmishes with police. Their authoritarian anti-authoritarianism often mimics the oppressive attitude and behavior of the powerholders they hate. They alienate not only the people who aren't involved in a social movement, but most movement activists as well — even though they need both groups to achieve their stated goals. An extreme form of the ineffective rebel is the negative rebel, who is described in the next section.

Ineffective change agent

Ineffective change agents adopt ideologies and undertake activities to achieve a better world, but they either oppose or are unconnected to the long-term process of building the social and political conditions needed to achieve their vision at the societal level. Ineffective change agents try to alleviate symptoms without promoting systemic change and a paradigm shift. They call for reform, not social change. For example, the "not in my back yard" *(NIMBY)* anti-toxic waste protesters oppose toxic waste dumped in their own neighborhood, but often do not oppose either the *growth and prosperity* system that causes toxic waste or the dumping of it elsewhere.

On the other hand, some ineffective change agents promote utopian ideas, but they don't engage in the hard work of grassroots organizing to achieve them. They believe that envisioning and proclaiming the new society is enough. Some anti-hunger projects of the 1970s, for example, envisioned a world without hunger without any concrete program for ending hunger. For over a decade, such organizations collected tremendous amounts of money, while world hunger escalated. Other utopians advocate personal growth or alternative rural lifestyles in ways that could only be achieved by society's privileged, highly educated, and over-consuming upper-middle and upper classes.

Ineffective reformer

Some reformer behaviors conflict with movement success. Many reformers are based in national and regional offices of POOs. These generally have traditional oppressive hierarchical organizational structures, large staffs and budgets, boards of directors, and large memberships. Their own organizational maintenance needs often take precedence over the political actions that the movement requires from them. Catering to big funders, foundations, and powerholder-laden boards of trustees inevitably leads to moderate or conservative politics that don't stray too far from the status quo. For some professional movement bureaucrats, the desire to preserve their career, high salary, and high-status job inhibits their advocacy of controversial social change.

When social movements get to the point where they have gained a majority of public opinion and are on the verge of achieving alternatives, powerholders and mainstream institutions try to split or undercut the movement by offering minor reforms. The ineffective reformers start making agreements in the name of "realistic politics," usually over the objections of the grassroots groups. Then they become cut off from the grassroots and the general public, whom they believe do not understand how "The System" works. For example, during the early 1980s, while the anti-nuclear weapons grassroots efforts staunchly opposed cruise and Pershing 2 nuclear weapons, the Washington-based movement lobbyists unilaterally and quietly refused to oppose these weapons. They thought such opposition was unacceptable even to liberal congressional Democrats and Republicans.

The staff of professional opposition organizations often act as self-appointed leaders of social movements. In coalition with staff of other POOs, they behave as if they represent the movement, deciding on strategies and programs for the entire movement and then sending directives down to the local levels. This oppressive hierarchical behavior, combined with conservative politics, splits the POOs off from grassroots activists, especially when the POO is a national or regional organization dictating to activists in local groups. By playing the role of movement bosses, the POO staff disempower the grassroots. They undercut the movement's power and success because all the power of social movements is based in the grassroots.

All of those who play ineffective roles believe that their approach is the only one that counts and regard activists in other roles, promoting other programs, as naive, unimportant, or even harmful. They fail to see that social change requires a complex, multi-dimensional web of approaches and coalitions that support each other, creating a united front.

The Negative Rebel

The negative rebel deserves special attention because it is the most confusing and potentially harmful of the roles of activism. Negative rebels are often self-defined radicals who advocate militant actions and revolutionary ideologies for fundamental change. Yet, their ideology, slogans, attitude, and activities are usually disconnected from any means of achieving their high goals. The activities of the negative rebel are mostly tactics oriented and are counterproductive to achieving their goal of radical social change. For example, they focus on militant activities at demonstrations, such as blockading a doorway for 30 minutes longer than the rest of the demonstrators, calling police derogatory names, or making surprise "attacks" on property so that the police will not discover them until after they are already on the site. The strategic question of whether these activities help or hinder the movement in achieving its long-term goals is not discussed.

Negative rebels tend to view themselves as being on the margins of both society and their social movement, challenging authorities, structural arrangements, decisions, and policies. They usually view the world as polarized between good and evil, revolutionary and reactionary — "we" who have the truth and are the vanguard of righteousness, against "them," the powerful enemy. Their attitudes, thoughts, and actions are dominated by deep feelings of outrage, anger, and hostility.

On the one hand, the negative rebel is widely accepted as a part of movement culture and many negative rebels claim to be the most radical and politically correct of activists. On the other hand, they can be so damaging that powerholders even hire infiltrators to play the negative rebel in an effort to subvert movements (these infiltrators are known as *agents provocateurs*). In addition, the mainstream media use the image of the negative rebel to characterize social movements so they can belittle and de-legitimize activists in the eyes of the public. Negative rebel activity makes such good headlines and copy that it usually overshadows the more positive movement efforts.

In the United States, many rebels define themselves as anti-American and passionately oppose the country, its symbols like the flag, and its traditions like the Fourth of July. They are the mirror image of the super-patriot. Anti-Americanism is devastatingly counterproductive to movements in the U.S. It alienates the 90 percent of Americans who are patriotic, often frightening them into supporting the powerholders and the status quo when they might have been persuaded to support the movement. Anti-Americanism turns off ordinary citizens and makes it almost impossible for them to listen to the movement's message. That is why FBI director J. Edgar Hoover continuously tried to portray Martin Luther King as anti-American. Richard Gilber identifies the fear of being seen as anti-American as the chief factor restricting participation in the anti-nuclear weapons movement.[2]

While negative rebels appear anytime, they are especially prevalent within a year of the movement's take-off stage. The extensive media coverage and popularity of a social movement during this time induces many opportunists to flock to the movement to promote their own ideology, organization, or personal rebelliousness. These people frequently end up filling the negative rebel role. Simultaneously, there is often a leadership vacuum and reduced discipline in the movement because many of the original leaders have either dropped out from exhaustion and depression or have moved on to new activities, such as public education, local organizing, promoting alternatives, or parliamentary politics.

Ironically, negative rebels interpret the movement's successful progression to the stage of acceptance by the majority of the public as an indication of the failure and demise of the movement. They become demoralized because the powerholders fail to change their policies, even though a majority of the public has adopted the movement's goals for change. This mistaken sense of failure causes negative rebels to call for desperate militant actions as a means of last resort. They may claim, "We tried nonviolence and the soft approach. The powerholders wouldn't listen. To achieve our goals we need to devise actions that are even more militant and forceful. We must use any means necessary." Other activists who have lost hope of success join the negative rebel, acting out their frustration, rage, and despair through aimless, violent militancy. An indicator of the futility of this approach is that most of the infamous negative rebels from the 1960s, including the Red Brigades of Germany, the Weather Underground, and the many violent radicals described in the film *Berkeley in the 1960s*, have recanted their actions as mistakes.

Types of negative rebels

There are many different kinds of negative rebels. Some fit into several categories.

- **True Believers.** Many activists believe that the negative rebel role is the most powerful and militant way to act out their strong feelings of anger and compassion regarding a grave social problem. Some might doubt its effectiveness, but emotionally they need to take this type of strong and dramatic action.
- **Hard Left.** Some negative rebels are members of far left-wing groups whose politics combine revolutionary and anarchistic anti-authority ideologies along with militant action. Although small in number, their flamboyant and arrogant style attracts naive negative rebels and often gets the most media coverage. Hard-left negative rebels are typically organized into small tightly knit groups that sometimes quietly join movements and other groups to disrupt, destroy, take over, or manipulate them for their own self-serving purposes.
- **Personal Rebels.** The negative rebel role is ideal for people who are in a rebellious stage of their personal life and want to establish their own identity. The movement may be the only place where these individuals can act out their anger and rebelliousness, flout authority, and trash property while they simultaneously claim to be acting in the name of a good cause, receive television coverage, and get positive feedback from others.
- **Naive Followers.** People who are new to social activism might join negative rebel activities at a movement event, not knowing that this kind of activity probably violates the guidelines for participants that were set out by the event's organizers.
- **Personal Opportunists.** The dramatic and individualistic nature of negative rebel activities is ideal for egocentric and narcissistic individuals to assume leadership roles and to get media attention at the expense of the goals of the movement. The loudest, pushiest, and most obnoxious can take center stage in the free-for-all of an ideology in which no one can tell anyone else what to do and everyone is free to do his or her own thing. This simply opens every demonstration and social movement up to being destroyed by agents provocateurs or other negative rebels.

- **Agents Provocateurs.** At least since the time of Machiavelli, powerholders have used agents provocateurs to subvert citizen-based opposition, and this practice has thrived in the modern era of social movements. In addition to gathering intelligence, a chief goal of agents provocateurs is to discredit movements in the eyes of the public and to destroy movement organizations from within by creating internal conflict, mistrust, confusion, dissension, disruption, mayhem, and general unhappiness.

In the United States, agents provocateurs have generally been undercover police officers who infiltrated movements and tried to make them appear violent and anti-American. The *COINTELPRO* Papers documents how the FBI hired thousands of people to infiltrate, disrupt, and discredit 215 dissident groups since the 1960s.[3] A noteworthy example was the use of police as agents provocateurs to perform militant actions that resulted in massive clashes with police at the 1968 Democratic convention in Chicago. Officials claim that one of every six demonstrators was an undercover agent,[4] including the shirtless radical with a red headband who climbed the flagpole in Chicago's Grant Park during the convention, tearing the American flag down in front of the world's television cameras. He was, in fact, a Chicago police officer.

Those disruptive, angry, radical activists who vehemently and militantly call for revolutionary change through any means necessary — disruption of meetings, property damage, battle with police, or the violent overthrow of authorities and the establishment — perform the same function as agents provocateurs. The irony of the negative rebel role is that it carries out the strategy and tactics of the powerholders and authorities it claims to oppose so strongly.

"Doing your own thing" – and its limits

Unfortunately, aspects of negative rebel activity are sometimes accepted as legitimate movement behavior and culture by people who believe the following stereotypes about social movements:

- Activists should use militant direct action that goes beyond traditional nonviolence, with no distinction between what is strategically effective or ineffective.
- Activists should freely express their anger and frustration because it is cathartic for people to act out their feelings and, after all, the personal is political.
- People should be free to "do their own thing" by whatever means they prefer, unfettered by movement authorities, rules, and structures.
- No one in the movement should tell others what to do; after all, isn't that the kind of authoritarianism that we oppose?

Negative rebels often justify their independent actions by claiming that the freedom to "do your own thing" is a sacrosanct cardinal principal of democracy and, by extension, of social movements. But this is not true in general and is particularly dangerous when applied to social activism. In a democracy, participants are not free to do whatever they want. Democracy requires a balance between individual freedom and responsibility to the whole group or society. Individuals are only free to act within agreed-upon boundaries, rules, and requirements. They must act in ways that do not violate the rights and privileges of other citizens or participants and that are necessary for the good of the whole group.

Negative rebels, however, commonly violate these principles of democracy. One typical way is by attending events organized by others and disrupting them with rowdy behavior, vandalism, and provocation of the police or other groups — acts that clearly flout the principles and agreements of the sponsoring organizations. These are subversive acts that constitute parasitic exploitation rather than democratic participation.

Interpreted this way, "do your own thing" (DYOT) not only violates the principles of democracy, but also makes social movements more vulnerable to the powerholder strategy of undermining movements through agents provocateurs. DYOT, moreover, is closer to the capitalist tenet of rugged individualism in the unfettered marketplace than it is to participatory democracy.

One of the recent examples of "do your own thingism" is the pro-violence groups, sometimes called the "black bloc," that have uniformly adopted the anarchist black dress code and have shown up at a series of anti-corporate globalism demonstrations around the world, beginning in Seattle in November 1999. While the organizers and at least 99 percent of the participants in those demonstrations clearly followed nonviolent principles, the tiny minority countered that DYOT was politically correct. They had a right, they claimed, to show up in the name of *pluralistic relativism*, and they argued that the imposition of nonviolence was authoritarian and hierarchical.

There is a critical difference between authority and authoritarian and between hierarchy and oppressive hierarchy. The organizers and the participants who wanted nonviolent demonstrations had the authority to call for total nonviolence because the decision came from the majority through a democratic process. They *were* acting in a hierarchical manner because they depended on the different levels of structure required for groups of people to work together. The DYOTers, however, were both authoritarian and oppressively hierarchical because they forced their decision to act violently on everyone else. The nonviolent demonstration organizers, on the other hand, were not allowed to do their own thing, that is, have a nonviolent demonstration.

The DYOTers were free to organize their own demonstration at another time or place and proclaim ahead of time that they would attack police and destroy property. This would never happen, however, because negative radicals doing their own thing need a mass of nonviolent people to hide behind and use as human shields — that is the real reason they come to nonviolent demonstrations.

But the responsibility for organizing a nonviolent demonstration ultimately falls on its organizers. They need to take a positive and direct stand ahead of time by proclaiming that the demonstration will be totally nonviolent and that only those willing to abide by the guidelines are invited to attend. Moreover, they need to have a clear position that they will denounce and oppose those who attempt to be violent. This position requires the organizers to include extensive plans and training in the organizing process to ensure the demonstration is totally nonviolent.

Negative rebels make bad revolutionaries

Despite their radical ideology and bravado, negative rebels usually act out of deep feelings of powerlessness, hopelessness, and desperation. Because they see the powerholders and system as all-powerful and themselves as relatively powerless, negative rebels have little hope of achieving success. Consequently, they promote rebellious tactics out of deep personal and political frustration and anger, and the resulting actions are disconnected from a practical strategy. There does not need to be strategy, accountability, or responsibility if one believes there is no chance of success. Many negative rebels act on the sense that "We have to do something; it doesn't matter what." As a result, many of their activities violate guidelines for achieving movement success, as the following examples show.

- **Negative rebels alienate the public.** Angry mob actions that include public violence, random trashing of property, skirmishes with the police, flouting the law, and interfering with the rights of others are widely viewed as intolerable. Negative rebel activities, therefore, not only turn the general public against the movement, but also scare many potentially sympathetic citizens into supporting the status quo and the powerholders.
- **Negative rebels reduce movement legitimacy and power.** A chief ingredient of movement success and power is convincing the majority of ordinary citizens that the movement, not the powerholders, is the true representative of widely held values, principles, and traditions of society. The actions of the negative rebel have just the opposite effect and turn the majority against social activism.
- **Negative rebels cause movement burnout, dropout, and dissipation.** While positive energy re-creates itself and stimulates movement growth, the negative rebel's energy does the opposite. Negative rebels dissipate movements by making activism unpleasant, inefficient, and ineffective.
- **Negative rebels legitimize fascistic tactics.** Mob street violence, clashes with the police, and property destruction are standard behaviors of fascism. An unintended impact of negative rebel behavior, therefore, might be the legitimization

of behavior that can be carried much further by future fascists, especially where there is economic depression, political oppression, or economic or ecological collapse. What moral or ethical defense could negative rebels have if fascistic groups brutally attacked them? Indeed, the presence of negative rebels takes the power of nonviolence away from all demonstrations they attend — that's why powerholders hire agents provocateurs.

- **Negative rebels provide an excuse for police to be violent and for legislators to pass laws contravening basic civil rights of protest.** This result is the opposite of engaging more citizens in civic life and building democracy, which is the goal of nonviolent social movements.

These are some of the reasons why Lillian Hellman, referring to herself and others, said, "Rebels make bad revolutionaries."

Curbing the negative rebel

Steps can be taken to reduce the harmful impact of negative rebels. Movement organizations need to establish clear, specific guidelines and standards of behavior for participants in both their internal affairs and their public events, based on the vision of a peaceful civil society. Similarly, individual activists need to take responsibility for their own movement participation by becoming more mature political activists. They need to ask themselves, "How am I playing the four roles? Am I a negative rebel? How can I become a more effective activist? Are my personal issues of rebelliousness, guilt, anger, or powerlessness or my self-image as a militant radical getting in the way of my effectiveness?" Such questions could be pursued with others in discussion groups. Finally, activists need to continue experimenting with participatory democracy, including learning how to balance individual freedom with responsibility and accountability within organizations and the movement in general.

MOVING FROM INEFFECTIVE TO EFFECTIVE ROLES

The effective ways of playing all four roles of activism have a common set of characteristics, as do all four ineffective roles (see Figure 2). Effective activists also respect those playing the other roles effectively and are allies with them, while appropriately challenging and negotiating with those playing the roles ineffectively. They also seek to play all four roles, as needed and appropriate.

Figure 2: Effective vs. Ineffective Activism

EFFECTIVE ROLES	INEFFECTIVE ROLES
Empowered and hopeful	Disempowered and hopeless
Positive attitude and energy	Negative attitude and energy
People power: Participatory democracy	Elitist: Self-identified leaders or vanguard
Coordinated strategy and tactics	Tactics in isolation from strategy
Nonviolence/means equals ends	Any means necessary
Promote realistic vision and social change	Unrealistic utopianism or minor reform
Assertive/cooperative (win-win)	Passive or overly aggressive/competitive
Feminist/relative truth/nurturer/adaptive	Patriarchal/absolute truth/rigid ideology
Faith in people	Put the "masses" down
Peace paradigm	Dominator paradigm

The mature activist

Successful movements require activists to be personally and politically mature. Activists need to act politically in a way that facilitates the long-term process of social movement success, while at the same time behaving personally in accordance with the model of peaceful human relationships. They should also keep the following guidelines in mind:

- **Play all roles of activism effectively.** There are many reasons why it is normal to play the four roles ineffectively, and many more reasons why it is hard to act effectively. First, being anti-authoritarian, oppressively hierarchical, or individualistic and self-righteous has long been accepted as standard social activist behavior. To switch from ineffective activism to effective behavior requires a high level of personal and political awareness and self-understanding. Second, because of the tremendous success of *"deconstructive analysis"* — that is, because they know what is wrong – activists often suffer strong feelings of hurt, sorrow, anger, and despair. These feelings are exacerbated because activists become keenly aware of the extent to which the official powerholders, those in whom the citizenry has placed its trust, violate the values of democracy, justice, and fairness. With these feelings of anger, despair, and disillusionment, it's easy to become self-righteous and bitter about the government. Finally, it is normal in our society to defend oneself and to react in kind when verbally or physically attacked. But to act effectively, activists need to be nonviolent at all times; they need to achieve a special level of personal development to respond nonviolently regardless of the severity of attack on them.

- **Be allies with activists who are playing the other roles.** There is a strong tendency to believe that the way *I* see and do things is the right and only way. Similarly, there is a long history of social activists believing their brand of activism is right while condemning activists with different approaches. It takes a new level of personal growth and self-transformation not only to recognize the need for other activists to play different roles of activism, but to consciously accept them and become an ally by praising, supporting, and cooperating with them.
- **Play all four roles.** For their movement to be successful, individual activists need to be able to play all four roles effectively. One day an activist might participate in a nonviolent civil disobedience action; the next day the same person could lobby for a bill in Congress and then give a talk to a civic group on why it should be involved in a social issue. This requires a range of skills and a well-developed, mature, and flexible personality. You need to be a rebel, able to resist, take risks, and put your body on the line and in the line of fire. You need to be a change agent, less egocentric than the resister and often invisible as you nurture and support other activists. Being a reformer requires another set of personality traits and political skills, as well as more mainstream attire and mannerisms that many rebels abhor.
- **Act on positive emotions.** Because they are often center stage, it is especially important that activists act on the positive emotions of compassion, love, and passion for a society that lives up to its highest values. Effective activists use the energy of their emotional distress, particularly their anger, fear, and frustration with powerholders, and strategically redirect it through imaginative and responsible nonviolent actions.
- **Achieve the vision of a good society.** Dysfunctional societies and organizations both produce and require dysfunctional people, who, in turn, create dysfunctional social movements. Conversely, the good society sought by social movements can only exist to the extent that its individual members have taken the path of personal transformation and developed into functional individuals whose beliefs, attitudes, behavior, and psychological and emotional levels are those of the good society. Social movements, therefore, need to be explicitly involved in the work of encouraging and supporting personal transformation.

Achieving political awareness and personal transformation

People do not need to wait until they are perfect before they become involved, but they do need to be committed to personal growth and transformation if they are to be effective citizen-activists. You can achieve political development through a wide variety of means:

- Become informed beyond the mainstream sources through the alternative media including books, magazines, videos, and Internet websites and email lists of key groups and issues.
- Become thoroughly acquainted with the groups and spokespeople of social movements who are working on issues that concern you.
- Attend workshops and lectures and discussion groups.
- Become involved. You need to act your way into thinking; you cannot think your way into acting.

There is also a wide range of ways to engage in the process of personal development and transformation. You can learn about conflict resolution, assertiveness training, group dynamics, co-counseling, twelve-step programs, personal support groups, and the many facets of multiculturalism. What is needed is a fundamental shift in our character from being dysfunctional and dominating, states that are normal for our culture and social systems, to being peaceful and consciously aware, which are the states needed in the good democratic society we seek.

3

The Eight Stages of Social Movements

SOCIAL MOVEMENTS DO NOT WIN OVERNIGHT. Successful social movements typically progress through a series of eight clearly definable stages, in a process that often takes years or even decades.[1] The Movement Action Plan's Eight Stages Model enables activists to identify the particular stage their social movement has reached, celebrate successes achieved by completing previous stages, and create effective strategies, tactics, and programs for completing the current stage and moving to the next. As they follow this process, activists are able to develop strategies to achieve short-term goals that are part of the long-term evolution to their ultimate objective. When they achieve the goals of one stage, activists can develop short-term goals, programs, and activities for the next stage, and so forth. This allows social movement organizers and activists to become social movement strategists.

Social movements usually address big issues, such as civil rights for African Americans, the war in Vietnam, universal health care, or corporation-dominated economic globalization. These noble goals, however, are too abstract to excite and mobilize people to action. Social movement strategists, therefore, divide their issues into a number of specific critical sub-issues and organize a sub-movement for each of them. For example, the anti-corporate economic globalization movement has been made up of numerous sub-movements including the sub-movement against the North American Free Trade Agreement (NAFTA), the sub-movement against the Multilateral Agreement on Investment (MAI), the sub-movement in favor of canceling Third World debt, the sub-movement against specific corporations that employ workers in sweat shop conditions, and the sub-movement that organizes fair trade programs, to name but a few.

The process of social movement success, therefore, involves many sub-movements that are progressing through the MAP eight stages of success. At any given time the overall movement can be identified as being in a specific MAP stage, while each of its sub-movements may be progressing through the eight stages at a different pace. This process ultimately affects the cultural, social, and political climate to the point where it becomes more costly for the powerholders to continue their policies than to change them. Even sub-movements that are defeated can contribute to this building process. Finally, when the whole movement achieves its major goal, many of the other sub-goals are automatically won, while others continue as part of a new movement.

The model in Figure 1, the Eight Stages of Successful Social Movements, provides a general description of each of these stages and the role that the movement, powerholders, and the public typically play in each stage. The model also delineates the goals for each stage, typical pitfalls, and the crisis that ends each stage and prepares the way for advancement to the next stage. Notice that until the opposition reaches Stage Four it typically is not recognized as being a social movement.

STAGE ONE: NORMAL TIMES

 Stagnation: It is a time of standstill and decline. The political and social environment is corrupt, insights or ideas from people of principle will be met with apathy or rejection, but they must remain true to their principles.

(From the *I Ching*, "Book of Changes")

There are many conditions that grossly violate democracy, freedom, justice, peace, a clean environment, the meeting of basic human needs, and society's other widely held and cherished fundamental values. These conditions do not exist in a vacuum. They are created and sustained by society's political, economic, and social systems, which are typically run by society's powerholders through private and public institutions. The two primary powerholders today are corporations and governments. Social problems are also sustained by various aspects of a society's culture, such as its beliefs, worldviews, myths and rituals, and the state of awareness of individual citizens.

In normal times these violations of society's sensibilities go mostly unnoticed. They are neither in the public spotlight nor on society's agenda of hotly contested issues. Normal times are politically quiet times. The great majority of the population either does not know the problem exists or supports the institutional policies and practices that cause the problem. Citizen opposition is too small in numbers and power and the divergent viewpoint is considered too radical or ridiculous to deserve credibility.

1. Normal Times
- A critical social problem exists that violates widely held values
- Powerholders support problem: Their "Official Policies" tout widely held values but the real "Operating Policies" violate those values
- Public is unaware of the problem and supports powerholders
- Problem/policies not a public issue

2. Prove the Failure of Official Institutions
- Many new local opposition groups
- Use official channels — courts, government offices, commissions, hearings, etc. — to prove they don't work
- Become experts; do research

Figure 1

Eight Stages of the Process of Social Movement Success

• Focus more on other sub-goals • Spin off new social movements

CHARACTERISTICS OF MOVEMENT PROCESS
- Social movements are composed of many sub-goals and sub-movements, each in their own MAP stage
- Strategy and tactics are different for each sub-movement, according to the MAP stage each is in
- Keep advancing sub-movements through the Eight Stages
- Each sub-movement is focused on a specific goal (e.g., for civil rights movements: restaurants, voting, public accommodation)
- All of the sub-movements promote the same paradigm shift (e.g., shift from hard to soft energy policy)

Public Must be Convinced Three Times
1. That there is a problem (Stage Four)
2. To oppose current conditions and policies (Stages Four, Six, Seven)
3. To want, no longer fear, alternatives (Stages Six, Seven)

8. Continuing the Struggle
- Extend successes (e.g., even stronger civil rights laws)
- Oppose attempts at backlash
- Promote paradigm shift
- Focus on other sub-issues
- Recognize/celebrate successes so far

3. Ripening Conditions

- Recognition of problem and victims grows
- Public sees victim's faces
- More active local groups
- Need pre-existing institutions and networks available to new movement
- 20 to 30 percent of public opposes powerholder policies

4. Take Off

- *TRIGGER EVENT*
- Dramatic nonviolent actions/campaigns
- Actions show public that conditions and policies violate widely held values
- Nonviolent actions repeated around country
- Problem put on the social agenda
- New social movement rapidly takes off
- 40 percent of public opposes current policies/conditions

PROTESTS

5. Perception of Failure

- See goals unachieved
- See powerholders unchanged
- See numbers down at demonstrations
- Despair, hopelessness, burnout, dropout, seems movement ended
- Emergence of negative rebel

POWERHOLDERS

6. Majority Public Opinion

- Majority oppose present conditions and powerholder policies
- Show how the problem and policies affect all sectors of society
- Involve mainstream citizens and institutions in addressing the problem
- Problem put on the political agenda
- Promote alternatives
- Counter each new powerholder strategy
- Demonology: Powerholders promote public's fear of alternatives and activism
- Promote a paradigm shift, not just reforms
- Re-trigger events happen, re-enacting Stage Four for a short period

7. Success

- Large majority oppose current policies and no longer fear alternative
- Many powerholders split off and change positions
- End-game process: Powerholders change policies (it's more costly to continue old policies than to change) are voted out of office, or slow, invisible attrition
- New laws and policies
- Powerholders try to make minimal reforms, while movement demands social change

The recent past offers vivid examples of unacknowledged problems in normal times: violations of African American civil rights in the South before 1950; the United States war against Vietnam before 1966; the dangers of nuclear power in Europe, Canada, and the United States before 1975; and corporate economic globalization before 1999.

Opposition

The opposition to these conditions and policies involves small numbers of people and is unnoticed. When the issues are brought to public attention, the opposition often receives more ridicule than support. For instance, women demanding women's rights in 1848 were dismissed as eccentric or crazy. Consequently, the opposition's efforts are relatively ineffective.

There are three major kinds of opposition groups:

• Professional opposition organizations (POOs)
• Ideological or principled dissent groups
• Grassroots groups that represent the victims

Professional opposition organizations are usually centralized, formal organizations located at the local, regional, or national level and headed by a strong central leader supported by a small, volunteer staff. Through diligent work, research, and critical analysis, POOs usually get access to information that contradicts what the public has been told and develop perspectives and analyses that radically contradict those of the powerholders and conventional wisdom.

The **principled dissent groups** are usually small, rarely noticed, and ineffective and appear far too radical at this time (for example, the first "ban the nuclear bomb" demonstrations at the White House, organized by the Quakers in 1959). In Stage One, these groups hold nonviolent demonstrations, rallies, pickets, and occasional civil disobedience actions. Because they support deeply held human values, the principled dissent groups often serve as a moral light in the darkness.

The **grassroots groups** are composed of local citizens who oppose present conditions and policies, but who do not yet have the support of the majority population, even at the local level. They promote a progressive view and represent the victims' perspective, provide direct services to victims, and may also carry out actions similar to those of the other two opposition groups.

Powerholders

The powerholders promote policies that favor the privileged and powerful corporate, economic, and political elites while violating the interests and values of the great majority of the population and the society as a whole. The powerholders work diligently to create and control the seemingly "normal" channels of the social systems, public and private institutions, and media through which they carry out their purposes. The powerholders maintain these abhorrent policies and practices primarily by keeping them away from public scrutiny, out of the public spotlight, and off society's agenda of contested issues.

This strategy of keeping their unprincipled policies and practices hidden from the public is deliberate, because the powerholders know full well that if the general population knew the truth, the people would be upset and demand change. The powerholders deceive the citizenry through the system of societal myths vs. societal secrets and official policy and practices vs. actual policy and practices.

Today, even the most brutal military dictatorships have a public façade of acceptable official policies and parliamentary democracy, complete with the pretense of public voting. Their actual practice however, involves oppression backed up by physical force, including intimidation, beatings, torture, imprisonment, and death, as well as social and economic sanctions against all opposition.

Public

In the United States and other industrialized societies with a tradition of democracy, the political and social consensus supports the powerholders' official policies and the status quo, because the general populace is unaware that the social conditions and the powerholders' actual policies and practices violate their values and self-interest. They believe the powerholders' explanations, which justify their policies in terms of society's highest principles. As a result, the public is usually unaware of serious social problems and the powerholders' involvement. In Stage One, only 5 to 10 percent of the population is upset by the social issue and disagrees with the powerholders' policies. In nations with more overt dictatorial governments, however, the great majority of the population may disagree with the government's policies and practices, but due to fear and the inability to organize safely, people take little overt action.

Goals

The goals of the opposition at this stage are –
• to become informed;
• to identify and document that a serious problem exists, how it violates widely held principles and values, and the specific role the powerholders play in it;
• to create active opposition organizations and infrastructure, no matter how small;
• to move on to the activities of Stage Two; and
• above all, to believe that social change is possible and that they can help create it.

Pitfalls

The main dangers in normal times are –
• feeling stuck; and

- believing that you are a powerless victim and there is nothing that you can do about it.

Political naivety, that is, having blind faith in the powerholders and the social system to address and solve social problems, will cause you to feel stuck. Powerholders promote the belief in powerlessness to keep the populace from acting to change the status quo.

Crisis

Small numbers of newly involved grassroots citizens realize that a critical problem exists and that neither the official powerholders nor many of the old POOs have the interest or ability to solve the problem through the normal channels of the established social system. They realize that they must confront the official institutions themselves and must use the official channels not only in an honest attempt to get policies and practices changed, but also to document that the normal channels for citizens to participate effectively in the democratic process are not working.

Conclusion

Normal times are politically quiet times because the powerholders successfully promote their official doctrines and policies while hiding their actual behavior. Thus, they keep their violations of societal principles out of the public consciousness and off society's agenda of issues. The opposition is tiny and feels hopeless because it believes that the problem will continue indefinitely, and it feels powerless to change it. Beneath the calm surface, however, the contradictions between the powerholders' actual practices and society's cherished principles and values hold the seeds for popular discontent that can ultimately create dramatic changes.

STAGE TWO: PROVE THE FAILURE OF OFFICIAL INSTITUTIONS

 Difficult Beginnings: The birth of every new venture begins in some confusion, because we are entering the realm of the unknown. It is our duty to act, but we lack sufficient power; we must take the first step.

(From the *I Ching*, "Book of Changes")

The intensity of public feeling, opinion and upset required for social movements to take off can happen only when the public realizes that governmental policies violate widely held beliefs, principles, and values. The public's upset is intensified when official authorities violate the public trust by using the power of office to deceive the public and govern unjustly and unlawfully. According to philosopher Hannah Arendt, "people are more likely driven to action by the unveiling of hypocrisy than by the prevailing conditions."[2]

Opposition

The opposition must prove that the problem exists and that the official power-holders and institutions actually participate in creating and perpetuating the problem. Therefore, the opposition must gather concrete facts and evidence through extensive research. It needs to prove that the actual practices of governmental powerholders and institutions violate society's values and the public trust.

The opposition must also attempt to use every official avenue, supposedly available for official citizen participation in the democratic process, to influence social policies and programs related to the problem being addressed. This includes going to every pertinent decision-making body, whether you are welcome or not, to prove that they do not work. It means testifying, challenging, and filing complaints in every branch of the bureaucratic machinery at the local, state, and federal levels of both public and private bodies. This effort may also include filing legal suits in the courts and taking concerns to city, state, and national legislators.

Don't expect positive results immediately. The goal is not to win the cases now, but to prove that the powerholders and the institutional bureaucracy are actually preventing the democratic system from working. Eventually, however, some of these legal or parliamentary cases might actually be won and create social change directly. After 20 years of filing cases in the courts, for example, the NAACP Legal Defense Fund's case of *Brown vs. Board of Education of Topeka* was won in the Supreme Court in 1954. It established the principle that "separate but equal" was no longer the law of the land and provided a legal basis for the school integration movement, as well as the broader civil rights movement that followed.

Powerholders

The powerholders fight the opposition through the normal channels, usually winning easily, while continuing their actual policies and programs. The power-holders do not feel threatened or concerned at this stage and treat the challenges using *bureaucratic management.* They deal quietly with citizen complaints by using the existing formal channels and offices, extending the "red tape" as far as needed. Normally, citizens eventually become frustrated and give up, ending the problem for the powerholders, who thereby successfully keep the whole potential problem out of the public's consciousness.

Public

Public opinion continues to support the government's official policies and the status quo, as the consciousness of the majority population remains unchanged. Yet even the low level of opposition causes public opinion against these policies to rise from about 10 to 20 percent. Except for the rare media coverage of opponents' activities, or the powerholders' condemnation of them, the problem is still neither in the public spotlight nor on society's agenda of contested issues.

Goals

The movement's goals in this stage are –
- to document the problem, including the extent to which the powerholders and institutions are involved;
- to record the attempts to use the normal channels for citizen participation in the democratic institutions related to the specific issue of concern, and to prove that they did not work;
- to become experts; and
- to build new opposition organizations that start small, grow, and spread to many new areas.

Pitfalls

The major movement pitfalls at this stage are –
- believing that social problems can be corrected solely by POOs using mainstream institutions and methods;
- not mobilizing widespread grassroots opposition; and
- continuing to feel powerless and hopeless because the system is not working the way it is supposed to and the powerholders and institutions seem so intractable.

Crisis

The crisis that ends Stage Two occurs when grassroots activists understand that the normal function of the powerholders, the political system, public institutions, and their procedures violates the public trust in them. Then they realize that extra-parliamentary political action will be needed to seriously address the problem and bring about social change.

Conclusions

This stage can be particularly disheartening. The problem and the policies of powerholders continue unabated, there is little public dissent or publicity, and the situation seems like it might continue indefinitely — as indeed it might. Yet the efforts of the opposition in this stage can eventually be used to prove that the emperor has no clothes and serve to bolster the movement in later stages. To survive this stage you must be stouthearted, determined, and persistent.

STAGE THREE: RIPENING CONDITIONS

 Assembling: This is a time of gathering together of people in communities. Strong bonds must be maintained by adherence to appropriate moral principles. Only collective moral force can unite the world.

(From the *I Ching*, "Book of Changes")

Before a new social movement "takes off," the appropriate conditions must build up over time, usually over many years. These conditions include the necessary context of historic developments; a growing, discontented population of victims and their allies; and a budding, autonomous, grassroots opposition. Together these elements work synergistically, or with more force than they would have separately, to encourage discontent with the present conditions and policies and raise expectations that they, as concerned citizens, can create change.

The historical forces are usually long-term, broad trends and events that worsen the problem, upset sub-populations, raise expectations, personify the problem, and promote the means for new activism. Some are outside the control of the opposition. For example, in the 1960s conditions were ripe for the black civil rights movement. The United States government was touting the ideology of freedom and democracy around the world in order to challenge communism and win over the newly emerged independent black African countries. In addition, a large northern migration of blacks, and the integration of blacks into the military at the end of World War II, made it increasingly difficult to maintain segregation. Finally, the 1954 Supreme Court's *Brown vs. Board of Education of Topeka* school integration decision provided a legal basis for full civil rights.

Opposition

A tremendous unheralded ripening process happens within the opposition movement. A growing consciousness and discontent arise among the sub-populations of victims and their allies. They achieve a new level of understanding the seriousness of the problem, the violations of critical widely held values, how they are affected, and the illicit involvement of the powerholders and their institutions.

This discontent can be caused by –

- **Perceived or actual worsening conditions:** For example, the building of hundreds of new atomic plant sites in the 1970s upset tens of millions of Americans who lived nearby.
- **Rising expectations:** For example, the new wave of black college students in the 1960s, who felt themselves to be full citizens, was refused the simple civil right of service at lunch counters.
- **Personalization of the problem:** For example, the Life magazine photographs of the 100 American soldiers killed in Vietnam or the murder of four church women in El Salvador in 1980 made these conflicts real to the mainstream majority population.

The growing numbers of discontented people across the country quietly start new, small, autonomous local groups, which together form a "new wave" of grassroots opposition that is independent from the established POOs. These groups soon become frustrated with the official institutions, channels, and powerholders, which they realize are biased in support of the status quo. Simultaneously, they become increasingly upset with many of the established POOs, which they come to see as working in a dead-end process with the powerholders.

In this stage, small local demonstrations and nonviolent action *campaigns* begin to dramatize the problem, placing a dim public spotlight on it. These demonstrations will serve as prototypes for direct action in the next stage. In addition, new websites, email listservs, and a few key traveling visionaries alert, arouse, inspire, and incite the broadening wave of local opposition groups with information, analyses, ideologies, strategy and tactics, training, networking, hope, and a vision of a rising opposition. It is also critical that pre-existing key networks and groups are available to provide support, resources, organizers and strategists, solidarity, and additional participants for the upcoming new movement. In the civil rights movement the black churches and colleges served this function. In the current anti-corporate globalization movement, pre-existing organizations such as Public Citizen, the Council of Canadians, Global Exchange, and the Ruckus Society, to name but a few, were available and jumped in.

Powerholders

Though irritated, the powerholders remain relatively unconcerned, believing that they can contain the opposition through strong management of the pertinent mainstream social, political, economic, and media institutions. The official policies remain unchallenged in the public arena, and the great majority of citizens therefore continue to believe in them, leaving the actual policies hidden from the general populace.

Public

The public consensus supports the powerholders' policies and practices, as the problem remains off society's agenda. Yet, primarily at the local level, there is a growing public awareness of the problem, a new wave of opposition, and a discontent regarding the powerholders. Consequently, public opinion opposing the current powerholder policies and practices quietly rises to 30 percent.

Goals

The purpose of this stage is to help create the conditions for the take-off phase of the social movement. The goals for the movement are –

- to help create and recognize the emergence of a variety of ripening conditions that set the stage for the movement to take off;
- to create, inspire, and prepare the new wave of individuals and groups by forming new networks, offering leadership training, and providing expertise;
- to prepare pre-existing networks and groups that will be concerned about the issue and involved in the upcoming movement;
- to personalize the problem by putting faces on the statistics about victims; and
- to create small, nonviolent demonstrations and campaigns that can serve as prototype models and a training ground for the take-off stages.

Pitfalls

Some of the key hazards of this stage include –
- becoming discouraged, and losing new activists, because the ripening conditions for a new social movement were not recognized; and
- allowing the bureaucracy, legalism, and centralized power of the leading POOs to squash the creativity, independence, and spontaneity of the new grassroots groups.

Crisis

The number of grassroots activists and groups grows larger, and people become increasingly upset and frustrated by both the problem they are concerned about and the mainstream educational and parliamentary methods they have been using to address it. Their upset and frustration grows to the bursting point.

Conclusions

The stage is set for the take-off of a new social movement. There is a critical problem that appears to be worsening, proven violations by the powerholders, many victims, spreading discontent, supportive historical conditions, pre-existing networks, and an emerging new wave of grassroots opposition. Yet no one — not the public, the powerholders, or even the new wave of activists — suspects the giant new social movement that is about to erupt onto the scene.

STAGE FOUR: TAKE-OFF

 Critical Mass: It is a momentous time of excess of strong elements. One takes courageous acts not by force, but by seeking true meaning to accomplish the task, no matter what happens. Maintain alliance with those below. It is like floodtimes, which are only temporary.

(From the *I Ching,* "Book of Changes")

New social movements surprise and shock everyone when they burst into the public spotlight on the evening TV news and in newspaper headlines. Overnight, a previously unrecognized social problem becomes a social issue that everyone is talking about. It starts with a highly publicized, shocking incident, a *trigger event,* followed by a nonviolent action campaign that includes large rallies, marches, and dramatic acts of civil disobedience that are soon repeated in local communities around the country or overseas.

The trigger event is an incident that dramatically reveals a critical social problem to the general public in a vivid way. It is like the arrest of Rosa Parks for refusing to move to the back of a bus in Montgomery, Alabama; like NATO's December 12, 1979, announcement that it would deploy American cruise and Pershing 2 nuclear weapons in Europe; or like the Seattle demonstrations against the World Trade Organization in November and December of 1999. Trigger events can be accidents or planned acts by the powerholders, individuals, or the movement.

The trigger event starkly reveals to the general public for the first time that a serious social problem exists and that deliberate policies and practices of the powerholders cause and perpetuate the problem by violating widely held societal values and the public's trust. The event instills a profound sense of moral outrage within a majority of the general citizenry. Consequently, the public responds with great passion, demanding an explanation from the powerholders, and is ready to hear more information from the movement. Many people join nonviolent demonstrations for the first time. The trigger event also acts like a trumpet's call to action for the new wave of local movement opposition groups that built up around the country during the previous stage.

Movement

The new social movement takes off when the activist opposition organizes a non-violent action campaign immediately following the trigger event, and the nonviolent actions are then repeated across the country and possibly in other nations as well. The nonviolent actions can take a variety of forms, such as mass rallies and marches, boycotts, strikes, and sit-ins, and often include civil disobedience at selected times and places. The nonviolent actions keep the public spotlight on the problem and build social tension over time. This "politics as theater" process creates a public social crisis that transforms a social problem into a critical public issue that is put on society's agenda of hotly debated issues.

The success of the movement in this stage is greatly enhanced by the use of *sociodrama action campaigns.* These are dramatic and exciting yet simple demonstrations in which participants put themselves physically into the gears and mechanisms of the means by which the powerholders actually carry out their policies related to the problem. Sociodrama demonstrations clearly reveal to the public how the powerholders violate society's widely held values and show that it is the movement, not the powerholders, that promotes and represents the values, principles, and traditions of the society. They usually conclude with nonviolent civil disobedience and are repeated in many different communities across the country and in other countries, if appropriate.

These are *dilemma demonstrations,* in which the powerholders lose public support regardless of their reaction. If they ignore the demonstrators, they are prevented from carrying out the policies. If, on the other hand, the demonstrators are harassed, attacked, or arrested by the police or military, the issue is kept in the public spotlight and public sympathy for the demonstrators increases, while disdain for the powerholders rises. The number of demonstrators often increases as more citizens are stirred to action.

For example, during the 1960s restaurant sit-ins, blacks sat at the segregated lunch counters throughout the U.S. South to eat. When white crowds attacked them and the police arrested them, the public got upset and sided with the demonstrators. However, if the police did nothing, the students either had to be served or would just sit there occupying the seats. The restaurant owners had to choose whether to serve the sit-in students or lose business and potentially go bankrupt.

This dynamic is sometimes called nonviolent jujitsu, because the overwhelming force of government sanctions and police power is turned around against the government itself. The more force the powerholders exert on the movement, the bigger the opposition to the powerholder institution that is initiating the attack. For this to work, however, activists must be totally nonviolent.

The new movement takes off as the nonviolent action campaigns and their sociodrama actions are repeated in communities across the country. The demonstration in Seattle, for example, was followed by demonstrations in Washington, D.C.; Philadelphia; Los Angeles; and elsewhere. The 1977 occupation of the Seabrook nuclear reactor site created spontaneous support and copycat demonstrations across the United States. Within months, hundreds of new grassroots anti-nuclear energy groups started up and soon began occupying their own local nuclear power plant sites.

Movement take-off is the result of thousands of people across the country taking spontaneous actions and forming new protest groups (or revitalizing old ones). These new groups usually adopt loose organizational structures that are based on direct participatory democracy, minimal formal structure, consensus decision-making, and loosely defined membership. Together these groups form a new nonviolent action wave of the movement; a new force that is not formally connected to either the established POOs or the traditional ideological dissent groups. Because the predominant method used at this time is protest and resistance, the take-off stage is often identified with the rebel role of activism.

Why do Social Movements Take Off?

First, social movements take off because the right conditions were created in the earlier three stages. Second, the trigger event and the nonviolent action campaigns alert the public that there is a problem, and the public becomes outraged at the contradiction between society's cherished values and principles and the actual policies and behavior of the powerholders. Third, a new climate of social crisis and public awakening gives hope to many latent citizen activists and inspires them to action. Fourth, the repeatability of the nonviolent actions gives the grassroots activists an effective means by which to be actively engaged on an issue. Finally, many people join because it gives meaning to their lives and gives them an opportunity to act on their beliefs.

There is a danger of POOs preventing movement take-off at this stage. The large budgets, professional staff, boards of directors that include or have direct or indirect connections with mainstream institutions and powerholders, and reliance on foundations for funding make almost all of the large POOs politically cautious and on the conservative side of the political spectrum of the left. Organizational maintenance needs may, understandably, take precedence over political action choices. In this regard, POOs are the opposite of the new wave rebels with their informal, low-budget groups that organize nonviolent actions and civil disobedience following the trigger event. POOs across the country can carve up the geographical turf of the nation, claim an ideological politically correct line, and accuse any rebel groups that arise of being politically incorrect, thereby undercutting their validity.

Powerholders

The powerholders are shocked, upset, and angry. The genie is out of the bottle. They realize that they have lost out on the three laws of political and social control:
- Keep the problem out of people's consciousness, out of the public spotlight, and off society's agenda of hotly contested issues.
- Keep the citizenry so discouraged and powerless that they believe it is futile to undertake social activism on the issue.
- Keep individual citizens isolated from each other and seeking personal gain rather than working for the common good.

Powerholders take a hard line in defending their policies and criticize the new movement, describing it as radical, dangerous, communist inspired, violent, led by outsiders, and irresponsible. A mere handful of elected politicians support the movement, while most mainstream politicians continue to support existing powerholder policies and programs.

Public

The public is alerted and educated by the movement through coverage in the media and by face-to-face contact with the new wave of activism at the grassroots level across the country. The extensive media coverage of the trigger event and the movement's dramatic nonviolent demonstrations not only makes the public aware of the social problem, but also conveys the social movement's position for the first time. Until now, the public has only heard the official line of the powerholders. Because of the stark contradiction, exposed during the take-off stage, between the powerholders' actual policies and society's widely held principles and values, public opinion rapidly rises to 40 percent and then over 50 percent against the powerholders' actual policies.

Goals

Some of the specific goals of this stage are –
- to create a new nationwide grassroots-based social movement;
- to put the powerholders' actual policies and practices in the public spotlight and on society's agenda of important issues;
- to create a public platform from which the movement can educate the general public;
- to create public dissonance on the issue by constantly presenting people with two contradictory views of reality — that of the movement and that of the powerholders;

- to win the sympathies and the opinions of a majority of the public; and
- to become recognized as the legitimate opposition.

It is *not* a goal or expectation to get the powerholders to change their minds, policies, or behavior in this stage.

Pitfalls

The chief movement pitfalls of this stage are –
- political naivety – expecting the powerholders to cave in because of the size of the opposition;
- burnout, depression, and dropout from the movement because of unrealistic expectations that the social movement would win in this stage;
- failure to see the take-off stage as a monumental success in the process of winning; and
- developing an attitude of arrogant self-righteousness, ideological absolutism, violence, and self-importance.

Crisis

The take-off stage is normally the shortest stage, typically lasting between six months to two years. After this dramatic and exciting period, an increasing number of activists realize the limits of protest and the rebel role as the movement's primary mode. In addition, the vast numbers of mainstream citizens joining the movement at the local level become engaged in the change agent work of local organizing and public education. At the same time, many of the rebel activists despair because their expectations of winning quickly through nonviolent direct actions were disappointed.

Conclusion

The take-off stage is an exciting time, with a trigger event, dramatic actions, high passion, a new social movement in the public spotlight, social tension that creates a crisis of society's values and principles, and high output of energy. It also is the signature stage of the rebel. A previously unrecognized social problem and the powerholders' actual policies both become known, creating a new public issue. Within two years the movement wins majority public opinion and progresses to Stage Six. Unfortunately, a large percentage of activists, particularly many rebels, don't recognize this process as success. Instead, they take it as a sign that the movement has failed and their own efforts have been futile. Consequently, many rebels and naive activists move to Stage Five.

STAGE FIVE: PERCEPTION OF FAILURE

 Retreat: You may now be suffering from an inner conflict based upon the misalignment of your ideals and reality. It is time to retreat and take a longer look to be able to advance later. Vengeance and hatred could cloud your judgment and prevent the necessary retreat.

(From the *I Ching*, "Book of Changes")

The perception of failure happens just when the movement is outrageously successful. By the end of Stage Four the movement as a whole has achieved all the goals of the take-off stage and has successfully progressed to Stage Six — Majority Public Opinion – but some movement activists do not share in this success.

Movement

After a year or two, the high hopes of instant victory in the movement take-off stage inevitably turn into despair as some activists begin to believe that their movement is failing. It has not achieved its goals and, in their eyes, it has not had any "real" victories. They come to believe that the powerholders are too strong and are determined not to change their policies. Moreover, the powerholders and the mass media report that the movement is dead, irrelevant, or nonexistent. Activists in Stage Five also believe that the movement is dead because it no longer looks like it did at the start of the take-off stage: the numbers at demonstrations and civil disobedience actions have dropped substantially. Many Stage Five activists develop cynical attitudes and some turn to destructive behavior.

The problem, however, is not that the movement has failed to achieve its goals, but that activists had unrealistic expectations that the long-term goals could be achieved in such a short time. The despairing activists are unable to look at the movement from this point of view and acknowledge the progress that it has made along the road of success — creating a massive grassroots-based social movement, putting the issue on society's agenda, and winning a majority of public opinion.

Ironically, involvement in the movement tends to reduce activists' ability to identify short-term successes. Through the movement, activists learn about the enormity of the problem, the agonizing suffering of the victims, and the complicity of the previously trusted powerholders. The intensity of this experience tends to increase despair and unwillingness to accept any successes short of achieving ultimate goals.

However, the powerholders' failure to change either their minds or their policies is a poor indicator of the movement's progress. The powerholders will be the last segment of society to change their minds and policies, but the longer the public sees the powerholders violating societal values and ignoring the democratic majority opinion, the higher the political costs will be for the powerholders continuing those policies.

The image that most people have of a vital and effective social movement is of the take-off stage — giant demonstrations, civil disobedience, media hype, crisis, and constant political theater — but this is always short-lived. Movements that are successful in take-off soon progress to the much more powerful, but more sedate, majority stage (described below). Although movements in the majority stage appear to be smaller and less effective as they move from high-profile mass actions to less visible grassroots organizing, they actually undergo enormous growth in size and power. The extensive, seemingly invisible involvement at the grassroots level gives the movement its power at the national and international levels.

At this time, many activists burn out or drop out because of exhaustion caused by overwork and long meetings; too many internal organizational crises and conflicts; extended militant actions; movement violence; and feelings of failure, hopelessness, and powerlessness. In addition, most are unable to pace themselves and give themselves adequate rest, leisure, fun, and attendance to personal needs. Another reason why many activists become depressed at this time is that they are unable to switch their view of the movement's process of success from protest and mass demonstrations to winning over the public. Some joined the movement for a quick fix, assuming it was for a short-term period of crisis, and they are not prepared for the long-term involvement and drudgery needed for grassroots organizing.

Consequently, as the majority of activists shifts into Stage Six organizing, many rebels believe that the real movement is being abandoned. In frustration, some adopt more aggressive and combative attitudes and macho behavior, including violence, because they believe nonviolence has failed to produce results. Some create splinter groups dedicated to combative actions, as the Committee for Direct Action at the Seabrook nuclear plant site did in 1979, alleging that the movement organization had itself become conservative or oppressive.

One of the mistaken arguments used to support negative rebel activities is that because rebels are so militant, they make the mainstream movement look mild and more acceptable to the general population. Quite the contrary is true. Destructive activities turn off both other activists and the public; they invariably do more harm than good for the movement. These methods are also advocated by agents provocateurs who want to destroy the movement or use it to pursue their own purposes.

Finally, many activists are unable to switch to Stage Six because they do not have the knowledge and skills required to understand, participate in, and organize the majority stage. For example, nonviolence trainers traditionally play a critical leadership and teaching role regarding nonviolent protest actions during movement take-off. Unfortunately, they virtually disappear in the majority stage, because they have neither the understanding nor the skills to train activists in how to participate in the next stages of social movement success.

Powerholders

The powerholders try to discredit the movement by publicly condemning the negative rebels and militant activities. They might alternate good cop and bad cop tactics. On some occasions, the police may adhere to a nonviolent strategy themselves to project a public image of restraint and to win public acceptance. At other times they will use massive and excessive force against the movement, especially against negative rebels or key leaders. This provokes more negative rebel responses and scares the general public, which, fearing the "dangerous" actions of the movement, continues to support the powerholders.

The mainstream media typically characterizes the movement as the negative rebel. If 10,000 people are in a nonviolent demonstration and 10 break a department store window or throw stones at the police, that movement violence will be the front-page photo in tomorrow's newspaper or the lead story on the television news. At this stage, powerholder agents provocateurs may infiltrate the movement to create dissension and discord and turn the public against the movement.

Public

The general populace experiences dissonance during the take-off stage, not knowing who or what to believe. While many agree with the movement's challenges, they also fear siding with dissidents and losing the security of the powerholders and the status quo. At this point, the general citizenry is about evenly divided between the powerholders and the movement.

Movement violence, rebelliousness, and, in the U.S., what seem to be anti-American attitudes tend to turn people off and frighten them back into supporting the powerholders. They cause many concerned people to drop out or not join the movement. The public does not distinguish between the negative rebels and the movement's nonviolent mainstream. Therefore, it is the conscious strategy of the powerholders and media to equate the negative rebels with the mainstream of the movement to discredit the movement in the eyes of the public and drive the citizenry back into supporting the existing order. This is one of the reasons why the negative rebel is so harmful and needs to be actively guarded against.

Goals

The primary goal of the movement is to help those activists stuck in Stage Five to catch up with their social movement and move on to Stage Six. Activists in Stage Five should –

- recognize that the movement has progressed to Stage Six and adopt a role that is appropriate to that stage; and
- use the strategic movement frameworks of MAP to evaluate the movement, identify successes, and develop short-term strategies and tactics that fit in with long-term goals and the normal process of success.

The movement itself should –

- create effective and efficient democratic organizational structures and group dynamic processes;
- train activists in the Four Roles Model so they learn the difference between effective and ineffective ways of playing the four roles and to respect those playing different roles;
- adopt a strict policy of nonviolence and counter the negative rebel tendencies that first arise late in Stage Four and bloom in Stage Five; and
- provide activists with training to help them switch from a controlling to a cooperative model of relationships.

In order to guide and train activists for the long haul, the movement needs to change its organizational structure. There are three organizational archetypes: hierarchical, loose or anarchistic, and participatory democratic

In their eagerness to stop being hierarchical and oppressive, groups mistakenly believe that the alternative is no structures or leaders. No structure or rules is not democracy, but disaster, in which the most oppressive and controlling people dominate the group.

At first the anarchistic loose structure provides the freedom for flexibility, creativity, participatory democracy, independence, and solidarity needed for quick decisions and radical nonviolent actions, including civil disobedience, especially at the beginning of the take-off stage. But it becomes a liability after three months. Thereafter, the loose organizational structure tends to cause excessive inefficiency, participant burnout, and group domination by the most domineering and oppressive participants. The decision-making process resembles capitalism's rugged individualism in the free market more than the ideology of participatory democracy. Democratic organizations need structure and rules, but ones that promote participation and leadership.

Pitfalls

There are many pitfalls for the movement in Stage Five, chiefly:

- People are unable to see that the movement is in the process of success.
- There are feelings of disempowerment, despair, and burnout.
- Negative rebel attitudes and actions take center stage.
- There is a tendency to ideological totalism, with some activists maintaining that their view is the politically correct belief and that their way is the only way.
- Some activists impose the "tyranny of structurelessness" with their belief that democracy and freedom mean no organizational structures or leadership.
- The movement fails to make the transition from a Stage Four protest to a Stage Six social change movement.

Crisis

This stage emerges while the movement is still in the take-off stage and continues for some years during the time that the rest of the movement progresses to the majority public opinion stage. The perception of failure has a heyday of one or two years, during which it garners a lot of media attention. It is a short stage, however. It rapidly fades away either because its members become burned out and drop out, or they recognize the futility or downright harmfulness of this approach and join the movement by adopting Stage Six-appropriate activities.

Conclusion

The crisis of identity and powerlessness is a personal experience for many activists who mistakenly believe that their movement has failed and do not realize that it is actually in the normal process of success. Movement leaders can reduce the feelings of despair and disempowerment by providing activists with a long-term strategic framework, such as the MAP Eight Stages Model, to help them realize that they are powerful and their movement is winning, not losing. The movement also needs to adopt clear guidelines of total nonviolence for participants, and these must be widely publicized and agreed to by everyone involved in movement-sponsored activities. Moreover, such nonviolent policies need to be enforced by arranging training in nonviolence for all demonstration participants and by having adequate "peacekeeping" structures and methods at all demonstrations.

Activists need to realize what the powerholders already know — that political and societal power ultimately lies with the people, not the powerholders. They need to recognize when their own social movement is powerful and progressing along the normal path of success. Negative rebels need to realize the harmful effects of this role and adopt a more effective manner of activism. Activists can help themselves mature by forming support groups to take care of their personal needs, reduce guilt, have fun, avoid isolation, and understand and help create the movement's strategy and tactics.

STAGE SIX: MAJORITY PUBLIC OPINION

Changing: The forces at work are in conflict, leaving the path open to change. Far-reaching clarity about the future and great devotion are required. The transformation should be made gradually, nonviolently, without discordant and excessive behavior. The results lead to a progressive new era but are not evident until the change has already occurred.

(From the *I Ching,* "Book of Changes")

In Stage Six, the movement's primary mission is transformed from protest in crisis to creating social change through a long-term grassroots struggle with the powerholders. The change agent replaces the rebel as the movement's predominant active player. Increasingly, the movement wins the backing of a larger share of the public, which now opposes current policies and considers alternatives. The majority stage is usually a long process of eroding the social, political, and economic supports that enable the powerholders to carry out their policies. It is a slow process of imperceptible social transformation that creates a new social climate and political consensus, reversing those that existed during the normal times stage.

Movement

The movement needs to wage a Stage Six grand strategy. Too often strategy has meant filling a calendar of events with a conglomeration of unconnected campaigns, educational activities, and reactions to new powerholder policies. An effective Stage Six grand strategy, however, also includes a set of strategic programs, new organization and leadership models, and strategic goals that will take the movement through twelve phases that lead to Stage Seven.

Strategic Program

- **Massive public education and conversion.** The basic purpose of the movement in this stage is to educate, convert, and involve all segments of the population. This is accomplished through a broad variety of means, including public speaking, information tables at supermarkets, leafleting, and demonstrations, all based on face-to-face education of citizens by their peers to keep the issue before the public.

- **Grassroots organizations.** The key to Stage Six success is ultimately the ongoing, day-in and day-out basic organizing efforts of local activists, which include constant outreach and involvement of the local citizenry. This can only be done by a wide variety of local organizations with relatively few paid staff but a large number of volunteers.
- **Redefine the problem to show how it affects all segments of society.** To win over the great majority of the population, the movement needs to show each segment of society that together they make up that majority. They need to show each of these constituencies – parents, students, workers, the unemployed, teachers, police, home owners, renters, homeless, elderly, women, racial minorities, etc. – how the current powerholder policies violate their particular values, principles, and self-interest, and what they can do about it.
- **Build a broad-based movement organizational structure.** The movement's organizational structure needs to be pluralistic, including all segments of society by involving organizations, coalitions, and networks in the movement in a wide variety of ways, sometimes alone, sometimes together by, for example, co-sponsoring events. The movement also needs to include people and organizations that are effectively performing all four roles of activism: citizen, rebel, change agent, and reformer.
- **Make effective use of mainstream political and social institutions and processes.** As the movement wins more support, it can successfully use the mainstream channels of political participation. Organizations and members can now approach city councils, government and private institutional officials, and candidates; attend commission meetings and hearings; and develop ballot measures with increasing effectiveness. While the use of mainstream institutional structures and procedures serves to educate the public and further build the movement, it also can win actual judicial, political, and legislative victories. These successes prepare the way for the movement's ultimate victory over many years. For example, nuclear energy plants have been halted at the local and state levels, even though the central government and the entire nuclear industry still maintain the goal of building more nuclear power plants.
- **Selective use of nonviolent action activities.** Although nonviolent actions sometimes result in immediate successes, their chief purpose is to help achieve the goals of the particular stage of the movement. By Stage Six the movement will have a wide range of methods and programs, but it must continue to use nonviolent actions, rallies, campaigns, and, occasionally, civil disobedience when necessary or helpful. Because people are involved in so many different programs in this stage, and many no longer see the need or purpose of nonviolent demonstrations, the numbers participating in any particular national or local demonstration usually drop well below the sizes of the big demonstrations

that occurred during the take-off stage. However, when movements are in the majority stage, the total number of people participating in demonstrations nationwide in any year actually increases because these actions are happening in hundreds of local communities around the country, on several different sub-issues.

- **Citizen involvement programs.** The movement needs to develop programs in which large numbers of mainstream citizens and institutions perform activities that directly violate the powerholders' policies and programs. Citizen involvement programs differ from traditional demonstrations. They may provide services to victims; challenge current traditions, policies, laws, and practices; promote the principles or values that lie at the heart of the issue; and model an alternative or carry out the alternatives being sought. This empowers citizens and energizes the movement because people can take ethical action on the issue without having to wait for the government or corporations to change their laws and policies.

The classic example of citizen involvement was Gandhi's program for Indians to make salt from the sea or spin their own thread and make their own clothes when the British forbade domestic manufacturing of salt and clothes. The Sanctuary Movement in the United States in the 1980s is another example. At great risk to themselves, hundreds of local individuals, groups, churches, and towns throughout the country committed civil disobedience by providing sanctuary for political refugees from Central America at a time when the United States government was tracking down, arresting, and deporting them. These citizen involvement programs educate and convert the public, demonstrate the alternative values and policies, publicly show the extent of popular opposition, undercut the authority of the powerholders to carry out their policy goals, and build change from the grassroots upwards.

- **Respond to "re-trigger events."** *Re-trigger events* are trigger events that happen in Stages Six, Seven, or Eight. Two examples are the nuclear power plant accidents at Three-Mile Island (1979) and Chernobyl (1986) that occurred two and nine years respectively after the 1977 occupation of the Seabrook reactor site launched the take-off of the anti-nuclear power movement. Re-trigger events touch off a replay of the take-off stage. The incident creates a public crisis that thrusts the issue back into the headlines and public spotlight. Activists quickly organize mass rallies and demonstrations, new levels of public education and conversion occur, and there is increased pressure on the powerholders to take remedial action. This replay of Stage Four may last for weeks or months; then the movement settles back into Stage Six at a higher level of public support and increased determination.

Organization and Leadership Models

As the movement progresses from take-off to majority public opinion, the organization and leadership styles need to be transformed to follow a participatory democratic model. This organizational arrangement maximizes the advantages and minimizes the disadvantages of both the oppressive hierarchical and the spontaneous anarchistic models. Participatory democratic organizations need *more* structures and effective process methods than the traditional models to be efficient, flexible, and enduring.

Similarly, Stage Six is a critical period for the staff and programs of the national, regional, and local organizations that have been created by the new movement to coordinate and consolidate the efforts of the numerous local groups. The danger lies in their becoming traditional POOs that put egos, careers, and organizational maintenance ahead of the needs of the movement. If the organization's staff behave as if *they* are the movement, the grassroots dry up and the movement loses its power. The primary goal of movement POOs, therefore, should be to serve, nurture, and empower the grassroots and to promote participatory democracy in their own organization and the movement as a whole.

Strategic Goals

To wage Stage Six effectively, activists need to know the strategic goals for this phase of the movement. If there is no viable set of strategic goals, activists will be unable to see a relationship between their day-to-day activities and the process to achieve the movement's ultimate goal. Each movement will have specific goals, but the following are strategies common to most movements.

- **Keep the issue in the public spotlight and on society's agenda over time.** A fundamental goal for the movement is to keep the powerholder policies and resulting social conditions that violate the principles, values, interests, and beliefs of the great majority of the populace in the public spotlight. Over time, this helps to build the social and political conditions for change, because telling the truth over and over serves to destroy social delusions. For example, for over ten years the anti-Vietnam war movement exposed the American public to the view that the United States was not fighting for democracy and freedom for the Vietnamese people, but was actually fighting against the people by supporting an oppressive military dictatorship. At the beginning, this view was ridiculed as being held by only the radical left fringe; eventually it became the majority opinion.

- **Remember that the movement's primary audience is the general citizenry, not the powerholders.** The movement's foremost goal is not to change the minds of the powerholders, but to convince and involve the general citizenry. The powerholders respond to the demands of an educated, upset, aroused, and active public, not to social activists, no matter how right they may be.

• **Identify each of the movement's key demands and their respective sub-movements and develop separate strategies and tactics for each.** Social movements usually have a broad, ultimate goal, such as to achieve universal health care, or win full civil and human rights for women, African Americans, disabled people, lesbians and gays, or children. It will take these social movements years and decades to achieve their ultimate goals. The process of success involves identifying and achieving sub-goals along the way, such as winning the right to vote, to eat at restaurants, to ride buses, and to receive equal education. Each of these sub-goals has its own sub-movement, which is in its own separate MAP stage. When a new social movement progresses to Stage Six, many more sub-goals emerge, each with its own sub-movement.

• **Guide the movement through the dynamics of conflict with the powerholders.** Waging a social movement is similar to playing chess. Activists and powerholders constantly engage in the tactics of moves and countermoves as part of a larger strategy to win the public and build conditions to support their own position. The movement tries to build moral and political conditions that will erode the public support that enables the powerholders to continue their policies. The powerholders, on the other hand, keep changing their policies to maintain the status quo. The movement's goal is to keep weakening the powerholders' position and raising the social, political, and economic cost that the powerholders must pay to continue their policies.

• **Promote alternatives that go beyond mere reforms and include a paradigm shift.** The movement not only needs to protest present policies, but must also propose specific alternatives. In the process of struggle, activists learn that the problem is much bigger than they had thought. They come to realize that their original concerns were merely symptoms of much bigger and deeper structural problems; consequently, the movement keeps making broader demands. This ultimately includes the necessity to advocate a whole new worldview or paradigm. For example, when the women's movement became aware of how many women were abused at home, it became clear that society's beliefs about intimate relationships needed to change as much as the limited social roles for women did.

Twelve Phases of Stage Six

Stage Six is often a difficult time for activists. The excitement, high hopes, big demonstrations, nonviolent actions, and media coverage of the take-off stage have subsided. The powerholders, experts, and even many activists claim that the movement has died. The vibrant rebel and the protest efforts have been replaced by a larger number of isolated organizations and events that many believe are not getting anywhere. The social problems and powerholder policies continue, or even worsen. Consequently, this can be a discouraging time, despite the beehive of activity and full calendar of events.

The reality of a successful movement in Stage Six is quite different from this common perception. In the majority public opinion stage, successful social movements progress through a series of twelve developmental phases in which the movement slowly, almost imperceptibly, builds the social conditions that will eventually lead to success in Stage Seven. That success is first reached by some of the critical sub-goals and their sub-movements. Eventually, the fundamental goal of the overall movement is won. Knowing the phases in this process can help activists be more hopeful, empowered, happy, and capable of deliberately creating appropriate strategies and tactics that will successfully guide the movement through Stage Six.

1. **The issue is put on society's social agenda — and kept there.** The key to democratization of an issue and the effectiveness of a social movement is to put the problem on both the social and political agendas and keep it there over a long period. Putting an issue in society's public spotlight and on the political agenda apparently takes the movement 75 percent of the way toward success.[3] With the problem in the public spotlight, time is on the side of the movement as people are being alerted to, educated on, and involved in the issue. These are all essential elements of the movement's democratization strategy for resolving a social problem.

    On the other hand, the powerholders' first line of defense for their policies and the status quo is anti-democratic. They aim to keep the issue out of the public spotlight and off the social and political agendas. They know that their position tends to deteriorate under long-term public scrutiny. Powerholders are most effective when issues are out of the public arena.

2. **The movement wins a majority of public opinion against current powerholder policies.** The public opinion polls show that a majority opposes the current conditions and the policies of the powerholders on the basic problem. It is important to recognize, though, that while the majority of people may oppose current conditions and policies, they may not yet be ready to support new policies and programs advocated by the movement. In fact, they may agree with the movement's opposition to one policy, but then still support other policies that the movement opposes. And they may not yet support the alternative advocated by the movement. For example, people might oppose a U.S. invasion of Nicaragua, but they still favor the U.S. plan to send aid to the Contra "freedom fighters" who are trying to overthrow the democratically elected, Sandinista-led government.

3. **The powerholders change their strategy.** As old policies become discredited and opposed by a public majority, the powerholders adopt new ones, while still maintaining their original purposes and goals. For example, when the public majority opposed the Vietnam War, the United States government brought American troops home, but increased bombing and support for South Vietnam's war effort.

4. **The movement counters each new powerholder strategy.** The movement must build a majority public opinion in opposition to each new powerholder strategy. This process of countering each new powerholder strategy continues over many years. At any given time, the powerholders have a number of different strategies and programs that are all opposed by the movement, which is why the movement has sub-goals, each with its own sub-movement, to oppose the powerholders' key strategic policies.

5. **Many of the powerholders' new strategies are more difficult for them to achieve, thereby weakening their ability to continue their policies in the long run.** As the movement and public opinion oppose their old strategies, the powerholders are forced to adopt new, higher-risk, stopgap strategies that usually weaken their position and are more difficult to maintain in the long run. This is because most new powerholder strategies and policies are more obvious violations of the values and sensibilities of the public and are more easily exposed by the movement.

    Ronald Reagan's administration, for example, was prevented from adopting the traditional method of direct U.S. military intervention to overthrow Nicaragua's Sandinista government in the 1980s. It was forced to adopt the new strategy of developing the Contras as a puppet force to overthrow the Sandinistas, which in addition to being extremely costly and deadly, was also more difficult to carry out.

6. **Create strategic campaigns.** The movement needs to identify critical supports that the powerholders rely on to carry out their policies and then devise creative social action campaigns that reduce or eliminate this support. For example, the powerholders' goal of building a thousand nuclear power plants depended on a continual increase in electrical consumption, citizen support for nuclear energy, massive government subsidies and protections, and hundreds of billions of dollars up front to build the reactors. The anti-nuclear movement strategically launched programs to address each of these.

7. **Expand the issue and goals.** Movements start with a specific problem that people see as particularly offensive to their sensibilities and that motivates them to begin acting against it. As activists get involved with this problem, however, they learn of many others, some even bigger and more devastating than the first. The movement to stop an impending U.S. invasion of

Nicaragua, for example, rapidly expanded its goal to oppose all forms of U.S. intervention — not only in Nicaragua, but also in all of Central America.

For many activists, however, issue expansion can be discouraging and depressing. Instead of solving a serious problem, their movement activity has led them to realize that conditions are even worse than they had first understood – and that the government and corporations are behind it. Activists can alleviate these feelings somewhat by realizing that issue expansion is normal when their movements are progressing satisfactorily along the usual path of success in Stage Six.

8. **Win solid public opinion against current powerholder policies.** After years of education, debate, and confronting the powerholders' series of new, bogus strategies and public relations gimmicks, both activists and the general citizenry develop a stronger, deeper, and more informed opposition to powerholder policies.

9. **Promote solutions and a paradigm shift.** There is an advantage to the movement not winning too soon after the take-off stage. Many activists have not deeply considered anything beyond their moral and ethical objections to current policies. They have not taken a close look at the alternatives and their implications. On many issues it might take activists several years of involvement to become fully educated and to become clear about the alternatives. Therefore, not achieving the goals of a movement right at the start gives both activists and society as a whole the time needed to think through the issue, reject the series of unacceptable alternatives the powerholders propose, and generate appropriate alternatives.

The movement not only needs to advocate reforms to redress symptoms of social problems, but it especially needs to promote a paradigm shift, a change in the larger worldview that causes and maintains the problem. For example, it is not enough to oppose U.S. development of nuclear power; activists must also argue that rather than promoting maximum use of fossil fuel energy, the nation's energy policy should advocate minimizing fossil fuel energy use through conservation, efficiency, and solar alternatives.

10. **Win a majority of public opinion on the movement's proposed alternatives.** After the movement convinces the majority of the public that there is a serious social problem and the powerholders' policies are wrong, it must then convince the public to support the appropriate solutions. This requires another massive public education effort, using every possible means including public meetings, petition drives, leafleting, tables in business districts, and persuading key people and organizations to publicly stand with the movement.

11. **Put the issue on the political and legal agendas.** Now that there is a solid majority public opinion that both opposes the powerholders' policies and

favors positive alternatives, the movement can effectively use the mainstream political and legal structures and instruments to challenge the status quo with increasing success. The movement can successfully lobby politicians and political parties, promote or challenge existing candidates, run its own candidates, use referenda at the ballot box, promote large petition drives, or introduce lawsuits.

12. **The powerholders make dramatic shifts in their positions.** They retract earlier positions and policies, propose new "official" policies, and demonize the movement and its proposed solutions. For example, the powerholders first said that nuclear power was safe and too cheap to meter, but after a majority of people became educated and opposed it, the powerholders agreed that it had some safety problems and was costly. But without nuclear energy, they said, there would be blackouts and the economy would fail and the United States would lose its superpower status.

Powerholders

When the social movement enters the majority stage, the powerholders become seriously worried and engage in a prolonged *crisis management* strategy to promote their own policies and programs while simultaneously countering those of the movement. As always, their ultimate target is the hearts and minds of the general citizenry.

The powerholders use a wide array of strategies. The following are some of the most common ones.

- They strongly defend their existing policies, perhaps using new rhetoric to justify their societal myths and official programs.
- They engage in a dynamic process similar to a chess match with the movement. Each side makes moves and countermoves as they vie to convince the public that they are right.
- Increasingly, both government and corporate powerholders hire public relations firms, particularly those that specialize in the new field of "issues management," using vast amounts of money to orchestrate public relations campaigns that go far beyond the ones organized by the old "spin doctors."
- By the middle of Stage Six, the powerholders often co-opt many of the movement's goals, ideas, or rhetoric. That is, they adopt the words and concepts, such as "sustainability," "green," or "organic food," but only to confuse the public and reduce the effectiveness of the movement's use of the terms.
- Next they try to co-opt movement groups that are either politically far left negative rebels or more conservative reformers on the right end of the political spectrum, usually by providing them with funding. In addition, the powerholders create new bogus organizations that either oppose or support a cause;

these are called "astroturf coalitions," because they can be spontaneously rolled out to make an immediate impact on an issue and then rolled back up when no longer needed.

- Typically, the powerholders hire scientific, academic, political, or other professional experts on the issue to proclaim that the powerholders' policies and views are consistent with the considered views of the professional field. For example, there are many experts for hire who will proclaim that corporate globalization is the surest way to peace and prosperity.

- Industry and government stop funding experiments that undercut their policies, while giving enormous funding to scientific experiments and expert investigative commissions that support their views, such as those that conclude tobacco has not been proven to cause lung cancer, there is no proof of global warming, or cell phones are perfectly safe.

- By the later phases of Stage Six, powerholders also begin to engage in a negotiation process with the movement and other affected groups. This is mainly for show and to confuse, defuse, split, and co-opt the opposition. Any serious negotiation will not happen until Stage Seven.

- At this time, the powerholders often increase their more direct countermovement strategies in the form of various means of surveillance and intelligence gathering and the use of agents provocateurs to gather intelligence, discredit the movement, cause internal disruption, or to control and steer the movement.

Even as their position on the issue deteriorates, the powerholders keep pronouncing that their policies are correct and they are winning. Throughout the Vietnam war, for example, the U.S. government kept claiming that it "saw the light at the end of the tunnel" and all it needed was more time or more money. It repeated the claim that it was winning up until it lost the war.

Finally, when the powerholders realize that they need to change their policies or risk losing office, status, or their political, economic, or social advantage, splits begin to appear within the power structure, and, over time, pressure from the opposition creates a new social and political consensus. Many mainstream political, economic, and social elites are forced to switch their positions. By late in Stage Six, some even openly oppose the policies of the central powerholders in order to protect their own self-interests. The issue then becomes hotly contested within the legislatures, the administration, the courts, and all other sectors of society – the stage is set for Stage Seven.

Public

Public opinion opposing the powerholders' policies can grow to as much as 60 percent within a few years, and then, on some issues, slowly swells to a large majority of up to 70 to 75 percent over many years. The populace, however, is evenly split over wanting a change in the status quo. Half the public fears the alternatives more than it opposes the present conditions and policies. To achieve success, the public still needs to be converted to supporting alternatives. By the early 1970s, for example, 80 percent of Americans called for an end to the Vietnam war, but there was no consensus on the alternative because of the fear of the government-created demon that the loss of Vietnam would result in communism taking over all of Southeast Asia (which did not happen).

Goals

Although movements need to organize both locally and nationally and, increasingly, internationally, they ultimately are only as powerful as their grassroots base. All that an American movement's national offices in Washington, D.C., can do is "cash in" on the social and political gains created at the community level all over the country. The movement's chief goal, therefore, is to nurture, support, and empower grassroots activism. The movement needs to –

* keep both the issue and the powerholders' violations of society's principles and values in the public spotlight and on society's social and political agendas;
* switch the movement's primary focus from rebel and protest to change agent and grassroots organizing for positive social change on the issue;
* adopt participatory democratic organization and leadership models;
* train activists in the MAP methods, especially how to wage Stage Six;
* create strategic campaigns; and
* keep winning an ever-larger majority of public opinion and involvement against present powerholder policies and in favor of alternatives, including a paradigm shift.

Pitfalls

Even at the height of Stage Six, the powerholders and mass media will not only report that the movement has failed, but will also refuse to acknowledge that a new, massive, popular movement has been created. Large demonstrations and majority public opposition are dismissed as "vaguely reminiscent of the Sixties," rather than recognized as modern social movements that are at least as big and relevant as those 35 years ago. And when movements do succeed, they are not given credit. We are told, for example, that no new nuclear energy plants were ordered to be built for the last 25 years because of cost over-runs, high lending rates, and inflation, rather than being told the truth: that they were stopped by the tremendous political and public opposition created by people power. The pitfalls are numerous:

* Activists become stuck in the protest stage, adopting violence, rebelliousness, and macho radicalism.

- Activists believe that the movement is losing and local efforts are futile, when they are actually moving along the normal road of success.
- National, regional, and local POOs and their key staff act as if they are the movement, making unilateral programs and decisions for the movement as a whole and thereby disenfranchising grassroots activists.
- The movement gets co-opted by the powerholders, either through collusion or compromises by reformer activists that undercut the achievement of critical movement goals.

Crisis

There is overwhelming public support for changing powerholder policies and many powerholders begin joining in the calls for change.

Conclusions

Over many years, even decades, public opinion against the powerholders' policies swells to an overwhelming majority, sometimes up to 80 percent, as in the case of opposition to the Vietnam War. Almost every sector of society — including most politicians — eventually wants to end the problem and change current policies. But strangely, nothing seems to change. Over the years, however, the weight of the massive public opposition, along with the defection of many elites, takes its toll. The political price that the powerholders have to pay to maintain their policies exceeds the benefits and the current policies become an untenable liability.

STAGE SEVEN: SUCCESS

 Resolution: Victory seems to have been achieved. Everything looks easy. Just there, however, lies the danger. If we are not on guard, evil will succeed in escaping and new misfortunes will develop. You cannot fight for righteousness with corrupt motives, self-serving interests or deceit.

(From the *I Ching,* "Book of Changes")

Stage Seven begins when the movement, after a long process of growing bigger and deeper, reaches a new plateau in which the societal consensus turns the tide of power against the powerholders, launching an *endgame* process that eventually leads to the movement succeeding in reaching its goal. This endgame process usually takes one of three forms: dramatic showdown, quiet showdown, or attrition.

Dramatic showdown resembles the take-off stage. A sudden re-trigger event sparks a mobilization of broad popular opposition and a social crisis. But this time, the overwhelming coercive force of the public and the movement succeeds in forcing changes in the powerholders' policies or leadership or both. This occurred, for example, in the black voting rights movement in Alabama when the 1965 Selma to Montgomery march was brutally attacked by police, creating worldwide outrage. President Johnson and the Congress were forced to pass the Voting Rights Act a few months later, despite their earlier rejection of the bill on the basis that it was impossible to get it passed in that session of Congress. The dramatic showdown is the only endgame form in which the activists believe that they played the key role in achieving the movement's goal.

A **quiet showdown** happens when powerholders realize that they can no longer continue their present policies and they launch a face-saving endgame process of "victorious retreat." Rather than admit defeat and praise the movement for its correct views and its principled stand, the powerholders adopt and carry out many of the goals and policies that were demanded by the movement. The powerholders claim credit for the victory, even though they have been forced to reverse their previously held hard-line policies. The mainstream media complies by reporting this as a success of the powerholders.

Attrition is when success is slowly, quietly, and seemingly invisibly achieved in a long-term process, which could take decades. The social and political machinery slowly evolves new policies and conditions, such as the winding down of nuclear energy in the United States. For the past 28 years there have been no new orders to build a nuclear power plant, while during this time approximately 160 previously made orders have been canceled. During the attrition ending process, activists usually have even more difficulty recognizing that they are in a protracted endgame process of success, perhaps because it is not a clear and acknowledged victory and the powerholders have not totally given up, as is the case with nuclear energy.

In all three forms, even after the endgame process starts, the movement's final success is not guaranteed. Until the change is actually accomplished, the process can be stopped or reversed. Stage Seven involves a continual struggle, but one in which the powerholders are on the offensive until the movement's specific goal is finally won.

Movement

The locus of social movement activism dramatically expands beyond the rebels and traditional social activists to include the typically inactive majority of the population, and many mainstream political, social, and economic groups and institutions become involved as well. Whole segments of mainstream society become involved in a broad range of social activity that keeps society's spotlight on the issue, reveals the ethical violations of present powerholder policies, and creates real political and economic penalties for them. The politicians face hostile voters and the business community can suffer loss of sales and profits through boycotts, sanctions, and disruption of the marketplace. Sometimes there is a general, worldwide insurrection that isolates the central powerholders and their dwindling support. This is what happened to the white South African apartheid regime in the 1980s and ultimately caused its downfall.

In Stage Seven, the movement uses all four roles of social activism, develops a broad-based opposition, counters a series of bogus claims by the powerholders that they have changed their ways, carries out more nonviolent actions when appropriate, and promotes alternatives, including a paradigm shift. The efforts of social movement participants during this stage vary according to the endgame form. In a dramatic showdown, the movement might resemble the take-off stage, in which it plays a publicly obvious role involving mass demonstrations in a time of crisis. Success is achieved in a relatively short time. The toppling of President Milosevic in Serbia in October 2000, or the achievement of the 1965 Voting Rights Act five months after the Selma nonviolent civil rights campaign, are examples of such almost-immediate successes. In a quiet showdown, activists have to work to recognize the victory and their own role in it. In the process of attrition, achievement of the movement's goal is often not recognized as success. Over the extended time period, the movement's role is much less visible and much of the effort is carried out quietly through the low-key work of mainstream institutions and POOs.

Powerholders

The viability of the central powerholders on the issue becomes eroded economically, socially, and politically. Eventually, many powerholders conclude that it is more expensive for them to continue supporting the status quo than it is to promote an alternative. The central powerholders are increasingly isolated as they carry out their policies and programs related to this issue, and eventually they are defeated. As their position deteriorates, the central powerholders are often forced into making fatal mistakes, such as when President Richard Nixon ordered the Watergate break-ins and other "dirty tricks" against the anti-war movement and the Democratic Party. Mississippi Governor Ross Barnett was forced into a fatal mistake when he stood in the doorway of the University of Mississippi to prevent the first black student from enrolling, creating a riot and federal intervention.

In addition, the powerholders are, increasingly, prevented from doing what they must do to continue carrying out their policies. They are forced to resort to extreme political, economic, or military acts, which spur increased public opposition. For example, when the Pentagon was prevented from implementing programs it felt were necessary to win the Vietnam War, such as keeping American ground forces involved in large numbers, it increased bombing. The economic, social, and political penalties for these escalated acts further erode the base of support that the powerholders need if they are to continue their policies or remain in office.

The central powerholders have three different *endgame strategies,* according to the type of ending.

In a dramatic showdown endgame, powerholders can make a kind of "Custer's last stand," holding out until their policies are defeated either in the mainstream political process or by extra-parliamentary means. An example is President Johnson's continued escalation of the war in Vietnam right up until he was forced to decline from running for a second term in 1968.

A victorious retreat in a quiet showdown endgame is where the powerholders lose on the issue, but in reversing their policies they declare victory for themselves. One well-known example was President Reagan's declaration of success when he removed cruise and Pershing II nuclear weapons from Europe in 1986, after deploying them a few years earlier.

In an attrition endgame, powerholders exhibit persistent stubbornness, holding out over many years in an increasingly losing cause, until one of the above two endings eventually occur. The powerholders who continue to promote nuclear energy despite general public opposition are an example.

Public

The great majority of the public demand change. The opposition to the power-holders is now so overwhelming that the whole issue is publicly recognized as the "good guys vs. the bad guys." One is either for democracy, justice, and decency or in favor of excluding blacks from voting, barring women from medical schools, the Vietnam war, President Ferdinand Marcos of the Philippines, or South African apartheid — all conditions that had previously been accepted by main-stream society.

The citizenry had not acted against these policies and conditions before because they accepted them as normal, did not know what to do, felt powerless to act, were not called to action by a trigger event and crisis, or feared the alternative. Citizens are now so repulsed by the unethical policies and social conditions that their desire for change outweighs their fear of the alternative. The power-holders' strategy to demonize the movement no longer works. The mass population is now ready to vote, demonstrate, and even support the powerhold-ers in changing present policies if they are willing to do so.

Goals

The movement's goals for this stage are –

• to wage a successful endgame strategy to achieve one or more major demands;

- to have activists recognize and celebrate their successes;
- to shift the energy of the movement to create the ongoing conditions for sustained and effective citizen-based democracy on other issues; and
- to convince both activists and the public about the need to change the fundamental paradigm that underlies the issue.

Pitfalls

It is amazing that so many activists get depressed at this time. They either believe that the powerholders, not the movement, are actually responsible for the success, or they are upset because the powerholders have been given the credit, while the movement goes unacknowledged. The movement needs to avoid the following pitfalls:

- Failing to recognize the tell-tale signs of the "endgame" process that the powerholders are pursuing
- Fearing to claim they are near victory because then people will drop out or funders will stop giving grants
- Failing to claim any success because there is still so much suffering in the world that is related to this or other issues and powerholder policies
- Compromising too many key demands and basic principles in order to gain a victory
- Feeling letdown after achieving success on an important sub-issue, which reduces the movement's ability to maintain its momentum
- Achieving an important reform without building toward a paradigm shift and basic social change

Crisis

The movement succeeds in winning on a major goal. However, the underlying paradigm has not shifted and other sub-issues remain.

Conclusion

Rather than folding up after its Stage Seven success, the movement needs to maintain processes, systems, and structures (i.e., groups or institutions) on an ongoing basis at the regional, state, national, and international levels so that citizens can continue to participate in decision-making on critical issues of society. Activists now need to address some hard questions: What is success? How can the success be protected from backlash and implemented in actual policies and practices? What else needs to be done? How can this success be built upon to establish true citizen-based democracy?

STAGE EIGHT: CONTINUING THE STRUGGLE

 Continuing: Success now comes through long-standing objectives, traditions and enduring values. Apply just enough consistent force to affect the situation. The movement turns into a new beginning.

(From the *I Ching*, "Book of Changes")

The success achieved in Stage Seven is not the end of the struggle, but merely a landmark in a long-term process of fundamental social change that moves the society closer to the ultimate goal of sustained citizen-based democracy based on justice, ecological sustainability, and the meeting of everyone's basic human needs.

Movement

In this period the movement has an opportunity to expand on its success, focus on other demands, promote new issues, and most importantly, move beyond reform to social change. A number of tasks are required to ensure that the victory remains a reality and that it serves as a launch-pad for expanding the success to new levels and areas.

- **Follow-up to protect and expand the success.** First, the movement needs to play a watchdog role to make sure that the new laws, agreements, promises, and policies won in Stage Seven are carried out. A typical powerholder strategy is to make agreements or laws to dissipate the opposition, then not implement them. After the famous Voting Rights Act of 1965 was passed, for example, years of on-the-ground effort were still needed to make sure that blacks were actually allowed to vote.

  Second, the movement needs to guard against backlash. Movement successes act as a wake-up call to the powerholders and other conservative or right-wing elements to launch vigorous counterattacks to roll back the gains made by the movement. For instance, when the U.S. Supreme Court delivered its Roe v. Wade decision that legalized abortion, the right wing responded with its own anti-abortion or, as they named it, "pro-life" countermovement.

  Third, the movement needs to capitalize on the power and momentum it has created to expand the demands that have already been won. These follow-up efforts are primarily carried out by professional opposition organizations and by activists in the reformer role. While POOs may take the leadership role in this process, it is important that they involve the grassroots.

- **Re-focus the movement on other demands.** The movement needs to focus on achieving other demands that are strategically appropriate. For example, after the civil rights movement desegregated restaurants in 1960, it led a series of similar social movements focused on buses, then public accommodations, voting rights, jobs, and housing.
- **Promote new social consciousness, new issues, and new social movements.** The student movement grew out of the civil rights movement, the anti-Vietnam war movement grew out of both of these movements, and the women's movement was inspired by and developed out of all three of these movements. These new movements were not pre-planned, but emerged organically from social movement activism.
- **Move beyond reform to social change.** Social movements need to go beyond merely achieving specific, immediate reforms, though these are indeed important. They also need to consciously build toward fundamental philosophical and structural changes. This task can be accomplished by –
  - increasing the conscious awareness of people and empowering them to become life-long change agents involved in citizen-based democracy;
  - creating ongoing grassroots action organizations and networks;
  - broadening the analysis, issues, and goals of all social movements;
  - advocating alternatives and a cultural worldview or paradigm shift consistent with the transformation from the growth and prosperity era to an era of ecological sustainability and justice.

Powerholders

The powerholders can adopt a wide range of reactions to a movement's success, including reactions that are contradictory. On the one hand, the powerholders might publicly accept the change, even claim that they brought it about. For example, after ending wars or military engagements with Cuba, Vietnam, Libya, and Iraq, the U.S. government created long-term embargoes and prevented the delivery of humanitarian aid to the countries, which caused extreme hardship and death for citizens in those small nations. After agreeing to end nuclear weapons testing, the U.S. government continued development by testing the weapons with computers. Another typical ploy after unwanted legislation is passed is for the government to simply reduce the funding and staff size of the related agency. This happened with the U.S. Environmental Protection Agency after the passage of landmark environmental legislation. The public saw the government passing meaningful environmental protection laws, but did not see that it was cutting back on the staff needed to make corporations comply. In addition, it is typical for the powerholders to challenge the decisions and attack movement groups and individuals that were responsible.

Public

The public adopts a new conventional wisdom that supports the movement demand that was successfully won. The new public consensus, however, is tenuous. It can be reversed by new events and conditions or by the backlash efforts of reactionary elements or powerholders, such as the anti-abortion movement that emerged after the Roe v. Wade court decision to legalize abortion. On the positive side, the new public consensus and belief system often carries over to other issues. For example, the principle of nondiscrimination and justice for blacks that was highlighted by the 1960s civil rights movement provided the impetus for the student rights, women's rights, and gay and lesbian rights movements. The anti-Vietnam War movement created within the citizenry what the powerholders called the "Vietnam Syndrome," in which the public refuses to support U.S. military intervention in other nations.

Goals

The movement's goals include:
- celebrating the successes and the movement's role in achieving them;
- making sure the movement's success is fully implemented and protected against counterattack; and
- maintaining the vitality of the movement by keeping the grassroots and national organizations and structures actively engaged in implementing the successful

Figure 2: Winning the Public Three Ways (Created by Tom Atlee)

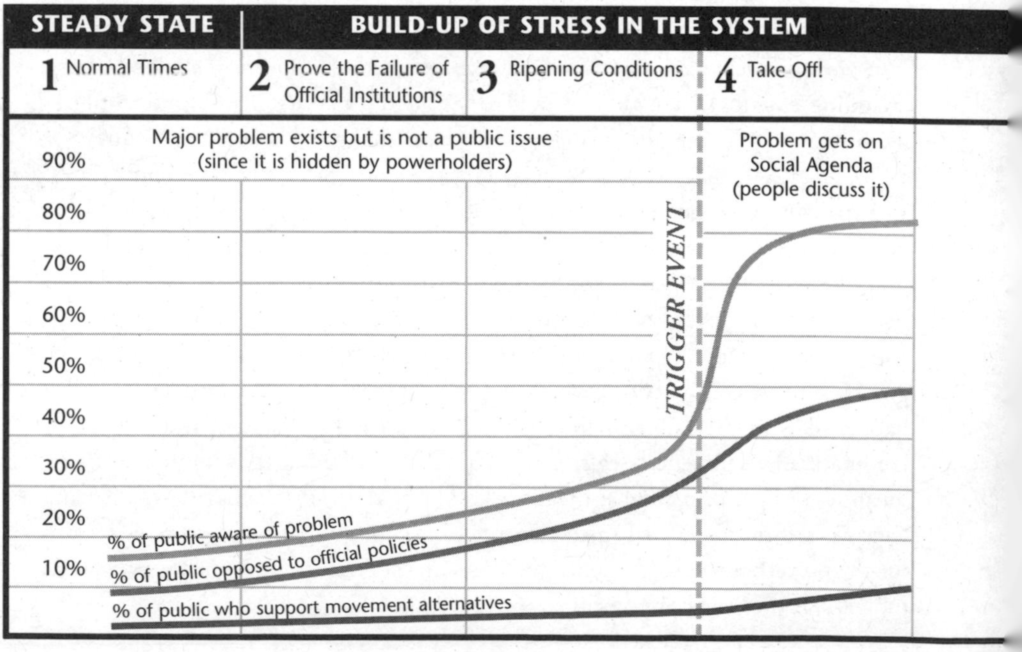

demands and engaged in sub-movements of the same issue or on other important issues; and
- promoting a paradigm shift, focusing on changing underlying beliefs and applying a similar analysis and strategic plan to other sub-movements on the same issue or to other important issues.

Pitfalls

The chief pitfalls of Stage Eight are:
- thinking that the movement is over without making sure that the victory is fully implemented or protected against backlash and counterattack; and
- allowing movement victories to be claimed by the powerholders as theirs and not the movement's.

Crisis

Many activists and organizations move on to work on other issues or drop out for a rest. However, this stage continues until all of the movement's demands are fully implemented and the danger of backlash is over.

Winning the Public Three Times

Social movements need to win the public three times during the process of success, not just once (see Figure 2). First, the public needs to become aware that

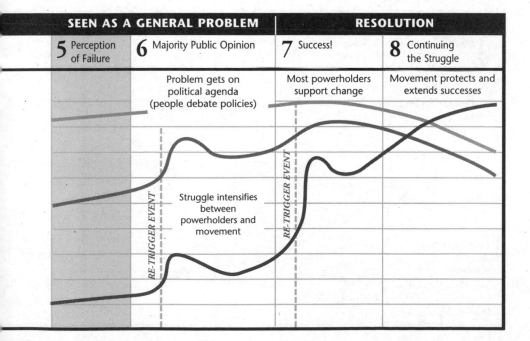

the social problem exists. Public awareness rises rapidly following the trigger event and throughout Stage Four. The public then needs to be convinced that the current powerholder policies and programs are undesirable and need to change. This happens primarily in Stage Six, majority public opinion.

But this is not enough for the movement to succeed in achieving its goal. This is another point in the social movement process where many activists become discouraged because they thought that having a majority of the public oppose current powerholder policies should be enough to convince the power-holders to change. It is at this point that the powerholders switch to a scare strategy in which they proclaim that life would be intolerable without the present policies in place.

For social movements to achieve social change on their issue, the public needs to be won over a third time: they need to believe that there is an acceptable solution or alternative to current policies and programs. This primarily occurs in the second half of Stage Six and in Stage Seven. For example, it was not enough for the public to become aware of the problem of nuclear power and then oppose it. At that point the powerholders agreed that nuclear power had some major faults, but without it, they claimed, the United States would have major electrical blackouts, the economy and jobs would collapse, and the country would lose its

Figure 3: The four roles of social movements in relation to the eight stages of social movements (Created by Tom Atlee)

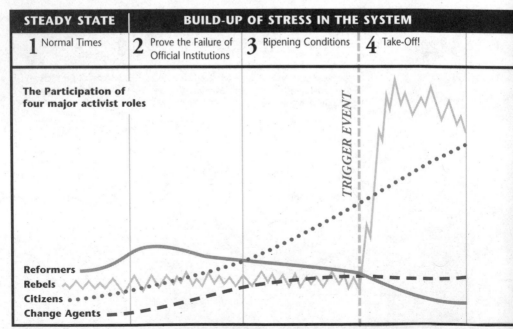

superpower status. The public had to be convinced that those things were either not going to happen or that there were acceptable alternatives to nuclear power.

Conclusion

There is no end. There is only the continuing cycle of social movements and their sub-issues and sub-movements. The process of winning one set of demands creates new levels of citizen awareness, involvement, and empowerment that generate new demands and movements on new issues. This process requires each role of activism and is why, although some roles are more prominent in some stages, all the roles are necessary and important (see Figure 3).

The long-term impact of social movements is more important than their immediate material successes. The 1960s civil rights movement, for example, not only achieved a broad array of immediate rights, but also created a new positive image of blacks among themselves and in the eyes of the rest of society. It established nonviolent action as a method for achieving people power and inspired new social movements around the world, including the student, women, and anti-Vietnam War movements.

Finally, people's social movements advance the world further along the path of meeting the spiritual, material, psychological, social, and political needs of humanity. Regardless of the material results, mere involvement can contribute to people's personal fulfillment. The emerging people power movements around the

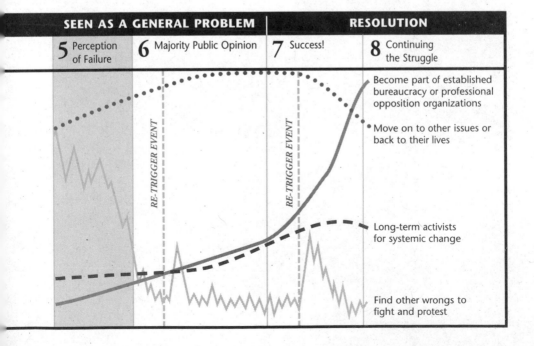

world today might well be transforming themselves and the planet from the present era of superpowers, materialism, environmental breakdown, disenfranchisement, abject poverty amidst opulence, and militarism to a new, more human era of democracy, freedom, justice, self-determination, human rights, peaceful coexistence, and ecological sustainability.

4

Believing in the Power of Social Movements

In order to be effective agents of social change, activists must first be open to the possibility that they are powerful and that their social movement might be progressing along the road to success. Even though grassroots activists and their social movements have been powerful and often successful throughout history, most activists still believe that they are powerless and feel that their movement is ineffective and failing. These beliefs and feelings can become self-fulfilling prophesies that create a chain reaction of hopelessness, low energy, depression, burnout, dropout, declining numbers of new participants, and disastrous strategies and tactics, born out of desperation, that ensure the movement's decline.

To achieve their full effectiveness, activists must avoid the powerlessness trap and believe in their own power and the power and successes of nonviolent social movements. They need to recognize, accept, and celebrate the progress and victories of their social movement as it travels the long road to success.

Three Unrealistic Beliefs — And How to Overcome Them

There are three ways that activists substantiate their belief that they are powerless and their social movement is a failure: "logical" reasons, buying into the social movement's "culture of failure" and an aversion to success.

Overcoming "logical reasons" for believing in movement failure

Activists at MAP workshops offer many reasons for believing that their movement is failing. Here are the most common reasons — along with an alternative perspective. While all of these may indeed be true if a movement is failing, they can also be true when movements are progressing along the road toward ultimate success. Consequently, by themselves they are false indicators of whether a social movement is failing or succeeding.

Reason 1. "Nothing has changed. The movement is merely 'treading water.'" After years of effort, activists might see little or no real change in the policies or practices of the powerholders or in the intolerable conditions that they oppose. The continuation of racism, sexism, corporate control, poverty in the midst of plenty, and environmental destruction seems to validate their feelings.

Response: Social change takes a long time. The status quo is deeply ingrained in the policies and interests of the official powerholders and is, initially, supported by a majority of the population.[1] It usually takes many years or decades to build up the social awareness and public conviction necessary to induce change. Because the powerholders will be among the last to change their minds and policies, their actions are a poor basis for judging how well the movement is doing.

Reason 2. "The powerholders are too powerful and will never listen to us." They pay no attention to either the movement or the public, even though the majority of public opinion may oppose current policies. The movement is like a mosquito attacking an elephant. Yes, movements have been successful before, but those were different times, and their issues were not as central to the powerholders' greed and privileged position as is our issue.

Response: The powerholders' strategy is to officially appear as though they are not being swayed by opposing social movements and public opinion. For example, President Nixon publicly claimed to be paying no attention to the anti-Vietnam War movement, even pretending that he was watching a football game on television during one of the big demonstrations in 1969. But after the war we learned that he backed down on many war plans – such as direct assaults on dikes in North Vietnam, which would have flooded much of the country, and the use of nuclear bombs — because of the anti-war movement.

Reason 3. "The movement is always reactive, not pro-active." The movement only does crisis management, merely reacting to the latest crisis rather than taking the initiative for positive change. The powerholders are totally in charge of the process.

Response: The dynamic struggle between social movements and powerholders is often like a chess match, in which both sides keep reacting to events and to the moves of each other in their effort to win the confidence of the public. Many activists only see one side of this give-and-take — the reactions of the movement. It is more accurate to perceive the whole interplay of both sides, including the reactive crisis management actions of the powerholders.

Reason 4. "The movement is not getting anywhere because it is focusing on an endless series of issues. Why doesn't everyone all work on the same issue?" The movement jumps from opposing one issue to another — nuclear testing, logging old-growth forests, immigration restrictions, corporate globalization, and so forth.

Response: There are many critical problems that need to be addressed immediately, so there needs to be many different social movements. Within each social problem there are many sub-issues that need to be simultaneously addressed, and more sub-issues are continually revealed. Different people and groups need to address the issues that they are most concerned about and that are closest to their lives and interests, as this is what gives them and the movement the energy for the enormous amounts of volunteer time and action required.

In addition, a large, centralized movement would inevitably get bogged down in bureaucracy and in-fighting over control. A hierarchy would develop that would sap the energy of the grassroots. It's better to have many local grassroots groups that are independent but voluntarily cooperate with each other, forming coalitions and organizing joint activities as needed. Moreover, such a decentralized style of movement organization is harder for powerholders and other self-interested groups to infiltrate and undermine.

Reason 5. "The experts, media commentators, TV, newspapers, and powerholders all say the movement is failing." Nowhere do we hear that the movement is powerful and succeeding.

Response: A mainstream "expert" is extremely capable of explaining the powerholders' position and justifying the status quo. The role of official analysts — such as government, academic, and mainstream media spokespeople — is also to explain that the powerholders are doing the best they possibly can and that opposition movement groups are illegitimate, nonexistent, communist or anarchist, violent, powerless, misguided, and failing. Activists need to be keenly aware of what the mainstream experts are saying in order to look for the kernel of truth and to be able to counter the propaganda being given to the public, but they should also make sure they do not fall for the powerholders' perspective.

Reason 6. "The movement is dead." After several years of intense energy, excitement, high hopes, media attention, and big demonstrations and meetings, many activists believe that their movement has dissipated into a state of low energy, hopelessness, cynicism, and despair. There are fewer people at demonstrations, the same few people attend meetings and lead different groups, there is little media coverage, and key people are lost to burnout or to newer, more exciting issues. How can we revive the movement and again have giant demonstrations and constant front-page coverage?

Response: When social movements progress from the take-off stage to the majority public opinion stage, many people believe that the movement has died. In the take-off stage there are big demonstrations and rallies, lots of media attention, a crisis atmosphere, high energy, and lots of excitement and expectation for immediate change. But the majority public opinion stage is more low-key and extends over many years, normally with fewer people at demonstrations and local meetings and with less flamboyant media attention. It reflects the change from the rebel role of Stage Four to the change agent role of Stage Six.

While it *appears* that the movement is waning, in reality it has grown tremendously by winning a majority public opinion and spreading throughout society's grassroots. The enormous amount of new local activity receives much less national media attention, and the hard political struggles using mainstream channels are far less exciting. The movement is only "dead" if one judges it using the criteria of take-off in Stage Four. To determine how well a majority movement is doing, you have to recognize the progress of the movement through the eight stages and judge it by the criteria of the appropriate stage.

Reason 7. "Any 'successes' that might have occurred were accomplished by events and powerful forces *outside* the movement." It was the Vietnamese who won the war, Reagan and Gorbachev who signed the Intermediate-Range Nuclear Forces (INF) Treaty that ended the deployment of land-based cruise and Pershing 2 missiles in Europe, and the French government decided on its own to stop nuclear tests in the Pacific and halt the Multilateral Agreement on Investment (MAI).

Response: Most positive developments that are related to social movement issues are connected in some way to the movement's actions. For example, the last thing on Ronald Reagan's mind during his 1980 election campaign was to make a deal with the Soviet Union; his campaign was based on building ever more nuclear weapons to "save the free world" from the "evil empire." Seven years later, after the new anti-nuclear weapons movement in the United States and Europe won over a great majority of people, Gorbachev was favored over Reagan in West German polls by 80 percent. Only then did Reagan decide to walk with his arm around "Darth Vader" in Moscow's Red Square and sign a nuclear weapons treaty.

Because movements usually neither recognize nor claim their own successes, they allow the powerholders to claim the successes for themselves. Even movement activists and groups often credit these successes to the powerholders. In 1988, the peace organization Beyond War gave its peace prize to Reagan and Gorbachev for the INF treaty, instead of giving it to the Western peace movements that really made it all happen. (This was rectified the following year, when the prize was given to local peace activists.)

Reason 8. "The movement has not achieved its (long-range) goals." Corporate globalization continues to expand, the United States still supports dictators, welfare reform has hurt women and children, and the rain forests are still being cut.

Response: Again, social movements take many years and need to be evaluated by how well they are progressing along the normal path of success, not by whether they have achieved their ultimate goal. The expansion of the movement to deal with new and larger purposes and goals is part of the process of social change. During that process, activists learn about problems that were unknown to them at the beginning of the movement and keep moving the goal posts farther away.

Reason 9. "The movement has not achieved any real victories." Most of the so-called victories were "phantom" successes, because they were replaced by new conditions or policies as bad as, or worse than, the old. For example, the invasion of Nicaragua was stopped, but the low-intensity warfare of the Contras began; atmospheric nuclear testing was stopped, only to be replaced by underground and then computerized testing; the MAI was stopped, but the World Trade Organization continues, and so forth.

Response: Given their proclivity to believe in failure and powerlessness, combined with the lack of a clear model of what the road to success looks like, activists have great difficulty identifying any short-range successes. Many political scientists report that the most significant step in social change is putting an issue on the social and political agendas and then keeping it there.[2] Yet movements never count this as a significant accomplishment. As they achieve short-term goals — like stopping a United States invasion of Nicaragua, bringing the U.S troops home from Vietnam, or ending French nuclear testing in the Pacific — movements see the policies they fought against replaced by other more devastating policies. They may even see the changes as ploys by the government to undercut the movement. Viewed from the standpoint of the Movement Action Plan eight stages, however, in each case mentioned the powerholders were forced to adopt new policies that weakened their position and were more difficult for them to carry out in the long run.

Overcoming the "culture of failure"

All groups, whether they are organizations or nations, have a collective set of assumptions about reality that is, to some degree, shared by most of their members and expressed in beliefs, values, attitudes, and behavior. Together, these compose the culture of a group, which is deeply rooted, generally unconscious, and rarely examined as to its validity and usefulness. Moreover, this culture sets narrow standards for acceptable thinking and behavior – in social movements this is sometimes called "political correctness."

The culture of social movements often includes a sense of powerlessness, despair, and failure that is consistent with – and sometimes produces – the "logical reasons" for believing that the movement is failing. The following are some of the common symptoms of social activism's culture of failure, with solutions.

Symptom 1. A focus on tactics that are isolated from a larger strategic context. The movement's activities are primarily seen as isolated activities, programs, and campaigns that are militant or fill up a calendar of events, but are unrelated to a long-range strategy for achieving the medium- and long-term goals of the movement. Over time, many participants despair because they cannot make any connection between their day-to-day efforts and achieving the larger goals they seek.

Solution: Placing the various movement activities within a strategic framework, such as the MAP Eight Stages and Four Roles Models, easily rectifies this. The issue can then be viewed in a larger context and the activities and events planned according to the guidelines suggested by the strategic model.

Symptom 2. The movement's analyses emphasize the problem, while excluding an analysis of the process of movement success. A movement's deconstructive analysis normally produces an ever-increasing and overwhelming abundance of evidence that the situation is bad and getting worse. It points out how deeply official powerholders and institutions are involved in corruption and lies, how powerful the powerholders really are, and how many people are being hurt or even killed. Producing deconstructive information and analysis about the gravity of a situation is an important strength of social movements; people need reliable information in order to act and make changes. However, a continuous barrage of devastating facts, with no way out, tends to sink people into despair, cynicism, inaction, and ineffective acts of desperation.

Solution: The focus on the problems can be balanced by including reconstructive analysis. Movement strategists and trainers need to include, as a standard part of social movements, the identification of specific objectives and a vision of the alternatives along the way. These milestones show how the movement is progressing along the normal path that successful social movements take in achieving their long-term goals.

Symptom 3. Over-emphasizing resistance and protest. Protest and dissent are critical aspects of social movements. However, over time, protest and resistance against the powerholders become wearing and can produce increased anger, burnout, and even self-defeating militaristic activities. Such movements increasingly attract "negative rebels," and that negative energy keeps more emotionally and politically mature people from joining, even when they would like to be active on a particular social issue.

Solution: In every social movement, the much-needed role of rebel, and its methods of protest and resistance, needs to be balanced with the roles of citizen, change agent, and reformer, as described in Chapter 2. Additionally, the day-to-day efforts of all these roles need to be seen within the eight-stage process for movement success and consciously acknowledged as being supportive of each other.

Symptom 4. An emphasis on guilt, rather than conscience, as the primary motivation for activists. A focus on how bad the situation is often implies how bad we are; we see ourselves as a major part of the problem. We let it happen, contribute to it, or benefit from it. In this way the movement increases feelings of guilt, which can trigger defensive responses of denial, anger, or internalized hatred directed at powerholders or other activists, or can trigger attempts to prove our innocence or goodness through a variety of ineffective or ultimately destructive attitudes and activities.

Solution: It is better to appeal to conscience than guilt. Asking people to act as guided by their conscience challenges them to express their highest values and principles. Acting from our inner spirit brings forth our true nature of caring, compassion, and connection with all people and the planet. This creates hope and positive energy that has staying power and attracts, rather than rejects, others. For example, when Nelson Mandela got out of jail, rather than condemning all whites for the evils of apartheid, he implored all blacks and whites to work together toward a nonracial society.

Symptom 5. Nostalgia for glorious past eras and movements, symbolized by the 1960s. Activists often express the wish that they were involved in the great movements of the past, such as the anti-Vietnam war and the civil rights movements of the 1960s. By comparison, their own movement seems low-key, confusing, undramatic, and ineffective.

Solution: What today's activists don't realize is that those past movements were quite similar to those of today and that activists, by and large, felt the same way then as activists today. For the first three years and the last four years of the anti-Vietnam war movement, activists felt powerless and depressed. From 1972 to the end of the war in 1975 (immediately following the high-energy years of 1967 to 1971), ever-fewer people attended demonstrations and the war raged as the killing and bombing increased. It seemed that the decade of movement opposition and the majority of public opinion against the war that the movement created were having no effect on the government's war policy. But after the war, much of the credit (and the blame) for the war ending was given to the anti-Vietnam war movement.

Ironically, in many ways conditions are more favorable for activists and social movements today than in the 1960s. Indeed, there are more and bigger movements, tens of thousands of ongoing groups working on social problems, a much more developed political and economic analysis, and a more favorable social and political climate for social change — due, in large part, to the legacy of past movements.

Overcoming the aversion to success

Particularly devastating symptoms of social activism's culture of failure are the attitudes and behaviors by which activists avoid movement success — success often seems to be unwanted, feared, and averted. Activists constantly snatch failure from the jaws of success. Some common examples of aversion to success – and the necessary attitude adjustments – follow.

Aversive attitude 1. Believing that the movement is failing because it has not won yet. After months or years of effort, activists often claim that their movement is failing because it has not achieved its ultimate goal, whether it is stopping the nuclear arms race, corporate globalization, domestic violence, or nuclear energy. They are unable to acknowledge any of their movement's short-term successes.

Attitude adjustment: Recognize that this line of reasoning is illogical and not used to judge other endeavors. Performance is normally judged by whether we are making satisfactory progress toward achieving a goal, not by whether we have already achieved it. Parents, for example, do not condemn their daughter for not graduating after the first year at university because they know it's a four-year process. Activists who judge that their movement is failing because it has not yet achieved its goal, even if it is highly successful in other ways, would continue to view it as a failure right up until it finally succeeds.

Aversive attitude 2. Discounting the accomplishment of previously important goals. To solve serious social problems, social movements set goals that could reasonably be expected to take five to ten years to accomplish. However, during the course of social activism, even more serious problems are discovered, and new goals that supplant the earlier goals are set every two or three years. When the older goals are achieved, they are now considered unimportant and are rarely celebrated or even recognized as successes. This not only denies activists the feeling of empowerment and success, but further demoralizes them and contributes to feelings of powerlessness and despair.

For example, in 1982, stopping deployment of the cruise and Pershing 2 nuclear missiles in Europe was the American peace movement's top goal. At the time, this goal seemed crucial, yet difficult to accomplish. Over the next few years, the movement adopted even bigger goals that were considered more important, including a freeze on building all nuclear weapons. When Reagan and Gorbachev signed the INF Treaty in 1986, ending the deployment of cruise and Pershing 2 nuclear missiles in Europe, the American movement hardly noticed. The following day, one activist at the Nuclear Freeze office in San Francisco said to me, "What is there to celebrate? They are building five nuclear bombs a day."

Attitude adjustment: Recognize the importance, power and success of the movement whenever it achieves any of its goals, including those that have been pursued for several years. Expect that it will take five to ten years to achieve social movement goals, and celebrate when they are achieved. This requires a willingness to go against activist cultural reluctance to identify and celebrate victories.

Aversive attitude 3. Animosity towards success. Activists commonly get upset, even angry, when told that their movement is winning,[3] but they become quite agreeable and friendly when told of new alarming facts about the grievous situation that they oppose. It is quite acceptable in movement circles to talk about the latest devastating environmental statistics, atrocities by dictators, or dastardly acts of the president, the CIA, or the World Trade Organization. But statements of movement power and success often draw emotionally laden protests and angry denials.

Attitude adjustment: Activists need to cultivate a sense of appreciation for the efforts of everyone — activists, citizens, and powerholders who change their policies.

Aversive attitude 4. Adopting the role of the victim. Many activists seem to have a psychological need to play the role of the victim: the powerless underdog who is helping other powerless victims: "poor me, poor them, poor planet." At the same time, they can adopt the role of world rescuer, the self-righteous moral hero who alone is working to save the world against all odds. This emotional need to be the powerless victim, underdog, or lone hero is a result of constantly facing major disasters and all-powerful powerholders. It is a form of co-dependency. If a problem is solved or a victory is won over the powerholders, then the activist loses his or her role of powerless victim, underdog, or lone hero. To maintain their self-image, therefore, these activists often unconsciously talk and act in ways that undercut positive and effective strategies and activities that might achieve movement success.

Attitude adjustment: To be effective, activists need to be committed to self-development and self-empowerment. They need to switch from playing the roles of victim and rescuer to becoming an empowered self who is emotionally, mentally, and physically centered, calm, and fulfilled as a human being.

Avoiding Self-Fulfilling Prophecies

Social movement activists need to be careful not to fall into the all-too-common trap of presuming that they are powerless and their movement is failing. The reasons activists use to support this presumption are poor indicators that a social movement is *actually* failing. But what is most devastating is that this line of thinking creates a self-fulfilling prophecy.

To a large extent we create our own reality by the way we interpret existing conditions. Just as we can see a glass that is either half full or half empty, we can see our movement as halfway toward success or half dead. If we believe our movement is failing — whether because of "logical" reasons, because we've bought into the culture of failure, or because we have an aversion to success — we can create the following unhealthy movement conditions and possibly produce a self-fulfilling prophecy of failure.

- **Discouragement and despair lead to movement dissipation.** Because they believe that their movement is failing and they are powerless, many movement participants and leadership become increasingly discouraged, hopeless, despairing, and burned out. These conditions contribute to a high movement drop-out rate and to lower levels of energy available to carry out programs.
- **There is a reduction in recruitment of new members.** The depressed state of the movement discourages new people from joining. Groups then sit around as their numbers decline and ask despairingly why there aren't more people present. But who wants to join a group with a negative attitude and low energy, in a state of collective depression?
- **Stuck in "protest" mode, activists are less able to work on strategies for achieving positive changes.** When activists believe that their movement cannot achieve change, they are more likely to become stuck in the rebel role of protester and resister, unable to balance this role with strategies and programs to bring about positive change and alternatives. One peace center staff member said in a workshop, "I never think about success. I guess I don't think it is possible."
- **Feelings of anger, hostility, and frustration lead to activities, including acts of violence, that turn the public against the movement.** Many movement participants begin by saying a healthy "no" to unjust conditions, but over time — as they become more informed about just how bad the conditions and power-holders are — they often become frustrated, hopeless, and angry. As they come to believe that their movement activity is having no effect, some turn to acts of desperation, without realizing that such activities hurt the movement by alienating the public.
- **Activists are unable to acknowledge and take credit for successes.** By believing their movement is powerless and failing, activists are less able to either recognize successes when they actually happen or give the movement credit for them. Instead, they allow powerholders to take credit for movement success. Obviously this deprives them of a major source of energy, enthusiasm, empowerment, and hope for the future.

Adopt a Realistic View of Power and Success

You might be more powerful than you know. Your social movement might well be succeeding. Most activists in most past social movements — including those that are now recognized as being extremely powerful and successful — believed at the time that their movement was failing. How do you know that you are not having a similar experience? This might be what success looks like and feels like. Your movement might be the most successful in decades. How do you know that it isn't?

To adopt a realistic view of social movement power and success, activists need to be open to the possibility that they are powerful and their movement is on the path of success. They also need to take the following steps.

Give up the "advantages" of powerlessness and movement failure

In order to adopt a new model of empowerment and success, activists first need to give up the "advantages" of believing that they are powerless and that their movement is failing. Many activists have a clear understanding of the usefulness of their own victim behavior — of believing that they are powerless and their movement is failing — and their fear of their movement succeeding. The following are some brainstormed responses by activists to the question: "What are the advantages to believing that your social movement is failing and you are powerless regarding the issue that you are concerned about?"

- "Powerlessness allows us to be unaccountable and not responsible for our actions. After all, if we are not going to be effective anyway, we can do whatever we like and it makes no difference."
- "In success, there is fear of us being co-opted and becoming like the establishment we hate."
- "As underdogs, we have moral superiority. The more oppressed and powerless we are, the more we can appeal to underdog feelings of self-righteous superiority and support. We can say it is only us, no one else really cares and is acting except us."
- "Being powerless allows us to avoid changing ourselves or our organization. We can maintain our old identity and be where we are most comfortable psychologically."
- "I will have to stop being the perennial rebel and become a change agent, or even a reformer."
- "I don't want the responsibility that goes with being powerful."
- "I don't want to grow up and be successful like my parents."
- "As a woman, I felt the same way when the feminist movement came along — that I was responsible for my situation and that I could change it. It challenged me to act powerfully."

Be willing to overcome the fear of success and strive for personal and political maturity

Allowing yourself and your movement to be successful requires personal and political maturity. The change from acting on an unrealistic model of failure to a realistic model of success requires a major emotional and cultural leap. Redefining your view of yourself and your social movement occurs at many levels, including mental, emotional, spiritual, and cultural.

- **Mental.** Activists need to change the way that they interpret the information they receive from their experience and consciously decide for themselves whether their movement is failing or progressing. As they give up the psychological "advantages" of the roles of victim and lone hero, they must identify themselves as empowered citizen-activists in a movement that is creating real social change.
- **Emotional.** Activists need to make the emotional changes required to transform themselves from victim to empowered citizen-activist. For example, they need to stop acting with self-righteous pride, anger, or rage. Instead, they need to focus on their highest values.
- **Spiritual.** Each activist needs to be committed to the inner journey of self-knowing and self-acceptance. Awareness and active exploration of the deeper dimensions of being human give us strength and appreciation of the goodness and potential that resides within all of us and our society. Social change has to include deep changes – not only in our society, but also within each activist and movement organization — that are consistent with the goals we seek. Our means of achieving goals are the ends in the making.

Use strategic social movement models, such as MAP

Social change is complex. Activists need to learn about not only their particular issue, but also how it connects with other issues and the larger social condition. Almost every human endeavor is accomplished through a set of instructions or a model. A model provides a framework for analysis and a structure for planning and acting. In Part I of this book I have described the Movement Action Plan, a practical strategic model that helps activists better understand, strategize, and organize social movements. In Part III we use five different social movements as case studies to demonstrate how MAP applies. In the next section, Part II, Mary Lou Finley and Steven Soifer provide a brief history of social movement theories and compare contemporary academic theories to MAP to make a closer connection between theory and practice.

Part II

Social Movement Theories and MAP

5

Social Movement Theories and MAP: Beginnings of a Dialogue

Mary Lou Finley and Steven Soifer

Social movement theory, whether the work of sociologists or political scientists, has largely been produced from the outside, looking in. In contrast, the Movement Action Plan (MAP) is both a theoretical model and an action guide developed through practice. Both activists and scholars can benefit from bridging the gap between theory and practice. To encourage this exchange of ideas and experience, in this chapter we provide a brief overview of social science theories on social movements, with a focus on contemporary theory. We also identify several key areas where MAP makes a contribution to social movement theory and parallels existing theoretical insights in the sociological literature on social movements from the activist perspective.

This is a dialogue that some sociologists may find heretical. Since the discipline began, there has been a split between scholars and practitioners that has not occurred in some other fields, such as psychology. Mary Jo Deegan, in *Jane Addams and the Men of the Chicago School,* attributes the split to the exclusionary practices in the 19th century that kept women sociologists out of academic positions and led to the development of a separate field dedicated to practice — social work.[1] This split has diminished somewhat in recent years as interest in applied sociology and clinical sociology has increased. However, these changes seem to have had little effect on the field of social movements. Even though some movement scholars have a personal interest in and are supportive of social movements, few scholarly works address both activists and academics.

Social work, on the other hand, generally relies on "practice theory." Simply defined, practice theory attempts to make sense of a practitioner's experience.

Practice theory proposes that theory is really only useful as it arises from experience and informs practice. We believe this approach is sorely needed in the social movement literature, and it is exactly the contribution that MAP makes.

MAP, which originated as a guide to action, is also a developmental, theoretical model of social movements. That is, it is a model that presents a theory of the stages of development of movements. It both theorizes aspects of social movements that have received little attention from movement scholars, and elaborates some perspectives found already in the literature. The methods that were used to develop MAP are similar to those used in grounded theory, introduced by sociologists Barney Glaser and Anselm Strauss in *The Discovery of Grounded Theory*.[2] Grounded theory is a method of analysis based on an **inductive** approach to theory building. According to social workers E.R. Babbie and A. Rubin, "Scientific inquiry in practice typically involves an alternation between deduction and induction. During the deductive phase, we reason toward observations; during the inductive phase, we reason from observations. In practice, both deduction and induction are routes to the construction of social theories."[3]

Like grounded theory, MAP takes an inductive approach: observations from Bill Moyer's decades of experience in social movements led to his construction of a model based on lived experience. To understand the contribution that MAP makes to social movement theory, we will first review frameworks proposed by past and contemporary theories.

Paradigms in the study of social movements

In his recent book, *The Art of Moral Protest*, James Jasper points out that each of the major classical schools of thought in social movement theory seems to be inspired by particular social movements:

> ... nineteenth century urban revolts gave us crowd theories; the Nazis inspired mass society theories; bureaucratized trade unions contributed rational choice models; the civil rights and labor movements yielded the strategic models of political process; the post-1960s cultural movements suggested identity theory [also known as New Social Movements theory]; religious movements were the paradigm for developing frame analysis.[4]

Jasper argues that each of these paradigms, or perspectives, sheds light on particular aspects of social movements — "what Robert Alford and Roger Freidland refer to as each paradigm's 'home domain'" — but represent "partial insights with little opportunity for synthesis."[5] We will discuss each of these major paradigms briefly, as well as three others: a value-added model, resource mobilization theory, and nonviolence theory.

The Crowd/Collective Behavior Paradigm

This model is based on studies launched by Gustave Le Bon's *The Crowd,* published in 1895, in which he described crowds as possessing a "collective mind" that enabled participants to carry out collective actions they would never do as individuals. Actions of crowd participants were perceived to be irrational, spontaneous, and often destructive.

Social movements were seen as similar phenomena, generally more long-term and more organized, but similar in nature to crowds, riots, fads, and other forms of collective behavior. These studies saw social movements from a psychological perspective, which "reduced protest to the release of pent-up frustration."[6]

Mass Society Theories

Efforts to explain the rise of fascist totalitarian movements in Europe resulted in the development of mass society theories.[7] Some scholars argued that a lack of ties to intermediary groups in society (such as churches, unions, clubs, and community groups) made citizens vulnerable to "mass behavior" and totalitarian movements.

Value-Added Model

Neil Smelser, in *Theory of Collective Behavior,* presents a more comprehensive scheme for understanding social movements. He broke with earlier psychological explanations of movements, arguing that collective behavior is basically a social phenomenon and must be understood by looking at the social context as well as the psychology of the participants. He identified what he termed the "determinants of collective behavior" — the conditions under which collective behavior arises — which included the following:

- Structural conduciveness (Does the basic organization of the society make collective behavior a possibility?)
- Structural strain (Is there something wrong?)
- Growth and spread of a generalized belief
- Precipitating factors (A dramatic event that sets things off)
- Mobilization of participants for action
- The operation of social control (Factors that minimize conduciveness or strain or, later, seek to limit the actions of movement participants by police action, injunctions, societal ridicule, and so on).[8]

While explanations from these early theories were somewhat useful, they gave little attention to the actors in the situation, and activists were still largely viewed as social deviants. It wasn't until the social movements of the 1960s — the civil rights movement and the anti-Vietnam War movement — that social scientists began to view things differently. It was no longer plausible to define activists as deviants after listening to Martin Luther King Jr. Movements and their participants came to be viewed as values-based, organized efforts to address serious social problems through non-traditional political and social channels.

Post-Sixties Theories of Social Movements

Rational Choice Theorists

In his 1965 book *The Logic of Collective Action,* Mancur Olson argued that activists joining social movements make a rational choice, based on a kind of "cost-benefit calculation." Drawing on perspectives from economic theory, he argued that people are motivated by and act on their own self-interest, and that they join social movements based on "selective incentives," not altruism or concern for the common good. Participants were seen by Olson in a more positive light, but this perspective stayed focused on the motives of participants and shed little light on what happened in the course of a social movement's history.[9]

Resource Mobilization Theory

Resource mobilization theory shifts the focus away from the motivation of participants to the resources that could be engaged by social movements. This perspective suggests that movements occur when participants are able to mobilize sufficient resources — including people, money, media, and information — to influence the political process. Based on the work of Lipsky and others, resource mobilization theory came to dominate the social science literature on social movements during the 1970s and early 1980s and is still a widely used theoretical framework.[10]

The Political Process Approach

Since the mid-1980s, the political process model, growing out of the work of Charles Tilly, and applied to the U.S. setting by Doug McAdam (in his study of the civil rights movement) and others such as Tarrow, Jenkins, and Perrow, has grown in importance, particularly in the United States. Political process theory has made two major contributions of importance from our perspective. First, it defined social movements as a part of the political process, but a part that operates at least partially outside political frameworks and institutions as commonly understood.[11] Sociologists with this perspective argued that social movements should be considered a part of political sociology and part of a society's political process, not just as a form of collective behavior. Secondly, political process theory suggests that to understand social movements, we need to look at what Peter Eisinger calls the "structures of political opportunity"[12] in the surrounding society.

This recognizes that new opportunities such as new potential allies, splits among the powerholders, new governmental processes, or new "ideological disposi- tions"[13]of those in power are important factors in movement emergence and development.

New Social Movements Theory

New Social Movements theory arose in Europe in the 1980s as a response to move- ments of the 1970s and 1980s. It is an attempt to explain the many social movements that emerged around women's issues, the environment, and similar concerns. These movements involved primarily middle-class people and were a major break with the worker-based movements, which had long been strong in Europe and had been based on social class differences. The new movements could not easily be explained by the kind of socialist and Marxist analyses that Europeans had typically applied to movements for social change. New Social Movements theory focuses on how culture influences and is influenced by social movements. Furthermore, it explores many of the dimensions of interest in the political process approach, such as political opportunity structure, using these concepts to compare the emergence of differing social movements in different European societies.[14]

Frame Analysis

In the mid-1980s David Snow, Robert Benford, and their colleagues used Erving Goffman's concept of frame analysis to explain the ways in which social move- ment activists conceptualize and publicly discuss ideas about social issues. They pointed out the importance of framing the problem and proposed solutions in ways that appeal to the public and motivate others to join the movement.[15] Their work suggested that a movement's success in framing the issues in appealing ways played a major role in its potential for conducting successful actions and winning over the public. This approach to theorizing was particularly important as it focused more attention on the work that activists do to create social movements.

Nonviolence Theory

Nonviolence theory has been developed primarily by practitioners and is not usually acknowledged by sociologists writing about social movements. Influenced by such diverse writers and practitioners as Henry David Thoreau, Leo Tolstoy, Gandhi, and Martin Luther King, the essential idea of nonviolence theory is that nonviolent strategies and tactics, practiced by large numbers of people, can create enormous pressure for change and even topple governments. For example, through non-cooperation with state authority and other forms of nonviolent protest, "people power" can put the authorities in a dilemma. Authorities can either negotiate with movement participants and begin a process of resolving the issue, or they can use violence against demonstrators, which may result in a loss of support for the authorities themselves. Nonviolence is based upon respect for every person, even one's opponents, and works by keeping open the relationship with opponents and seeking to convert them.

Gene's Sharp's three-volume work *The Politics of Nonviolent Action* is still a key articulation of nonviolence theory. He puts forward a theory of political power that focuses on the need for consent of the governed, with the attendant implication that by withdrawing that consent, ordinary people can have a power that they might not expect to have. He lists over 400 methods of nonviolent protest and describes situations in which they have been used, thus providing a catalogue of strategies and tactics for social activists to consider. He also describes, with cogency and insight, the dynamics of nonviolent action in the interaction between the movement and the powerholders, calling nonviolent strategies a kind of political jujitsu.[16]

There is much in this work that can help activists as they consider different ways to achieve success and think about how to handle the various responses of the authorities to movement demands and actions. However, Sharp doesn't give us much help in understanding how movements develop over time or the various kinds of work that activists must be prepared to do.

The Movement Action Plan grows out of the practice of nonviolence. It has been influenced by previous thinking and work on nonviolence and can be seen as a contribution to the literature on nonviolence theory.

Key Concepts in Contemporary Social Movement Theory

In the last decade, contemporary social movement theorists have been creating a synthesis that weaves together insights from resource mobilization theory and the political process model, as well as the recent work of European scholars identified with New Social Movement theory. This synthesis uses three dimensions of social movements as a framework: movement emergence, movement dynamics (including movement strategies and tactics, media response, and interaction with the opposition), and movement outcomes. This new synthesis is grounded in the political process model, which means that it is based in an understanding that social movements are a part of the larger political process. These theorists argue that social movements arise when three factors are present: [17]

- Political opportunities
- Mobilizing structures
- Framing processes

Political opportunities

Theorists who developed this concept, including Peter Eisinger and Sidney

Tarrow, point out that a key factor in the emergence of social movements is often a change in the political context in which the movement operates, such as the openness or repressiveness of the government, the nature of the party in power, or the openness of current elected officials to the movement's point of view. For example, in 1989 when the USSR signaled it would no longer use armed force to keep Eastern Europe within the Communist fold, a nonviolent movement in East Germany, which had been building "underground" for some time, mounted massive demonstrations that were successful in bringing a total change of government within a few weeks.[18]

This perspective has been used to help understand the timing of movement emergence, as well as, in comparative studies, to explain why a movement emerged in one place, but not in another with similar attributes. While this has been an illuminating concept, studies of political opportunities tend to focus on system-level structural conditions that may either facilitate or constrain movement activity, but give little emphasis to the activities of movement activists. From this perspective it may sometimes seem as if a movement is inevitable, a view that ignores the fact any movement is an accomplishment brought about by the work of activists. Tarrow's discussion of political opportunity structures is instructive:

> ... while they [political opportunities] do not on their own "explain" social movements, they play the strongest role in triggering general episodes of contention in which elites reveal their vulnerability, new social actors and forms of conflict appear, alliances are struck, and repression becomes sluggish or inconsistent ... Some dimensions of opportunity, like state strength or repressiveness, are more permanent than others, but the outbreak of episodes of contention is not based on stable structure alone.[19]

Mobilizing structures

The means and manner and vehicles through which social movements mobilize participants is another key factor. Research in this area has identified the importance of pre-existing networks in movement mobilization,[20] the complexity of factors affecting the decision to become an activist or remain a "free rider"[21](someone who receives benefits without being a member of the organization — for example, a labor union — that achieves them) and the contribution of what Aldon Morris calls "movement halfway houses" (training and education centers such as the Highlander Research and Education Center in Tennessee, Peace Action Centers, trade union schools, and Women's Centers) in developing and training networks of social activists.[22] This concept elaborates one of the key insights of resource mobilization theory, which suggested that movements emerge when they are successful in mobilizing sufficient resources; one major resource is, of course, participants. Studies of mobilizing structures have shed light on patterns of recruitment of participants and investigated motivations of participants.[23] There has, however, been less work on what it takes to retain membership in movement groups over time, although some studies have noted a pattern of discouragement and dropout in many movements.[24] MAP addresses this problem specifically.

Framing processes

This refers to the way in which social movements define, or articulate, the issues with which they are concerned. Snow and Benford, who introduced this concept to the social movement literature, propose that movements:

> ... are actively engaged in the production of meaning for partic-
> ipants, antagonists, and observers ... They frame or assign mean-
> ing to and interpret relevant events and conditions in ways that
> are intended to mobilize potential adherents and constituents, to
> garner bystander support, and to demobilize antagonists.[25]

Doug McAdam argues that the concept of framing is an important correc-
tive to structural theories, which often seem to suggest that movements are inevitable byproducts of certain structural conditions. For example, he points to Martin Luther King's work in the civil rights movement as a classic example of successful framing: "In his unique blending of familiar Christian themes, conventional democratic theory, and the philosophy of nonviolence, King brought an unusually compelling yet accessible frame to the struggle."[26] McAdam argues that this meaning-making work is a key part of movement activists' strategy: they must analyze the problem in such a way as to motivate participants and legitimate their efforts in the eyes of the general public.

To these widely used concepts, Tarrow adds three others that he believes are critical to understanding the trajectory of social movements:

- **Repertoires of action.** Movement activists, at a given place and time, have an
array of strategies and tactics. New tactics or strategies may be invented and then spread, and this invention of new, successful tactics can be an important component of movement growth. We suggest, for example, that the massive occu-
pation of the Seabrook, New Hampshire, nuclear power plant site in 1977 by the Clamshell Alliance, which led to the arrest of over 1,400 activists who were jailed in armories all over New Hampshire for two weeks, was such a new tactic for the anti-nuclear power movement. It sparked a series of similar, nonviolent, direct actions at nuclear power plant sites around the U.S. and elsewhere, as well as the proliferation of activist groups with a similar agenda, signified by the use

of parallel names such as the Abalone Alliance (California), the Crabshell Alliance (Seattle), and the Keystone Alliance (Philadelphia).

- **Cycles of contention or protest.** Protest activities tend to run in cycles, particularly as a new strategy or tactic is developed and is copied by other movement groups. This can result in rapid growth of the movement as it spreads to new communities.
- **Institutional response.** In order to understand the course of a social movement, it is important to study the response of the powerholders, as well as the response of the police and the media.

Limitations of contemporary social movement theory

Despite the additional frameworks and concepts proposed by these researchers, most remain focused on the most publicly visible aspects of a movement's work. The central problem is that researchers do not explore the full spectrum of a movement's activity. To conduct a more complete analysis they would need to look at both movement organizations and their activities and at movement-oriented activities taking place within regular, institutionalized political channels. This would require, as one movement scholar put it: "a degree of methodological syncretism that runs across the grain of the division of labor in contemporary social science."[27] Because most research stays within sharply defined academic disciplines, such as sociology or political science, it is difficult for researchers to see the depth and breadth of movement activity.

Doug McAdam has offered a critique of the limitations of contemporary social movement theory. After identifying six "strategic hurdles" for social movements, McAdam argues that theorists must examine movement effectiveness in overcoming these hurdles in order to understand movement successes and failures. The strategic hurdles are: [28]

- Attract new recruits
- Sustain the morale and commitment of current adherents
- Generate media coverage, preferably, but not necessarily, of a favorable sort
- Mobilize the support of various "bystander publics"
- Constrain the social control options of its opponents
- Ultimately shape public policy and state action

In his critique, McAdam says that social movement theory has not paid enough attention to the following issues, which bear on the six strategic hurdles.

- **Lack of study of movement dynamics and movement outcomes.** While there has been considerable attention to movement emergence issues, there has been comparatively little work on movement dynamics and movement outcomes, which include the last four hurdles on the list. He notes that there has been much work on the first two topics because of the strong theoretical interest in who joins social movements.[29]

- **Too little focus on activities of activists, particularly in framing processes.** In studies of the emergence of social movements there has been more emphasis on structural factors (for example, political opportunities structures) that facilitate and constrain movement emergence, and less focus on the actual activities of activists who create social movements. In particular, activist efforts to frame issues in such a way as to build the support of various constituent publics has received little research attention.

- **Absence of a focus on activists' work that creates social movements, that is, the agency of activists.** McAdam notes that "the everyday activities of movement participants" have been, ironically, "a neglected topic in the study of social movements." "We know little about the lived experience of activism or the everyday strategic concerns of movement groups" he says.[30] Similarly there has been a lack of focus on what Noel Sturgeon calls "direct theory" — the movement's own "theorizing through practice."[31]

- **Insufficient focus on movement actions in the framing process.** Social movements convey their framing of an issue to the public in two ways: through public statements and through their public actions. For example, during the civil rights movement, when activists sat in a restaurant and were refused service, it framed the issue of discrimination in public places through a powerful public action. In work on framing processes, according to McAdam, there has been too much focus on the verbal and written words of social movements and not enough focus on the way in which the actions themselves frame issues. He discusses what he calls "the framing function of movement tactics" in his work on the civil rights movement, noting, "It was the compelling dramaturgy of King's tactics rather than his formal pronouncements" that framed these issues for the public.[32]

- **Insufficient attention to non-movement actors.** Research has tended to be too movement-centered and has not paid sufficient attention to the other actors in the situation, for example, the government, the media, and other "bystander publics."

To these critiques offered by McAdam, we would like to add two of our own. First, the study of movement outcomes or results is hampered by confusion about the end point of a movement. Many researchers have looked for outcomes at the end of protest cycles and found that the movement often seemed to have little effect at that point. Some have noted depression and despair among activists as a movement "ends." Others, especially Tarrow, have noted what they consider a peculiar phenomenon: that although the movement is not successful at its conclusion, it often turns out that the goals of the movement are mysteriously enacted two to three years later, after the movement seems to be over. Tarrow, writing about movement outcomes, says:

Cycles of contention are a season for sowing, but the reaping is often done in the periods of demobilization that follow, by late-comers to the cause, by elites and authorities. The response to cycles of contention is often repressive, but even repression is often mixed with reform. Particularly when elites within the system see the opportunity to aggrandize themselves in alliance with challengers, rulers are placed in a vulnerable position [to] which reformism is a frequent response.[33]

Expecting successful outcomes immediately after a protest cycle is unrealistic, as the MAP model shows. Further stages must be allowed to unfurl before one seeks to determine if the movement has been successful. Looking for outcomes at the end of the protest phase can seriously underestimate the impact of social movements.

Second, no comprehensive theory exists that both explains the overall growth process of social movements and provides a framework for understanding the day-to-day dynamics of social movements. As we have noted earlier, most theories focus on particular aspects of the life of social movements, such as factors necessary for the emergence of a movement or the motivations of participants, but do not provide a comprehensive overview. Particularly significant is the tendency for studies to focus on the protest phase of a movement, but not to include in the definition of a social movement what MAP would consider the later phases of the movement. Some theorists, such as Gamson and Tilly, even suggest that "once a social movement begins to succeed by mobilizing a constituency or gaining formal representation, it ceases to be a movement, even if its goal, membership and tactics do not change."[34]

Tarrow frames it somewhat differently, as he sees that movements sometimes act like traditional interest groups, lobbying government bodies, but that when this occurs the study of their activities falls within the purview of political scientists. He acknowledges that the limited definition of social movements can be a problem, but notes that it is an artifact of the disciplinary boundaries within the social sciences and is difficult to overcome in scholarly work.[35] Ronald Libby, a political scientist writing about ecological movements, notes this same problem of disjuncture between the work of sociologists and political scientists. He describes what he calls "expressive interest groups," which he identifies as outgrowths of social movements that have the properties of both interest groups – such as money, expertise, and a political agenda — and the properties of social movement organizations, in that they mobilize citizens for social change. He argues that "the final stage of social movement activity — political campaigns by expressive groups — is often omitted from the analysis."[36]

These conceptual limitations and the traditional division of labor between the academic disciplines within the social sciences have been obstacles to the emergence of a comprehensive theory within the social sciences.

MAP and Contemporary Social Movement Theory

MAP makes significant contributions to social movement theory, providing:

- a comprehensive theoretical model of social movements;
- a framework for understanding movement outcomes;
- a framework for understanding movement dynamics;
- a focus on the agency of activists, including the differing roles played by activists at various points in the movement's development;
- an analysis of what is needed to sustain the morale and commitment of activists;
- an analysis of the importance of framing issues in terms of violations of widely held values; and
- an analysis of the potential for social movements to transform society so it becomes more fully based on a vision of compassion and respect, like that put forward by Gandhi and by Martin Luther King's "beloved community," and an understanding of how democracy can be a vehicle for that transformation.

These are the areas where there has been little previous research and theorizing.

- **MAP provides a comprehensive theory of social movements.** Bill Moyer defines social movements as "collective actions in which the populace is alerted, educated, and mobilized, sometimes over years and decades, to challenge the power holders and the whole society to redress social problems or grievances and restore critical social values." The key phrase to note is "over years and decades." Moyer views the movement as one entity, which uses various types of strategies over the course of its life — which may extend even for decades. The stages themselves are based on the degree of public support for the movement's goals (see Chapter 3).

MAP incorporates a more extensive definition of social movements than some theorists do, as it includes activities that are both institutionalized, such as lobbying, and non-institutionalized, such as direct action. In contrast, sociologists interested in protest tend to study Stage Four (and perhaps the stages leading up to it), while political scientists tend to study lobbying efforts, which are more typically Stage Six activities.

As we noted above, early social movement theorists were concerned particularly with the collective action aspects of social movements and identified movements as a type of collective behavior. Even recent theorists, such as Tarrow, seem wedded to this perspective. He writes about movements as "contentious politics" and focuses on the collective action. While much other research describes only one aspect or component of a movement's lifespan, the MAP Eight Stages Model provides a picture of "the whole elephant." This is a crucial matter when it comes to understanding movement outcomes.

MAP gives a framework for understanding movement outcomes. MAP makes an important contribution to understanding movement outcomes. By defining social movements as encompassing much more than the direct action /contentious politics stage, it suggests that we must examine movement outcomes not at the end of the direct action phase (or cycle of contention, to use Tarrow's term), but at a later point in the process, as the issues make their way through legislative bodies or other decision-making bodies of the powerholders. When a movement has gained the support of a majority of the populace, activists can then effectively use institutionalized channels to bring about change, though at this point the movement may look more like an interest group participating in lobbying than a protest group. The Eight Stages Model makes it clear that this is all part of the movement's history and is to be expected in a successful movement. It provides an alternative frame to Tarrow's description of cycles of contention as the "season for sowing," with the reaping occurring later by "elites and authorities."[37]

MAP gives a framework for understanding movement dynamics. MAP addresses many key areas of movement dynamics. The central thrust of the model is that appropriate tactics and strategy will vary depending on the stage of the movement. For example, in MAP Stage Two, activists need to develop strategies and tactics appropriate to Stage Two goals: working through existing channels and proving the failure of official institutions. The civil rights movement filed lawsuits and attempted to bring change through the courts; the anti-nuclear power movement made presentations at public hearings sponsored by the Nuclear Regulatory Commission; the women's movement, protesting society's treatment of rape victims, attempted to get local hospitals to serve rape victims more effectively and to get the courts to prosecute suspected rapists.

MAP also sees movements in terms of non-movement players — such as media, opposition, general public, government, and powerholders — and specific target sub-groups of the populace. It also suggests what activists must accomplish in order to be successful in the chess game of moves and countermoves between the movement and the powerholders for support of the public over time.

MAP places a focus on the agency of activists, including the differing roles played by activists at various points in a movement's development. The agency of activists is central to the MAP framework; the Eight Stages Model is intended to serve as an activist's guide for decision-making and for devising tactics and strategies. It addresses matters that are of great concern to those who are inventing and constructing social movements. There is a clear focus on, in McAdam's terms, "the everyday activities of movement participants."[38]

MAP analyzes how to sustain the morale and commitment of activists. A premise underlying MAP is that the morale and commitment of activists is strengthened when they have an understanding of the larger framework of social movements. Activists are nurtured by understanding the need for long-term work, the benefit of changing tactics and strategy depending on movement stage, and, perhaps most importantly, that "victory" is seldom won at the time of movement take-off. Sustained action of varying types is still required for a movement to be ultimately successful. Activists need to understand that protest is in the middle of a long-term process, with important actions also required both prior to and after the protest stage.

Researchers have identified a particular morale problem that often emerges after major protest activities. James Downton and Paul Wehr note that movement activists think they are failing and get discouraged. John Lofland writes about the soar and slump of polite protest.[39] MAP describes why demoralization emerges and what needs to be done by activists to avoid remaining in this state. In particular, activists playing the "rebel" role may become burned out at the end of the Stage Four take-off. The MAP model's Stage Five, "Perception of Failure," fits with the observation of these other theorists (see the Stage 5 discussion in Chapter 3).

In MAP, Moyer proposes that depression and drops in morale occur when activists do not have sufficient understanding of the long-term process of social movement success. They may also have difficulty switching from protest to the different actions required for mobilizing the general public to act (see the discussion on the four roles of activists in Chapter 2). MAP makes it clear that it is a major strategic mistake to try to win during the movement take-off stage.

MAP shows the importance of framing issues in terms of violations of widely held values. An important component of the power of social movements lies in activists' ability to show how powerholder policies violate widely held values such as freedom, democracy, the right to vote, fair treatment, sustainability, preservation of the environment for the next generation, equality, justice. The public can be aroused and will be supportive of movement goals when a movement shows that these cherished beliefs are being violated. For example, activists on both sides of the abortion issue have struggled for a framing that would provide them with the strongest public support. Anti-abortion activists have organized under the slogan "the right to life," while those supporting women's right to have an abortion have articulated their position as "women's right to choose." MAP articulates how the power of a social movement comes from such an aroused public, concerned about the violation of its cherished values.

MAP emphasizes the role of social movements to transform society to a more compassionate community, and the use of democracy as a vehicle for that change. MAP shares a Gandhian, Kingian vision that there is a basic urge in the universe for connection to one another, for compassion, for the building of "the good society," "the beloved community." Social movements can be a vehicle for that transformation, and democracy, in its broadest sense, can be a vehicle for accomplishing that. In this sense, MAP differs from more traditional academic frameworks, which generally do not take a strong value position. However, it is consistent with academic work in areas such as women's studies and African American studies, which do have an explicit values base.

MAP encourages the social construction of meaning. It has been argued by Alberto Melucci and others that one of the important tasks of social movements is to construct meaning for social movement activists themselves.[40] MAP has played a role in this work for over 20 years. Since it was first presented to activists in the anti-nuclear power movement in 1977, MAP has lived a life within social movements for peace and justice, serving as a training tool for nonviolent activists. In its function as a training tool for movement activists MAP helps activists examine the meaning of their movement experience. It has provided a context — a longer time frame, a definition of the tasks of social movements, a description of specific roles activists can play, and a theoretical model that makes sense of the movement's unfolding — that is more empowering and which places setbacks in a larger picture. Activists' ability to define and understand their situation has an impact on their ability to remain involved in and enthusiastic about a social movement, and this in turn affects the sustainability of their movement.

Conclusion

MAP provides a comprehensive theory that addresses many key aspects of social movements. The Eight Stages Model is a framework for understanding strategies, tactics, and other aspects of movement dynamics, as well as a framework for understanding movement outcomes or results. MAP helps to illuminate the work activists do in the creation of social movements and shows how that work must be adapted and modified as the movement gains more popular support (and thus moves from one stage to the next, in MAP terms). It addresses questions of the self-confidence and commitment of activists by identifying pitfalls that can cause morale problems if not sufficiently dealt with by the movement. Finally, MAP goes beyond the usual terrain of social movement theorizing to argue that social movements can be vehicles for revitalizing our democracies, calling us back to our most cherished values and transforming our societies into more compassionate and sustainable communities.

We hope that MAP contributes to the dialogue between scholars and activists, providing theoretical insights grounded in the practice of social movement activists. It would be good if we, as activist scholars and scholar activists, can find ways to work together toward the social transformations our societies so desperately need.

Part III

Case
Studies

6

The U.S. Civil Rights Movement

Bill Moyer[1]

The U.S. civil rights movement of the 1960s succeeded in achieving most of its goals and inspired a wave of nonviolent social movements around the world. The movement's goal was to gain for African Americans those rights that are guaranteed by the Constitution and Bill of Rights, and which, therefore, could be contested in the court system. Obviously, securing those rights is only one part of the larger effort to achieve full freedom and opportunity for blacks equal to that of white Americans.

It was as a participant in the civil rights movement that I first began to think about the process of social movements. This experience provided a model for the development of the MAP four roles of activism and eight stages of successful social movements.

Stage One: Normal Times (1940–1953)

During this period, the southern United States was a bastion of racism. Schools, public accommodations, jobs, housing, and political participation were segregated. Although racism thrived throughout the country, "Jim Crow" was the name given to the legal edifice of total racism that existed in the South and was openly advocated and enforced by the dominant white culture at all levels of local and state government and by social, economic, and religious institutions. It was backed up by strong social sanctions that included loss of employment, physical violence, and murder.

Mainstream America accepted this blatant violation of the Constitution and the Bill of Rights as the "Southern Way of Life." Neither the Democratic nor Republican parties considered this American-style apartheid a social problem or political issue. In 1938, for example, after over 100 Negro lynchings had occurred in that decade, Congress failed to pass an anti-lynching bill.

116

Clearly, even the most severe social problems, by themselves, do not cause a positive institutional response.

However, during this Stage One period, a number of movement activities emerged that achieved some specific changes and set the stage for future events. For example, in 1941, A. Philip Randolph threatened a massive black march on Washington to protest job discrimination and the segregation of the military. Fearing it would split the country and encourage the enemy in time of war, President Roosevelt issued an executive order to end discrimination in defense industry jobs and established the Fair Employment Commission. Although some blacks were employed, the Commission was ineffective. This was the first time that the tactic of threatening a mass demonstration was successfully used at the national level, and it served as a precedent for the future movement.

In 1942, members of the pacifist organization Fellowship of Reconciliation (FOR), including staffers James Farmer and Bayard Rustin, used Gandhi's method of nonviolent direct action, holding small "sit-ins" to successfully desegregate several restaurants in Chicago. Similar action groups formed in a few other northern cities, resulting in the formation of the Congress of Racial Equality (CORE) in 1943. For the next decade, CORE'S small-scale, localized, direct action activities helped to reduce blatant segregation in public accommodations in the North.

In 1946, Jackie Robinson and the Brooklyn Dodgers integrated baseball.[2] The following year, CORE organized the Journey of Reconciliation in which an interracial group violated segregation laws by traveling in buses to the South, serving as a model for later "freedom rides." In 1948, President Truman integrated the U.S. military. There were two main reasons for this. Military integration was a small step to end the blatant contradiction of so many blacks fighting and dying in World War II to preserve democracy and freedom that they were not granted at home. As well, it improved the U.S. image in the eyes of the black African colonies, many of which became nations immediately following the war. The U.S. and the rest of the "free world" needed to win these new nations to their sphere of influence in the Cold War with the U.S.S.R. and the Eastern Bloc nations.

None of these efforts precipitated a civil rights movement or a flurry of additional challenges to racism in other areas, because they were not grounded in a grassroots struggle. However, beginning in the 1930s, a cadre of black lawyers had affiliated with Howard Law School and the National Association for the Advancement of Colored People (eventually named the NAACP Legal Defense Fund) and developed a legal strategy for integrating public schools in the South. The group ultimately consolidated its many school discrimination lawsuits into the *Brown v. Board of Education of Topeka* case, which went to the Supreme Court. It was this act that precipitated the emergence of Stage Two.

Stage Two: Prove the Failure of Official Institutions (1954–1956)
On May 17, 1954, the U.S. Supreme Court rocked the nation with its decision that separate school facilities were not equal under the Constitution. The Court ordered public schools to be integrated "at all deliberate speed." At first this was hailed as a great victory for ending racism in education, supporting the NAACP's claim that racism could be eliminated through normal legal channels by reformers. But this conclusion was soon tested.

The federal government's decision to "force" white children to attend integrated schools affected all whites throughout the South, and most were appalled at the idea. It challenged the dominant racist white culture, the racist-based power structure, and the Jim Crow laws that ensured white supremacy. As a result, Southern whites mobilized a massive resistance movement against the NAACP and the court-ordered attempts to integrate the schools.

State and local governments and even the Congress and executive branch of the federal government refused to enforce the integration of schools. President Eisenhower called for "gradualism," arguing that each state had the right to create its own plan of school integration. Both the Democratic and Republican parties were vying for support from the racist, all white, southern Democrats. The Supreme Court decision itself did not call for immediate implementation, but specified that integration should occur at "all deliberate speed," which it left to the racist local governments to interpret. Another reaction to the Supreme Court decision was a resurgence of the Ku Klux Klan and the White Citizens Councils, which used inflammatory racist rhetoric, violence, and mob actions against any efforts to support the integration of the schools.[3]

The failure to implement the Supreme Court decision proved to the southern black community that the reformer role, and its method of using normal governmental, administrative, and legal channels alone, could not work in the South without the demands of an aroused citizenry.

In the city of Montgomery, however, the stage was set for a new type of civil rights activity. On Thursday, December 1, 1955, on her way home from work as a seamstress, Rosa Parks refused to give up her seat to a white person, was arrested and taken to jail. This led the black Women's Political Council to call for a boycott of the city's buses on Monday. A.D. Nixon, a local black civil rights advocate, called an emergency meeting of about 40 black ministers and civic leaders the next evening. They agreed to support the boycott, thousands of promotional leaflets were distributed, and the ministers announced the boycott from their pulpits on Sunday.[4] The boycott was 100 percent effective. The young Dr. Martin Luther King Jr. was chosen to head up the new organization/movement, the Montgomery Improvement Association (MIA), because he had recently arrived in town and was not involved in the stultifying feuds among the ministers.

King's speech at the Monday night rally following the successful boycott set the tone not only for the Montgomery boycott, but for the emerging civil rights movement. He called for a combination of militancy and moderation, grounded in both the Christian values of the black community and the democratic values of the nation. He said that they were full American citizens with a deep-seated belief in democracy, and that their campaign was to highlight the flagrant discrepancy between American ideals and practice. King said that the militant actions of their boycott would be carried out with total love and nonviolence toward the white community, that they were there to "fulfill the American dream, not to condemn it."

The boycott lasted for 381 days. The entire black community of 50,000 people was involved. There were weekly mass meetings and an organized carpooling system for people to get to work and school. There was also a strong commitment to love and nonviolence based on the words of Gandhi and of the Bible.

The city's powerholders and racist white community reacted with a series of strategies. MIA car-pool drivers were constantly ticketed by police, and building inspectors placed notices of housing code violations on the buildings used by the movement. When local underwriters refused to give insurance to MIA drivers, Lloyds of London did. About 100 leaders, including Dr. King, were arrested for violating the state's anti-boycotting laws. King's house was bombed.

The drama of the struggle in the heart of Dixie, sustained over time, drew not only national, but worldwide attention. Funding flowed in from around the country. In the heat of the campaign, the MIA raised its demands to a call for total desegregation of the buses. The boycott eventually ended with total success when the U.S. Supreme Court overturned the Alabama state and local bus segregation laws in October 1956. After days of mass nonviolence workshops in which blacks received training on how to remain peaceful in the face of provocative attacks, King and others led the peaceful integration of the buses on December 21, 1956.

The Montgomery Bus Boycott arose because the movement in Montgomery was in MAP's third stage, Ripening Conditions. Montgomery's black community was a highly politicized environment. The city buses were a daily symbol of segregation and humiliation. The city's Jim Crow laws required blacks to sit in the back of the bus and to give up their seats as the number of white passengers increased. This bus segregation system had a multitude of weaknesses: it violated the U.S. Constitution and Bill of Rights; it violated the widely held values of the American people and the image of America that the U.S. government was trying to project around the world as it vied for superpower leadership of the "free" world; the bus company was economically dependent on black riders, who made up about 70 percent of the passengers; and the entire black community of Montgomery was offended by it.

Furthermore, the key actors were well prepared. Rosa Parks had been a past secretary of the local NAACP, and a month earlier she had attended a two-week training conference at the Highlander Folk School, a Tennessee training center for community social change activists. A.D. Nixon was an officer in a militant union, the Brotherhood of Sleeping Car Porters, was a past state president of the NAACP, and had been involved in the threatened March on Washington a few years before. He and Jo Ann Robinson of the Women's Political Council had talked about a boycott of the segregated Montgomery bus system months earlier — they even had made a sample flyer for a bus boycott. Martin Luther King had studied Gandhian nonviolence at university, attended local NAACP meetings, and had just established social and political action committees in his church. The black church was the central pre-existing institution that was available to support the new movement as it took off, as were civic groups such as the Women's Political Council.

The boycott effectively used all four MAP roles. The citizens kept the campaign grounded in the nation's widely held values of democracy and freedom, and their demands were based on the civil rights guaranteed by the U.S. Constitution. Many of the citizens were based in the Christian church, which was revered by the large majority of whites in Montgomery and within mainstream America. The rebels brought attention to the movement with the nonviolent bus boycott campaign. The entire black community of Montgomery filled the social change agent role by its involvement in the boycott, mass meetings, and car-pooling. Finally, the reformers ultimately won the day through the court case, which was decided favorably by the U.S. Supreme Court.

The Montgomery Bus Boycott was the first successful effort that combined both the Gandhian nonviolent action, mass movement approach with the NAACP-type legal tactics. Such mass movements can use political, economic, and legal strategies, or any combination of the three, to achieve their goals. The Montgomery movement was unable to apply either *political* pressure on the racist city government, especially since most blacks could not vote, or effective *economic* pressure on the business community, which was not much tied to the city bus company. Ultimately, it was the *legal* strategy that brought victory.

Rosa Parks' arrest was the trigger event for the Montgomery bus integration movement, but it did not serve as the trigger event for the launching of the larger civil rights movement because that was still in Stage Two, Proving the Failure of Official Institutions. The Montgomery bus integration campaign was a successful sub-movement of the larger civil rights movement, and it demonstrated that it was possible to change the South's Jim Crow laws by combining the mass movement nonviolent action method with a legal strategy.

Stage Three: Ripening Conditions (1956–1959)

During the last half of the 1950s, three developments made the social movement of the 1960s inevitable. First, the black community became disenchanted with elite leaders' efforts to end Jim Crow using official channels, such as the courts and lobbying government officials. Second, the effectiveness of the NAACP, which championed this "institutional politics" approach, was greatly reduced in the South due to the white racist system's backlash attacks resulting from the *Brown* decision. And third, new civil rights groups committed to the mass movement method of direct action sprouted in black communities across the South following the Montgomery Bus Boycott.

Ever since its founding in 1909, the NAACP had been the dominant black protest organization in the United States. It was a classic professional opposition organization — highly bureaucratic, with key staff and leadership drawn from the professional class, including ministers, teachers, lawyers, and doctors. Its primary activity was limited to the elite-led institutional politics method of educational persuasion and legal challenge. Although it was widely respected by the black community, it did not involve a mass base of ordinary citizens.

Following the NAACP's startling school integration victory at the Supreme Court in 1954, the southern white racist community and power structure set out to destroy the civil rights organization they feared was about to end the "Southern Way of Life." The all-out war of repression against both the NAACP organization and associated individuals included repressive laws, legal actions, intimidation, loss of employment, physical violence, and murder. In Alabama, the organization was made illegal for nine years. As a result, between 1955 and 1958 the NAACP lost 246 branches and over 49,000 members in the South.[5]

During this period, the NAACP not only lost its hegemony over southern civil rights efforts, but the reformer role and its bureaucratic style of organizing lost favor in the black community as well. The stage was set for the emergence of a new style of civil rights activism that was based on mass movements and the rebel and social change agent roles of nonviolent direct action and grassroots organizing.

Inspired by the Montgomery movement, bus boycott campaigns and other civil rights activities sprang up in dozens of black communities across the South, starting in 1956.[6] They were invigorated by a new hope that change was possible in the South, and by a realization that the nonviolent mass movement method gave them a powerful organizing tool. The new strategy also allowed them to overcome the traditional divisions within the black community's leadership by bringing together younger inspired leaders, mostly clergy and students, who were ready to take bold action. Moreover, the nonviolent mass movement approach allowed everyone to actively participate, old and young, men and women, rich and poor, white and black, professionals and working class.

Sociologist Aldon Morris called these autonomous, civil rights action communities Local Movement Centers (LMCs).[7] Based in local black churches, they organized a wide variety of activities — demonstrations, sit-ins, boycotts, education, voter registration, nonviolent action training, legal cases, organization development, fundraising, and regular mass meetings — and were also just a place to hang out with others who were ready to be involved in this new effort. Some of the action-experienced people, such as Martin Luther King, traveled extensively to help inspire, organize, and train activists in the multitude of LMCs.

In January 1957, leaders of these LMCs from 11 states met at Dr. Martin Luther King Sr.'s Ebenezer Baptist church in Atlanta and formed an organization that became the Southern Christian Leadership Conference (SCLC). Thereafter, SCLC provided communication, coordination, and support for and between the dozens of local protest movements that were previously autonomous. One of SCLC's principle requirements for membership was that groups agree to promote mass-based, nonviolent, direct action movements. Dr. Martin Luther King Jr. was chosen to lead the new organization.

The Crusade for Citizenship was one of SCLC's first projects. Its purpose was to educate and register blacks to vote, taking advantage of the 1957 Civil Rights Act that supported the right to vote. Due to massive white resistance (and the lack of sufficient organization in the black community), the Crusade failed to enfranchise blacks, proving again that the normal racist political system did not work for blacks. However, it did serve to further educate, train, organize, and prepare the black community in the method and the necessity for taking the more militant direct action mass movement approach.

The Gandhian nonviolent mass movement method's connection to the black southern civil rights movement was strengthened when both King and the Reverend James Lawson made separate trips to India to learn directly from Gandhi's followers. After two years in India, Lawson returned in 1959 and ran a nonviolent action training program Saturday mornings for black divinity school students in Nashville, Tennessee. Members of this class, such as James Bevel, Diane Nash, Bernard Lafayette, and John Lewis, later became leaders of the 1960s movement. Their group not only studied the theory and practice of nonviolence, but they also experimented with sit-ins and protests against Jim Crow laws in Nashville. Moreover, they planned to begin a full-fledged sit-in campaign early in 1960.

At the same time, NAACP Youth Division members Floyd McKissick and Douglas Moore began conducting trial sit-ins in the restaurants, bus station, and ice cream parlors in Durham, North Carolina. The NAACP did not support these efforts. There were also a number of "outside" sources of support for the new budding movement, including the Highlander Folk School, which helped by training organizers of the new movement; the Fellowship of Reconciliation and CORE, which provided nonviolence training; and northern black churches and white liberals, which provided some funding.

The stage was set. The black community was organized and trained for a new social movement, expectations were high, local groups committed to mass movement direct action were established across the South, nonviolent direct action was a proven method, the black church and black students were part of the established institutions and existing networks, coordinated by SCLC, that were in place. People were ready to go.

Stage Four: Take-Off (1960–1963)

The widely acknowledged trigger event of the 1960s Civil Rights movement occurred on February 1, 1960, when four black freshmen at North Carolina Agricultural and Technical College in Greensboro, N.C., violated the law by "spontaneously" sitting down at Woolworth's whites-only lunch counter. They were refused service, but remained seated until closing time. That night they held a meeting with other students in their dormitory, and the next day 30 students resumed the sit-in. Soon hundreds of students from the ten Greensboro-area black colleges joined in, waiting in shifts to be served, starting the lunch counter sit-in movement.[8]

Typical of Stage Four take-off, students across the South repeated the sit-in tactic at their local eating establishments. Demonstrators underwent extensive nonviolence action training to prepare them for harassment, arrest, and jail time. Each sit-in was carefully planned and timed. It soon became clear to demonstrators and white authorities alike that the traditional powerholder method of controlling the black community by intimidation and arrest did not work against the mass movement method. In fact, most demonstrators welcomed arrest as a symbol of their involvement in the new freedom movement. And the arrests and physical violence by the powerholders only served to inspire more participants and to promote the cause to the rest of the nation and the world as it was covered by the media. By mid-April, an estimated 50,000 demonstrators had participated in sit-ins in 78 communities, and 2,000 had been arrested.[9] Moreover, support demonstrations were soon organized at 100 mostly white colleges in the North.

Ella Baker, SCLC's executive director, organized a conference, The Southwide Student Leadership Conference on Nonviolent Resistance to Segregation, in Raleigh, North Carolina, on April 15 to 17, 1960. About 120 students, representatives from sit-ins throughout the South, attended, and there were another 100 observers, mostly white students active in the North. On the advice of Baker, the students formed a new independent organization, the Student Nonviolent Coordinating Committee (SNCC).

SNCC had a small national staff and office and a decentralized structure, giving total autonomy to the local groups. They believed that the traditional bureaucratic organizations of many adult-led civil rights groups were too hierarchical for the mass movement direct action method to work. On the other hand, they feared a totally spontaneous, "structureless" model was too loose and chaotic and would be ripe for takeover by activists with strong egos or by agents provocateurs. Consequently, they developed a third organizational model — a decentralized, participatory democratic model that used Quaker consensus. This contrasted with SCLC's model, which gave autonomy to its affiliate groups but left final decisions to the minister at the top of each organization.

The sit-in movement again showed that the nonviolent direct action and mass movement strategy was an effective method for the black civil rights movement, especially when accompanied with an effective economic, political, or legal strategy. Woolworth's, for example, adopted a total integration policy because it suffered economically from the combination of lost black business in the South and the secondary picketing and boycott of its northern stores. On the other hand, the Nashville sit-in movement of 1960 hurt the profits not only of the restaurants but of all the white downtown businessmen. It ended with a gigantic march to the steps of city hall, where the mayor told the movement's spokesperson, Diane Nash, that he agreed to desegregate the lunch counters. This nonviolent mass movement strategy was adopted by the rest of the civil rights movement and by many social movements around the world in the years following.

By the end of 1960, dozens of cities in the "Upper South" had their eating establishments integrated, but much of the "Deep South" remained unmoved. The demolition of the Jim Crow system and the achievement of basic civil rights had only begun to take off. Ultimately, it would require the awakening of the majority of the American people to demand federal intervention through new laws that were seriously enforced.

The following year, in a strategic attempt to force the federal government into the civil rights struggle, CORE launched the Freedom Rides campaign to test the federal laws that guaranteed the integration of the nation's interstate bus and train terminals. The simple plan was for integrated groups to sit in the front seats of public buses as they went to the Deep South, thereby deliberately violating Jim Crow bus segregation laws. The first bus, with James Farmer, CORE's executive director, on board, left Washington, D.C., on May 4, 1961. Ten days later, a white mob burned the bus outside of Aniston, Georgia. On May 21, Freedom Riders were physically attacked and beaten by a white mob as they arrived at the Montgomery, Alabama, bus terminal. That night an aggressive white mob threatened King and the Freedom Riders as they held a mass meeting in a church. The next day the federal government was forced to intervene, providing National

Guard protection as a new wave of Freedom Riders left on a bus. However, this group was arrested and imprisoned when the bus arrived in Jackson, Mississippi. During the next months, 300 Freedom Riders were arrested and put in Parchman, Mississippi, jail for up to 50 days each.

The sustained Gandhian-type sociodrama campaign of arrests and imprisonment of people attempting to integrate bus terminals drew media attention over the summer. The entire nation was upset by the white mob brutality, the violations of the legal civil right of interstate travel, and the complicity of the police as well as the local and federal governments. The social pressure built up to the point that by September, the Freedom Rides succeeded in their goal: the federal Interstate Commerce Commission made a new ruling to desegregate interstate bus and train stations, establishing new penalties for violators, effective November 1, 1961.

Beginning on that date, SNCC sent waves of activists to Albany, Georgia, to test the new law. Their arrests, when they arrived in Albany, were the catalyst for the local adults to respond by creating a new broad action coalition, the Albany Movement. This movement conducted a series of demonstrations, culminating in the arrest of Martin Luther King and 250 others on a "prayer march" on their way to city hall. The town's powerholders were forced to make a verbal promise to obey the federal law by desegregating the terminals. Martin Luther King and the others were let out of jail and agreed to call a halt to the demonstrations.

Albany appeared to be a great success. It was, therefore, a tremendous embarrassment to King and the movement when the city failed to keep its promise. For the next six months the movement unsuccessfully tried to resume its campaign of boycotts and demonstrations, but the broken agreement had taken away its momentum. When Dr. King returned to Albany for his court trial in August 1962, the activists again attempted to rejuvenate the movement by staging marches, rallies, picketing, sit-ins, and other kinds of demonstrations. Over a thousand demonstrators went to jail, including 70 northern clergy. However, police chief Laurie Pritchett adopted a new and effective police strategy. He responded by appearing to be reasonable and with minimal violence, dispersing those arrested to jails in surrounding counties so that the movement ran out of demonstrators before the police ran out of cells. The movement dissipated.

While the movement succeeded in putting severe economic pressure on the downtown businessmen, ending the campaign on the powerholders' mere promise to meet the movement's demands for integration was a fatal mistake. This was a lesson well learned, which King and the movement were intent on not repeating.

Despite failure to achieve its stated goals, the Albany Movement successfully used the mass movement method to mobilize the entire local black community.

Through the national and worldwide publicity that it focused on Albany's Jim Crow segregation, the movement alerted, educated, and won the sympathy of the majority of northern public opinion. With the campaign in Albany, the civil rights movement advanced to MAP's Stage Six, Majority Public Opinion.

Stage Five: Perception of Failure (1964–1968)

Since the Montgomery Bus Boycott, the civil rights movement's culture, organization, and leadership were based in the black Christian church. The movement was characterized by a clear ethic of love and nonviolence, strong clergy leadership, and Gandhi's method of nonviolent mass movement. Its purpose was integrationist. Black Americans should have the status of full citizens, with equal rights, responsibilities, and privileges, and the opportunity to participate in American life. Their vision was that blacks be integrated into the society just as previous oppressed groups, such as the Irish, Jews, and Poles, had been. As Martin Luther King was fond of saying, the aim was to fulfill the American Dream of equality, democracy, and justice, not to condemn it.

When CORE and SNCC joined with SCLC in 1960 as the primary organizations involved in the southern civil rights movement, they were in full agreement with the principles of achieving integration through nonviolent action. These two groups, however, were secular and organizationally separate from SCLC's network of church-based Local Movement Centers.

Four years later, when hundreds of northern white students (including myself) participated in the Mississippi Freedom Summer Project of 1964, we expected to encounter anger and hostility from white Mississippi racists, but we were shocked and dismayed to receive a similar response from many (though not all) of the SNCC and CORE staff and volunteers. This was the beginning of an ideological split that festered inside the movement for the next few years. The split became national news during James Meredith's Mississippi March Against Fear in 1966, when SNCC leaders Willie Ricks, Stokely Carmichael, and H. Rap Brown began shouting "Black Power,"[10] challenging the movement's "Freedom Now" slogan as the ideological basis for the black people's movement.

The emergent Carmichael/SNCC-led faction of the movement cited the need for a more militant strategy, abandoning nonviolence. They said that the white powerholders and racist whites would continue to resist violently and would never allow blacks full and equal citizenship. Consequently, they advocated black separatism and black independence by any means necessary, including violence. H. Rap Brown frequently received national publicity as he justified their advocacy of violence, saying things like "Violence is as American as apple pie." This call was connected to an appeal for black pride, empowerment, and black consciousness, mainly drawn from the activities of Malcolm X and the Black Nationalism movement, which had gained some popularity at the time. Though a leading figure in the black struggle, Malcolm X played no part in the southern civil rights movement. He advocated separatism, violence, and hostility towards whites, all of which were at odds with the nonviolent integration movement.[11]

In the face of calls for violence, Martin Luther King said:

> I could imagine nothing more impractical and disastrous than for any of us ... to precipitate a violent confrontation in Mississippi. We had neither the resources nor the techniques to win ... Many Mississippi whites, from the government on down, would enjoy nothing more than for us to turn to violence in order to use this as an excuse to wipe out scores of Negroes in and out of the march ...

> The problem with hatred and violence is that they intensify the fears of the white majority and leave them less ashamed of their prejudices toward Negroes ... Violence only adds to the chaos. It deepens the brutality of the oppressor and increases the bitterness of the oppressed. Violence is the antithesis of creativity and wholeness.[12]

At the same time, King realized that the movement needed a "strategy for change, a tactical program that will bring the Negro into the mainstream of American life as quickly as possible. Nonviolent action already has a remarkable record of achievements from buses, lunch counters, public accommodations and voting rights."[13]

Stage Six: Majority Public Opinion (1963–1964)

The majority public opinion stage began in 1963 with the Birmingham Movement, the most successful civil rights campaign to date. For seven years, protests had totally failed in Birmingham, Alabama, where the infamous Public Safety Commissioner "Bull" Connor enforced total white supremacy in one of the most racist cities in the South. That changed in April, when Dr. King and SCLC were invited to lead a new civil rights effort in Birmingham. It was a huge endeavor and met with brutal resistance. There were daily demonstrations for 65 days, mass meetings of sometimes over 5,000 people, and thousands of demonstrators were arrested, at times filling the jails. There, King wrote his famous "Letter from a Birmingham Jail" to the local clergy.

But what most stirred the moral conscience of the nation and the world was the TV and newspaper coverage of police clubs, water hoses, attack dogs turned on young and old demonstrators, the violence by the state national guard, and the series of bombings, including the bombing of a church where four little girls attending Sunday school were killed, which caused Birmingham to be nicknamed "Bombingham." In spite of such deliberate provocations, the movement remained nonviolent. Finally, on May 10, 1963, the movement ended successfully when the Birmingham political and business powerholders agreed to desegregate the business district and also hire blacks.

The Birmingham movement's success can be attributed to a number of factors:

- It used the nonviolent mass movement method effectively, involving the entire local black population.
- It maintained a sociodrama action campaign for 65 consecutive days, with nightly mass meetings and demonstrations that exposed Birmingham's brutal enforcement of segregation.
- The black community's demands for basic legal rights won worldwide support through continuous media coverage.
- It remained nonviolent, despite extreme efforts by the police and state national guard to provoke demonstrators to violence, which would have obscured the discrimination issues and taken away the movement's moral high ground.
- Its strategy of putting economic pressure on downtown businesses succeeded, as a sustained boycott and demonstrations in the business section kept even white patrons away.
- It had very narrow and focused demands with a specific target group, as opposed to the Albany campaign, which made very general demands.
- It did not give in to the powerholders' first verbal offer of unsubstantiated promises, as it did in Albany.
- Worldwide news coverage embarrassed the Kennedy administration into pressuring the Birmingham powerholders to capitulate.

The Birmingham campaign completed the movement's process to put civil rights on society's agenda and won a larger majority of public opinion in support of its cause. The strength of public support became immediately apparent at the conclusion of the Birmingham movement when Martin Luther King and others made triumphant tours of key northern cities. King estimated that over a million people attended those first white-majority mass meetings of the civil rights movement that occurred in Cleveland; St. Louis; New York; Washington, D.C.; Chicago; Los Angeles; and Detroit, to name but a few.[14]

In the ten weeks after Birmingham, the U. S. Justice Department recorded 1,412 separate demonstrations and 12,500 arrests — and that 275 of the 574 larger southern communities desegregated at least some of their facilities.[15] The number of SCLC affiliates grew from 85 to 110. On June 11, President Kennedy urged Congress to pass an administration bill that would prohibit discrimination in public accommodations. By the end of the summer, King concluded that the movement was responsible for thousands of integrated restaurants, hotels, parks, swimming pools and new job openings. King's assessment was:

> For hundreds of years the quiet sobbing of an oppressed people had been unheard by millions of white Americans ... The lament became a shout and then a roar and for months no American, white or Negro, was insulated or unaware ... White America was forced to face the ugly facts of life as the Negro thrust himself onto the consciousness of the country and dramatized his grievances on a thousand brightly lighted stages.[16]

On August 28, 1963, the civil rights movement held what A. Philip Randolf called the largest march in U.S. history. The March on Washington had over 250,000 black and white participants. That historic event, in which King delivered his "I have a dream" speech, demonstrated that the civil rights movement was well into MAP's majority public opinion stage. Moreover, the media treated the march as a significant occasion by giving it sympathetic, banner-headline newspaper coverage and live television and radio coverage nationally and overseas. Tens of millions of white Americans saw black Americans portrayed in the media in a positive light for the first time. Observing the friendly demonstrators and hearing the persuasive logic and wisdom of a series of black leaders, culminating with King, inspired blacks and informed and won over millions more white Americans.

By the end of the summer, a *Newsweek* survey reported that an overwhelming majority of whites in the North and South supported laws to guarantee voting rights, job opportunities, good housing, and integrated travel facilities. A large majority in the North and almost a majority in the South favored integrated schools and lunch counters.[17] Moreover, King concluded that the biggest reason for hope was the massive alliance for civil rights created among the various segments of the country during the summer.[18] Thousands of student, civil, labor, political, and religious groups engaged in either direct involvement or support efforts for blacks to gain full civil rights in the United States.

The desegregation movement in 1963 created such public political pressure that the federal government was on the defensive. It felt forced to take some kind of decisive action, at least against blatant segregation and Jim Crow laws in the South. Therefore, with King and other civil rights leaders in attendance, President Johnson signed the milestone 1964 Civil Rights Act before a national radio and television audience on July 2, 1964. The Act outlawed segregation and discrimination in public accommodations — such as hotels, restaurants, movie theaters, public parks, drinking fountains, and other places that provided public services — and in some specific aspects of voter registration and employment. It removed one of the most overt aspects of racism, the "Whites Only" signs.

Although President Johnson told the civil rights leaders present at the signing that the Act removed the need for any more direct action protest demonstrations, they recognized that the law was no cure-all. It contained lots of holes. It did not guarantee the right to vote, nor did it provide federal government protection, nondiscriminatory housing, or relief from poverty.

The logical next target of the movement was the right to register and to vote. Full participation in the political process had long been recognized by the movement as the key to blacks achieving justice and equality in the South; it was also thought to be the most difficult goal. Because the black vote was feared by the racist southern powerholders, it was fiercely opposed. There were local legal obstacles, racist violence, and black fear and apathy regarding voting. But there was also a "hands off" policy on the part of the federal government, including the FBI, which meant the feds would not interfere with racism of any kind that occurred in the southern states. Consequently, it was only now, when the overall civil rights movement was solidly in the majority public opinion stage, that the voting rights sub-movement reached the ripening conditions phase and was ready for take-off.

Mississippi was chosen as the target for the voting rights campaign because it represented the heart of the Deep South and had several years of solid grassroots organizing for voter registration. In November 1963, a statewide umbrella civil rights organization called the Council of Federated Organizations (COFO) ran its own "freedom candidates" in a symbolic alternative election, since they were excluded from the official election process. Then on April 26, 1964, COFO established the Mississippi Freedom Democratic Party (MFDP) to hold its own unofficial Democratic Party primary elections that summer for the purpose of selecting alternative Democratic candidates who were elected in an open, non-racist process that was in keeping with the U.S. Constitution and the Bill of Rights. This process challenged the official Democratic Party convention in Atlantic City in September, where candidates were elected in a racist process in which blacks were not allowed to run for office.

The trigger event that launched the take-off stage of the voting rights sub-movement was the 1964 Mississippi Summer Project, which was sponsored by four major civil rights organizations: SNCC, CORE, SCLC, and the NAACP.[19] Over 700 students, mostly northern and white, were recruited, trained, and dispersed to work with MFDP groups across Mississippi. Because the project was enormous in size, was an ongoing dramatic event, and put the lives of northern white students at risk, the Summer Project received major media coverage. For the first time, the attention of the entire nation was fixed on the state of Mississippi and its violent racist opposition to black citizens' right to vote.

Over the summer, four participants were killed and 80 were beaten. Over a thousand arrests were made and 67 homes, churches, and business were bombed or burned.[20] The FBI's six-week hunt for the bodies of three civil rights workers highlighted the extent of violent opposition to black voting rights. Nevertheless, the MFDP registered over 80,000 people during the summer, and in its unofficial alternative Democratic primary the MFDP elected 68 delegates to the Democratic National Convention. The Democratic Party refused to seat those delegates at the Atlantic City convention. However, the party made a landmark decision that for the 1968 convention, racial discrimination in selecting state party delegates would be prohibited. Members of the MFDP and SNCC were extremely angry and disillusioned, and a split occurred between them and the more established civil rights groups, such as SCLC and the NAACP, which were more willing to accept the less than ideal compromises offered by the Democratic Party.

Then on December 10, 1964, Martin Luther King received the Nobel Peace Prize, which not only promoted his personal status, but also increased the credibility of the entire civil rights movement. All the pieces were finally lined up for the Civil Rights Movement's end-game challenge to achieve the right to vote.

Stage Seven: Success (1965–1968)

In 1965 the movement launched a voting rights campaign in remote Selma, Alabama. Like Mississippi, Selma represented entrenched racist "bitter end" resistance to black civil rights. The city of Selma, for example, had imposed an injunction against all civil rights public meetings since the failed attempts to integrate its public accommodations the previous July. Strategists thought that a sociodrama campaign against Selma's severe resistance could evoke such sympathy and outrage that the entire nation would demand a federal voting rights act.

The Selma Campaign was organized jointly by SCLC, SNCC, and the local coalition called the Dallas County Voters League (DCVL). It began with a mass meeting on January 2, 1965, addressed by King. This was soon followed by daily marches to the county courthouse, where blacks tried, mostly unsuccessfully, to register to vote. Continuous confrontations with the authorities led to several thousand arrests. On March 7, in what became known as Bloody Sunday, state troopers and sheriff's deputies, many on horseback, attacked, beat, and gassed hundreds of demonstrators as they crossed the Pettus Bridge, attempting to march from Selma to the state capitol of Montgomery.

The nation was outraged when the event was highlighted on the TV news and in every newspaper. Sympathy marches were held across the country, and over a thousand people demonstrated outside the White House. Hundreds of clergy and others responded to an emergency call to join the next attempted Selma marches. One northern clergyman, Reverend James Reeb, was beaten and killed by whites outside a Selma restaurant. In response to these events, on March 15, President Johnson submitted a Voting Rights Bill to Congress. He delivered a stirring special address to Congress, viewed on television by 70 million Americans, in which he pleaded that "their cause must be our cause, too," and ended by repeating the movement's theme, "We Shall Overcome." Protected by 1,800 Alabama national guardsmen, the march from Selma to Montgomery finally occurred between March 21 and 25. The power of an aroused and outraged public sped up the political process, and President Johnson signed the historic 1965 Voting Rights Act on August 6.

There was one last sub-movement led by Dr. King that was clearly focused on black civil rights. After being stymied in their End Slums community organizing effort, SCLC and the local Coordinating Council of Community Organizations (CCCO) launched the Chicago Open Housing Movement. On July 30, 1966, at a mass meeting, Dr. King announced the beginning of a series of marches out to the real estate offices in the whites-only neighborhoods to demand that they serve blacks on a nondiscriminatory basis. Real estate offices were seen as similar to discriminatory restaurants; both were businesses open to serve the public.

During the next four weeks, three days each week, between 200 and 1,000 black and white demonstrators marched (or sometimes rode in cars) from churches in the black community out to the distant white neighborhoods, such as Gage Park and Marquette Park. The marchers were met with the jeers, bricks, bottles, racist signs, Confederate flags, knives, firecrackers, Nazi insignias, and fists of thousands of angry white people. On one occasion, dozens of demonstrators' cars were blown up (while guarded by Chicago police) and 28 demonstrators were sent to emergency care. The blocks where marchers stopped at real estate offices often looked like war zones, with the large front windows of most of the businesses broken by flying objects. On August 5, in the middle of a march in Marquette Park, Dr. King was hit on the head by a brick. He later commented, "I've been in many demonstrations all across the South, but I can say that I have never seen — even in Mississippi and Alabama — mobs as hostile and as hate-filled as I've seen in Chicago."[21]

Initially, Mayor Richard Daley's police, though present, provided little protection for the marchers because the racist white community was a basis of Daley's political power. Eventually, the continuous negative publicity from the national and worldwide television coverage of the carnage led Daley to provide massive and ample police protection for the demonstrators. Moreover, the ongoing exposure of the segregated and racist housing policies in Chicago and, finally, the expected violence against the movement's impending march to the town of Cicero, known for its violent racism, forced Mayor Daley to make an open housing agreement with CCCO on August 26, 1966. The Summit Agreement included a list of specific steps the city and other business, labor, and governmental organizations pledged to take for fair housing. An independent organization, the Leadership Council for Metropolitan Housing, was established to assure the agreement's implementation. The Chicago Open Housing Movement also made a critical contribution to the passage of the 1968 Civil Rights Act, which outlawed racial discrimination in housing.

By the end of 1966, the civil rights movement had achieved its primary goal of removing all of the overt racist Jim Crow laws in the South and North. Moreover, it had forced the passage of a series of federal laws and executive orders that legally assured blacks of their civil rights that were guaranteed them by the United States Constitution.

Stage Eight: Continuing the Struggle (1966 to the future)

The civil rights movement was astoundingly successful, especially considering where it started. It created a revolution in the civil rights of African Americans, particularly by ending the racist Jim Crow laws and customs in the South. Moreover, the reverberations of the civil rights movement continue to be felt not only throughout the United States, but worldwide. The movement's eighth stage, Continuation, in which it expands its successes while simultaneously protecting against backlash, has been going on since the 1960s.

The continuing expansion of the civil rights movement achievements is evident in both the North and South. The most dramatic changes can be seen in the South in the integration of politics, public accommodations, buses, restaurants, schools, universities, sports teams, and the workforce. In her 1994 article "The Fruits of Freedom Summer," for example, Bell Gale Chevigny reported some indications of the fundamental changes in Mississippi to that date. Mississippi then led the nation with 890 black elected officials. There was a changed racial climate, indicated by the integration of the local police forces and the state highway patrol. The first black law graduate of Ole Miss, 1960s civil rights activist Constance Slaughter-Harvey, was the general counsel to the Secretary of State. Mississippi adopted mandatory attendance in school, the last state to do so. Infant mortality was drastically reduced, and gross hunger and malnutrition, gross anemia, and parasites had all but disappeared according to Dr. Robert Smith, an African American Mississippian who was co-founder of the Medical Committee for Human Rights in 1964.[22]

Sub-Movements — From Civil Rights to Anti-Vietnam War and Economic Justice

By the summer of 1965, the civil rights movement had swelled in numbers and stature. Dr. King and the movement were seen by many as representative of the nation's highest values. Yet with President Johnson's signing of the 1965 Voting Rights Act, SCLC staffer Jim Bevel ominously concluded, "There is no more civil rights movement."[23] A. Philip Randolph called it a "crisis of victory," because the next barriers to black equality and justice were beyond civil rights; they were issues demanding the radical transformation of the nation's social and economic structures. That is to say, in MAP theory, they were not strictly sub-movements of the black civil rights movements.

Martin Luther King also understood that the problems of both black America and the nation as a whole required solutions far beyond civil rights. Moreover, King was well aware of the risks when he took leadership in promoting the unpopular anti-Vietnam war view and the issue of economic justice. Consequently, during the last two years of his life, King was often vilified by blacks and whites, conservatives and liberals, and civil rights leaders and racists. In addition, he was the target of the fury of President Johnson and the harassment of J. Edger Hoover's FBI.[24]

Anti-Vietnam War

King felt that morally, ethically, and strategically he had to take a public stand and leadership against the United States' war in Vietnam, regardless of the consequences. He said he could not split himself to support violence against Asians and nonviolence at home. He saw that black soldiers were not only slaughtering Vietnamese, but were being killed themselves, and at twice the rate of white soldiers. Moreover, King asserted that the money to end poverty at home was "being squandered on the Vietnam War"[25] and that the bombs that were dropped in Vietnam were landing in the streets of American cities.

Martin Luther King was the first leading public figure to come out against the Vietnam War. He delivered a stirring speech at New York's Riverside church on April 4, 1967. At that time, while there was a small opposition to the war, there was no anti-war social movement. Moreover, one poll showed that 75 percent of Americans and 48 percent of black Americans supported the war. Consequently, King's worst fears were fulfilled. There was overwhelming hostility to his anti-war stand. Even northern white liberals were so furious with him that they virtually stopped their contributions, which were a critical source of SCLC's funding. Clearly, most people did not view the anti-Vietnam war effort as a sub-movement of the black civil rights movement, but as a sub-movement of the peace movement, which they did not support.

However, with King's public support and with two ex-SCLC staff, James Bevel and Bernard Lafayette, as key organizers, the anti-Vietnam Spring Mobilization campaign escalated into a full-blown mass movement. The trigger events for the movement's take-off stage were the first giant marches against the war: on April 15, 1967, 50,000 people marched in San Francisco and over 100,000 in New York City, where Coretta King and Martin Luther King respectively spoke.

By the time King was killed 12 months later, a majority of Americans were converted and the anti-Vietnam war movement had advanced to MAP's Majority Public Opinion Stage. It took another eight years, however, to end the war.

Economic Justice

By 1965, King realized that achieving full civil rights for blacks, though an important milestone, would only be a first step. Even if statutory racial discrimination ended, it would not affect the quality of the lives of most poor black people in either the rural areas or northern city ghettos. Moreover, he believed that the problems of blacks were the result of the economic system, not individual effort alone, and that the problems of poor black people could not be resolved in isolation from solving the plight of all poor Americans, most of whom were white.

King had recognized that poverty was not strictly a civil rights issue, because no American had "economic rights." The Constitution and Bill of Rights provide only "political rights." The Poor People's Campaign, therefore, was a sub-movement of a much-needed economic rights movement. King saw that poverty was a "structural part of the economic system" and that "there is a need for a radical restructuring of the architecture of American society."[26] He wanted an economic bill of rights for America's poor people, similar to that set forth in the Marshall Plan for Europe after World War II.[27]

To achieve these goals, Dr. King and his SCLC organized the Poor People's Campaign in January 1968. The campaign called for thousands of poor blacks, Chicanos, Native Americans, and whites to march together from across America to Washington, D.C., where they would challenge Congress and hold massive nonviolent actions until their demands were met. Tragically, just before the caravans of poor arrived in Washington, Dr. King was assassinated. The campaign went ahead, with thousands of poor people living in wooden A-frame huts in "Resurrection City," along the reflecting pool behind the White House. The campaign ended after three months, with none of its demands met, when a thousand police arrested the demonstrators and destroyed their housing.

The Poor People's Campaign did, however, invigorate a variety of efforts and social movements focused on structurally based economic issues, and it can be considered a precursor to the current anti-corporate globalization movement.

Legacy

Finally, the civil rights movement amply demonstrated another facet of movements that successfully complete Stage Eight: it had a social impact far beyond its immediate goals. Black Americans gained a new sense of self-esteem, empowerment, and belief in themselves as equal citizens. And the Gandhian method of nonviolent action and mass movements based on love was established as a valid and effective means by which ordinary people could address their social problems. The civil rights movement inspired and was used as a model for virtually all the social movements that followed in the United States and many other places in the world, including the student's, women's, anti-Vietnam war, anti-nuclear energy, peace, gay and lesbian, economic, and environmental movements.

7

The Anti-Nuclear Energy Movement

Bill Moyer

AFTER A FRUSTRATING decade of opposing nuclear weapons, in 1970 I decided to help create an anti-nuclear energy movement for three reasons:
- Nuclear power was going to become a major danger
- Particular conditions made it especially ripe for the creation of a viable social movement
- A successful anti-nuclear energy movement could be used as a stepping-stone to create an effective anti-nuclear weapons movement.

In 1970, developing both nuclear weapons and nuclear energy was a top priority of the official powerholders and was supported by a majority of the public. However, unlike nuclear weapons, nuclear energy had three characteristics that made it especially susceptible to the creation of a new nationwide, grassroots, "not-in-my-backyard" social movement:
- The decision to build nuclear power plants was made at the local and state levels by private utility companies and state energy commissions, and these institutions could be made responsive to an inspired and organized local citizens effort.
- There was an enormous and immediate direct economic and safety impact on those who lived near nuclear reactors and who had to pay for them through their utility bills.
- Nuclear reactor sites provided an ideal target for social movement nonviolent direct actions, similar to the restaurants, buses, and voting registrar offices of the 1960s civil rights movement. Moreover, they existed across the country, so similar strategies and actions could be carried out everywhere simultaneously.

The anti-nuclear energy movement provides a good example of the MAP Eight Stages Model. It also demonstrates both the attrition end-game process of success in Stage Seven and the tenacity of the powerholders who persist when the issue is central for them. While the movement has stopped the first wave of nuclear reactors, the government and private profit-making utilities are creating a new strategy for energy production that requires a revival of the movement. The anti-nuclear energy movement also raises the question "What is success?"

Stage One: Normal Times (1940s–1960s)

The United States government dropped nuclear bombs on Hiroshima and Nagasaki during World War II with the intention of stopping the war. Developing nuclear weapons was also a cornerstone of the powerholders' campaign to make the U.S. the dominant world super-power. This goal required that the country establish a scientific community with nuclear expertise and a positive nuclear public image. To that end, President Eisenhower and the federal government promoted the nuclear energy industry with the Atoms For Peace program in 1953. This new energy policy was initiated without democratic public debate, and in 1954 the Atomic Energy Act, a law still on the books today, allowed the government to prioritize the development of nuclear power, using the argument that it was in the interests of "national security" to overrule state and local concerns.

The government created a new societal myth that described nuclear energy as a modern miracle that would provide clean, safe, and unlimited electricity. It would be too cheap to meter and would launch a new era of affluence for everyone. The actual policy, however, was hidden from the public and presented a different story. To make nuclear energy possible, the federal government provided massive financial, legal, and developmental support. At the same time, all information about the reality of nuclear energy — that it was actually dangerous, dirty, unbelievably expensive, unnecessary, and finite — was suppressed until the 1970s.

Private electrical companies jumped on the nuclear energy bandwagon only after being given outrageous financial incentives that guaranteed enormous profits for merely building reactors. The final incentive was the 1957 Price-Anderson Act, which limited the nuclear industry's liability in the case of nuclear accidents. The first nuclear reactor, converted from a nuclear submarine, was rushed into commercial service in Shippingport, Pennsylvania, in 1957. With government support it was only 13 years before nuclear energy took off, and by 1970 there were 40 operating nuclear reactors and another 100 being constructed (see Figure 1).

The Atomic Energy Commission (AEC) was the federal government's official nuclear watchdog agency, assigned to look after the public's welfare. Instead, it promoted nuclear energy at any price, overriding laws, rules, costs, and safety considerations while suppressing all critical information and internal opposition. For example, the public was told nothing about the nuclear accident at Detroit's Fermi reactor in 1966, an incident similar to the later disaster at Three Mile

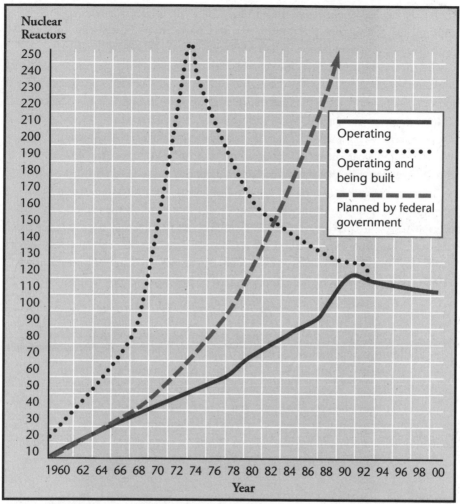

Figure 1: Number of Nuclear Reactors in the United States — Planned, Operating, and Under Construction (1960-1999)

Island. During normal times (MAP Stage One), such trigger events usually have no impact.

Believing the powerholders' societal myths, the public gave its enthusiastic support. Nuclear power had a glowing future. Even the budding anti-nuclear bomb movement either ignored nuclear energy or supported it outright.

At this time, any opposition seemed hopeless. It is, therefore, easy to understand why the handful of people who questioned nuclear power were viewed as crazies, Luddites, or communists who wanted to end our way of life and return us to the stone age. Yet isolated pockets of individuals across the country began to doubt the nuclear energy fairy tale and formed small, local, reformer-type organizations that began gathering information and educating themselves and others.

Even during normal times, however, activists can occasionally organize successful campaigns around specific sub-issues that more blatantly contradict public sensibilities, which quickly race through the eight stages. For example, during this period groups stopped the plans to dump nuclear waste at Cape Cod and to build a nuclear reactor in Queens, New York. On the West Coast, from 1958 to 1963 young Sierra Club members waged a successful campaign that stopped the Bodega Bay nuclear energy complex, which was to be located at the epicenter of the 1906 earthquake that destroyed San Francisco.

The impact of the powerholders' influence on professional opposition organizations, even in this first stage, was demonstrated when the Pacific Gas and Electric Company persuaded the Sierra Club's board of directors not to oppose its plans for building the Diablo Canyon nuclear reactor in San Luis Obispo, California. In response, the club's founder, David Bower, resigned and founded Friends of the Earth to be more independent of powerholder control.

Stage Two: Prove the Failure of Official Institutions (1970–1975)

During this period I began my decade-long role as an anti-nuclear energy Paul Revere, alerting the citizenry, especially progressive groups and individuals, and rousing people to action. In 1972 I gave a presentation at an international ecology conference in The Netherlands, sponsored by the Club of Rome, in which I listed the dangers of nuclear power and predicted a forthcoming social movement against nuclear energy that would be launched by a massive nonviolent blockade of a nuclear reactor site and would then spread to all the other reactor sites.[1] (This later happened in Whyl, Germany, in 1976, and Seabrook, New Hampshire, in 1977.)

Between 1970 and 1975, the nuclear energy era accelerated. The number of operating nuclear reactors grew from 40 to 55, but more importantly, there were 131 orders for new reactors, a rate of 23 new orders each year. The total number of reactors already operating and being built rose from 140 to 254. Project Independence was well on its way to achieving the goals that President Nixon set in 1974 — 1,000 operating nuclear power plants by the year 2000. By then, it was promised, nuclear power would provide 50 percent of America's demand for electrical energy, which was expected to double every ten years.

Although all of the nation's powerholders and an overwhelming public majority favored nuclear energy, new conditions spurred a sudden growth in small, independent, grassroots opposition groups across the country. By the mid-1970s, I estimated that close to 100 million people lived within 100 miles of new nuclear reactor sites, and there were always a few locals, especially those nearby and downwind, who were concerned enough to get their neighbors together to start asking questions.

They created small, "not-in-my-backyard" reformer groups that did research and held meetings with neighbors, government, and local nuclear utility companies. Most dramatically, they challenged the building of the reactors at the long and laborious AEC licensing hearings that, by law, had to be held near every reactor site. While many of these opposition efforts were doomed to failure, they clearly demonstrated that the AEC hearings were merely a charade, a blatant pretense of citizen participation, actually set up to rubber stamp the government's approval without seriously considering dissenting opinions, safety, and financial costs for local residents. This violation of democratic values served as a rallying point for opposition.

Participating in the licensing process forced the local opposition activists to undertake extensive research and self-education about nuclear energy; they became experts on the issue. Challenging the powerholders in the licensing process also enabled the groups to document negative aspects of nuclear energy and the failure of official institutions, establish their own public credibility, and start educating their neighbors and the general public. Some opposition groups held statewide citizen *initiatives* on ballots. Although most of these initiatives lost by a two-to-one margin, they served to educate the public, and a stronger opposition began to form. And a ballot referendum did succeed in stopping a nuclear plant in politically and environmentally sophisticated Eugene, Oregon.

From the beginning, activists discovered that the nuclear energy establishment had made no effective plans for dealing with the critical problem of disposal and storage of nuclear waste, which had to be kept totally separate from the environment for thousands of years. Consequently, the movement made safe nuclear waste disposal a central sub-issue.

In an example of the typical move-countermove process between social movements and powerholders, the nuclear industry contributed to its own failure through its efforts to defeat a California ballot initiative against nuclear power. The California initiative was defeated by a close margin, but to undercut the movement's anti-nuclear energy initiative, Pacific Gas and Electric and other powerholders launched a countermove, promoting a state law, passed in 1975, that ruled no new nuclear power plants would be built until a solution was found for the problem of high-level nuclear waste disposal and storage. This strategy would come back to haunt them as it triggered a process that ultimately led to the curtailment of nuclear energy, first in California, then nationwide..

By the end of this stage, the great majority of public opinion still favored nuclear energy, but public opposition to nuclear energy grew to between 20 and 30 percent, as measured by polls and the results of various referenda.

Stage Three: Ripening Conditions (1975–1976)

During these two years, it appeared to most activists that nothing could stop the nuclear behemoth, as six new nuclear plants began operating, raising the total of operating reactors to 58. Moreover, in 1975 alone there were 21 new orders for nuclear reactors, raising the total of nuclear plants being built or already operating to 254. The nuclear industry seemed to be on track to meet Operation Independent's goal of 1,000 plants by the millennium, and the Nuclear Regulatory Commission (NRC) continued granting reactor construction and operating licenses to utility companies, despite convincing evidence presented by the growing number of increasingly frustrated opposition groups.

Alongside these gloomy developments, there were many signs that conditions were becoming ripe for the take-off of a full-blown anti-nuclear energy movement and the possible demise of the nuclear industry, though most activists were either unaware of them or gave them little credence. The end of the Vietnam War in 1975 meant the anti-war activists and their organizations were available for a new social movement. Grassroots groups continued to grow in size and numbers to become a substantial new wave of opposition, as tens of millions more citizens were upset to learn that they lived within 100 miles of a new reactor site, making them susceptible to its costs and dangers. And a serious accident at the Browns Ferry, Alabama, reactor, though little publicized, demonstrated the potential dangers of nuclear power.

In 1976, a powerful new anti-nuclear energy strategy succeeded in the state of Missouri. A statewide referendum ended the state's Construction Work In Progress (CWIP) law by a two to one margin. Utilities were counting on the CWIP laws that existed in all the states to pay for the enormous cost of building nuclear power plants. CWIP allowed utilities to collect the billions of dollars needed for construction from their rate-paying customers via their monthly electric bills during the 10 to 20 years it took to build them. Without CWIP, the cost of building nuclear reactors would be an almost insurmountable obstacle, as the nuclear utility companies would have to borrow money at steep interest rates over a long period of time, increasing the actual cost of building each reactor many times over.

At the same time, two events further undercut the nuclear energy industry. There was a dramatic rise in bank interest rates, which greatly increased the cost of building reactors, and a decrease in electricity demand reduced the need for the generating capacity. Indeed, in 1976 there were no new orders for nuclear reactors and 17 existing orders were canceled, reversing, for the first time, the growth in the total number of reactors being built and operating. The 1975 peak of 254 dropped to 237, and the federal government quietly reduced its planned number of operating reactors for the year 2000 from 1,000 to 500.

While the federal government and the nuclear energy industry continued to promote nuclear energy at the national level, the anti-nuclear energy opposition grew in numbers and determined resistance at the local, regional, and state levels, because that's where the decisions regarding nuclear plants were made and where the economic, safety, and political impacts were felt by citizens. In 1976, a series of events in California and New England primed these two regions of the country for the take-off of new anti-nuclear energy movements.

In California, citizens challenged the planned Diablo Canyon reactor for three years, not only for the usual reasons, but also because it was sited on an earthquake fault line. When the licensing hearings gave the green light to begin construction, this blatant decision infuriated the local opposition and incited it to the next level of resistance: nonviolent direct action.

In the Northeast, the AEC, ignoring the overwhelming rational and legal arguments advanced by local opponents, decided to license the construction of the Seabrook nuclear plant in New Hampshire. In response, the opponents also turned to nonviolent direct action as a last resort. A few weeks after the AEC decision, a small number of Clamshell Alliance members held the first civil disobedience occupation of a nuclear plant site in the United States. Then, inspired by the 1976 blockade of a nuclear plant site in Whyl, Germany, by 25,000 people, the Clamshell Alliance announced its plan to organize a Whyl-type blockade of the Seabrook site, starting the next spring.

Typical of the successful ripening conditions stage, all of the above situations were silently growing to the bursting point, like an overblown balloon, ready to explode with the right pinprick. But still, the conditions seemed far short of what was needed to stop the expanding number of operating nuclear reactors, while the government and electric utility industry continued promoting the glories of nuclear energy. Although public opinion against nuclear energy rose to about 30 percent, the question of nuclear energy still was not on society's agenda of hotly contested issues, and all the powerholders and a large public majority supported it.

Stage Four: Take-Off (1977–78)

In the spring of 1977, the opposition to nuclear power turned into a full-blown, nationwide social movement. The trigger event was the arrest and jailing of 1,414 Clamshell Alliance protesters who were blockading the Seabrook nuclear reactor's construction site. For two weeks, the civil disobedience action and subsequent jailing were the top news story across the United States and in many other parts of the world. Through daily national television and radio interviews, many emanating from jails across New Hampshire, the protesters were able to educate the public about the follies of nuclear energy and for the first time were publicly recognized as a legitimate opposition.[2]

During the incarceration, demonstrations sprang up across the country in support of the jailed protesters. True to take-off stage dynamics, within weeks the Seabrook action inspired the formation of hundreds of new anti-nuclear energy groups, which rapidly became organized into scores of alliances that conducted similar demonstrations and blockades at the nuclear reactor sites near their homes.[3] By August, thousands protested and 500 people were arrested at the Diablo Canyon nuclear reactor construction site in California.

The anti-nuclear energy movement was led by a wave of independent local and regional groups and individuals. It brought together several different constituencies that effectively carried out the rebel role of nonviolent direct action, including civil disobedience. The primary constituencies included:

- Not-in-my-back-yard (NIMBY) anti-nuclear energy activists and inspired local citizens, who were taking the last-resort action of civil disobedience
- A large number of energetic, politically radical young people, often from universities and high schools, who swelled the numbers participating in civil disobedience
- A small in number, yet critical collection of preexisting groups devoted to nonviolent social change, such as the American Friends Service Committee and the Movement for a New Society, which provided much of the guidance and training for the nonviolent demonstrations, campaigns, and civil disobedience

These anti-nuclear energy rebel activists created new methods of working for fundamental social change that combined Gandhian-Kingian nonviolence, a radical political-economic-environmental analysis, the energy of youth, and new democratic methods of participatory democracy, such as consensus decision-making and the *affinity group* method of collective organization. This new social action style was later carried into succeeding movements on other issues, such as the anti-nuclear weapons and non-intervention in Central America movements.

In this stage, the movement achieved important concrete successes. In 1978, some local and statewide referenda against nuclear energy succeeded. Kern County, California, for example, defeated the planned Wasco nuclear plant by reversing the two-to-one vote of 1976. New Hampshire, home state of the Seabrook site, voted against CWIP and also voted out pro-nuclear, anti-Clamshell Alliance incumbent Governor Meldrim Thomson Jr. There was also a turnaround in national public opinion. Polls showed that in June 1977, 61 percent were in favor of nuclear power and 22 percent were against, but in the fall of 1978 only 39 percent were in favor and 52 percent were against — a gain of 30 percent opposing nuclear energy in one year!

Moreover, in this 1977–78 period there were again no new orders for nuclear power reactors, while 42 previously ordered reactors were canceled, further reducing the total number of reactors already operating or being planned from 237 to 195. The nuclear industry was in a quiet tailspin. Despite these setbacks, the powerholders fervently maintained their promotion of nuclear energy, publicized the start-up of six new reactors and the take-off of the nuclear energy era, warned about future blackouts and a weakened America without nuclear energy, and attacked the new movement as naive, violent, and anti-American.

Many exuberant activists had high expectations that the new movement's size, the extensive media coverage, and the rightness of their cause, along with the new majority of public opinion, would force the powerholders to end nuclear power soon.

Stage Five: Perception of Failure (1978–1982)

While the anti-nuclear energy movement achieved the goals of Stage Four and progressed to Stage Six, beginning in 1978 some activists became stuck in Stage Five. Less than a year after dramatic demonstrations and mass arrests, and with a narrow majority of public opinion against nuclear energy, some rebel activists mistakenly believed the movement was ineffective, powerless, losing, and dying out. They became disheartened by some of the facts: not one reactor had been directly stopped by nonviolent action, six new reactors had been started up, and the targets of the movement's biggest demonstrations — the Diablo Canyon and Seabrook reactors — were still being constructed. In addition, the number of people attending blockades had drastically decreased and fewer people were willing to get arrested.

Because they mistakenly believed that nuclear power would be immediately stopped by ever increasing numbers of people doing massive civil disobedience blockades of construction sites, these rebels were devastated when reactor construction continued. What they didn't know was that this pattern was typical of the process of success of Stage Four. They mistakenly judged that the movement was losing because it had not achieved its goal of stopping nuclear power or even stopping Diablo Canyon and Seabrook, when they should have based their judgment on whether or not the movement had achieved the goals of Stage Four and was progressing along the normal road of movement success to Stage Six.

Some in this small minority of activists assumed the role of ineffective rebels. They mistakenly believed in the romantic myth that nuclear power could be stopped in Stage Four by radicalizing masses of people, 10 to 20,000, who would use militant, disruptive tactics to blockade construction sites. For several years the ineffective rebels broke off from the mainstream anti-nuclear energy groups. In New England's Clamshell Alliance, for example, they formed the Coalition for Direct Action, were called Hard Clams, and claimed they used "direct action" instead of the "milquetoast" nonviolent actions that had been used by the Soft

Clams. After several years of ineffective attempts at harassing the police through direct action tactical maneuvering, this strategy waned.

The Soft Clams, on the other hand, had already understood that they could not stop the Seabrook plant through direct action alone. They planned and pursued a social change agent role with a Stage Six strategy of educating, involving, and mobilizing the general public in a long-term social movement process, while still using nonviolent actions when strategically appropriate.

Stage Six: Majority Public Opinion (1978–1990)

By 1978, a strong anti-nuclear energy social movement emerged that had grassroots groups, organized into regional and statewide alliances, challenging every nuclear reactor site in the country. Because the issue was now on the public agenda with majority public support, the movement was not only able to continue its nonviolent protest actions (though on a lower scale), but was also able to take an assertive role in challenging the social foundations of nuclear power and advocating alternatives.

Most of the recent anti-nuclear energy converts, both individuals and organizations, began using the power of their new majority to pursue mainstream methods for social change. The primary role of the anti-nuclear energy movement changed from the rebel to the Stage Six-appropriate social change agent and reformer. Instead of direct action, the movement focused on mobilizing the local groups and the general public in a wide variety of political, social, legal, and economic strategies to coerce both the state governments and electrical utilities to stop nuclear energy and replace it with sustainable, safe alternatives.

The most critical of the economic strategies was a challenge to the Construction Work In Progress laws that still existed in most states. Movement groups across the country had astonishing success in eliminating CWIP in almost every state. Consequently, there was a complete reversal in the economics of nuclear power. Nuclear energy went from being "too cheap to meter" to being too expensive for utilities to provide because they suddenly had to borrow billions of dollars, at high interest rates, to build reactors. This was a major reason why the cost of constructing nuclear plants increased by three to ten times the original estimates.

The anti-nuclear energy movement then countered the utilities' efforts to raise the vast sums of money they needed to construct new reactors. The movement organized campaigns to stop potential loans from reactor investors, such as non-nuclear utilities, banks, municipalities, and individuals.

The movement also used a number of political strategies. With a majority of the public now opposing nuclear energy, state and local referenda against nuclear power were more likely to succeed. The Rancho Seco reactor was closed in 1988, shortly after a close vote by the people in Sacramento, California, and referenda also closed several reactors near Seattle, Washington.

Over the next decade, two reactor accidents served as powerful re-trigger events: Three Mile Island (1979) and Chernobyl (1986). Each accident was followed by months of Stage Four-like protest demonstrations, new levels of public fear, and increased public opinion against nuclear power. Demonstrations across the county culminated when 125,000 protesters marched to the nation's Capitol on May 6, 1979.

A West Coast re-trigger event occurred in California in 1981 when the AEC decided to allow low-power testing at the Diablo Canyon reactor. This precipitated the biggest anti-nuclear demonstration since 1977, which included 1,905 arrests over several weeks, the largest civil disobedience action ever at any reactor site. This proved to be the peak of the rebel protests. When the NRC again announced the low-power start-up of Diablo Canyon in 1984, 500 people were arrested, a significant, but lower number. This was the last of the big civil disobedience actions at reactor sites.

Following several years of concerted effort, movement lobbyists in Washington defeated the Clinch River breeder reactor by a 52 to 46 vote in the Senate on October 23, 1983, taking away a key source that the nuclear industry counted on for fuel for nuclear power plants. The U.S. Supreme Court placed another huge nail in the coffin of nuclear power with its 1983 decision to uphold the California law prohibiting new nuclear power plants until there was an adequate method in place for storing nuclear waste.

The national outcry following the Three Mile Island accident put a public spotlight on the federal government's Nuclear Regulatory Commission, which was responsible for the safety of nuclear power. As a result of public and social movement pressure, the NRC quickly adopted new, stronger safety regulations for the design and construction of nuclear power plants that far exceeded the requirements in existence at the time. This greatly increased the cost and prolonged the construction time for all of the reactors being built. For some, however, it spelled the end. For example, in January of 1984, the NRC denied an operating license to the almost completed Byron, Illinois, nuclear plant because of faulty construction, and Commonwealth Edison then canceled the $3.7 billion plant. Three days later, Public Service of Indiana canceled its half-completed Marble Hill reactor at a cost of $2.5 billion, and Cincinnati Gas and Electric then canceled its 97 percent complete Zimmer reactor in Ohio.[4]

Throughout this stage, activists in the reformer role continued to challenge the NRC on many issues. One strategy focused on getting the NRC to enforce its requirement that in order to be licensed to operate, every nuclear plant must have in place an effective community evacuation plan that had the acceptance and cooperation of the proper local authorities. This put the power to accept or reject nuclear reactors in the hands of local governments, which were much more politically responsive to their constituents. Consequently, the national powerholders became split from many of the local governments and state governors, who were compelled to challenge the licensing of reactors because of the violation of this requirement.

During this stage, dozens of nuclear utility companies had to cut back or abandon their nuclear reactor plans due to severe financial crises — even bankruptcy in some cases. The economic crunch on nuclear utilities was caused by a wide array of interconnected and accumulating factors including:

- reactor construction costs that were five to ten times the original estimates;
- high interest rates on the billion-dollar loans that were needed for each reactor;
- construction times that were 10 to 15 years longer than expected;
- faulty design and construction of reactors;
- a cost-plus mentality on the part of contractors;
- poor business management;
- · stricter safety regulations and enforcement by the NRC; and
- years of delay caused by citizen-based legal and political challenges.

The situation of the Long Island Lighting Co.'s Shoreham reactor illustrates these factors. In 1987 it was over a decade behind schedule, and costs had risen to 15 times the original estimate; the company was paying $2 million a day just in interest on the loans.[5] In 1989 the Seabrook I reactor finally started up, but its owner went bankrupt and canceled Seabrook II. These were all victories resulting from the movement's reformer efforts. On top of this string of defeats, the demand for electricity dropped from a 7 percent to a 1 percent annual increase, making most of the proposed nuclear plants unnecessary since most areas already had enough generating capacity for the foreseeable future.

Despite the anti-nuclear energy movement's dramatic progress on so many fronts, there were also signs that discouraged activists. First, typical to successful movements in Stage Six, there was a dramatic decline in both the numbers and size of nonviolent demonstrations against nuclear power since the 1977–79 heyday. Even after the 1986 Chernobyl accident, only 200 people marched in Washington, D.C., and a mere 74 were arrested at the nearly completed Seabrook reactor site.[6]

A second, and perhaps more serious, discouraging sign for activists was that from 1978 to 1990, 42 new nuclear power plants started up — one every 18 weeks! — raising the total number of operating reactors from 71 to 113. Moreover, both Diablo Canyon and Seabrook, the two reactors that most publicly defined the movement's opposition to nuclear power, started operating.

However, there had not been a new order for a reactor (that was not subsequently canceled) since 1973. All indications were that the number of operating reactors in the United States would steadily decline. The four reactors listed as "under construction" were set for cancellation, and there were no prospects for new reactors being ordered in the foreseeable future. Nuclear power was seen not only by the public, but also by banks and utilities, as too expensive, and uneconomical compared to alternatives, unnecessary, too risky, politically unpopular, and too dangerous.

Stage Seven: Attrition Success (1991 to the future)

Within 30 years, the anti-nuclear energy movement has achieved astonishing success, reversing the nuclear energy era that was promoted by the nation's powerholders and supported by the public. The movement advanced to the success stage in 1991, when the number of operating nuclear power plants dropped for the first time, from 113 to 112. The number of operating nuclear reactors continued to steadily decline throughout the decade, reaching 103 by 1999. The remaining reactors are expected to close down as they complete their life expectancy or are shut down for economic, safety, or other reasons. This will spell the end of this generation of nuclear power, because there are no more reactors under construction and there has not been a sale for a new nuclear plant in the U.S. for 28 years. Pro-nuclear energy forces are suffering a colossal defeat, but the movement is engaged in a long-term process of attrition that may last another 30 years until all of the present reactors are closed. This protracted demise is guaranteed by the fact that hundreds of billions of dollars have been invested in operating reactors that provide 20 percent of the nation's electricity. In addition, the government and the nuclear power industry still strongly advocate nuclear power as the future centerpiece of a strong America.

The powerholders have a multifaceted strategy to revive and re-invent domestic nuclear power. The George H. W. Bush administration, for example, created the National Energy Strategy in 1991. This initiative called for the revival and massive proliferation of nuclear power plants. It promoted new societal myths claiming that nuclear power was the main "alternative" to Middle Eastern oil and would also prevent global warming caused by fossil fuel plants. The Bush administration also canceled the nuclear industry's billion-dollar debt to the government for uranium enrichment and in 1992 lobbied Congress to permit "fast track" licensing for reactors. The Department of Energy also produced a pro-nuclear energy curriculum for secondary schools, called "Science, Society and America's Nuclear Waste." Finally, the nuclear industry's U.S. Council for Energy Awareness spends $20 million a year to promote nuclear energy.[7]

The anti-nuclear energy movement continues its efforts to shut down operating nuclear reactors and also to oppose powerholder attempts to extend their legally allowed life. The Citizens Awareness Network, for example, has groups in

New York and throughout New England that helped shut down four reactors since 1992 — Yankee Rowe, Maine Yankee, Haddam Neck, and Millstone-1.

Stage Eight: Continuing the Struggle (1992 to the future)

The anti-nuclear energy movement is in the long-term attrition process of achieving total success in its original goal of defeating the first generation of nuclear power plants. Its work, however, is far from done. It needs to continue working on ongoing sub-issues, such as closing existing reactors and opposing nuclear waste transportation and waste sites. It needs to combat the powerholders' new strategies to revive nuclear energy, while simultaneously promoting its larger goal of achieving a paradigm shift in the nation's energy policy.

Some of the other key sub-issues, each requiring its own sub-movement, that have emerged in Stage Eight are the following:

- **Deregulation of electricity.** The powerholders want to deregulate electricity generation so that they can control electrical production and the price for all sources of energy production, raise electricity rates to make ever-bigger profits, and avoid state control in a new unregulated "free market" energy system.

- **Conglomerate control of the energy industry.** The powerholders also launched a grand strategy to reconfigure the energy industry into mega-conglomerates that will take the decision-making away from local communities, local utilities, and statewide utility commissions. This means the powerholders alone can decide whether to build reactors and raise electrical rates.

- **Reactor debt bailout.** Unbelievably, nuclear utilities want states to have electrical consumers pay for the $135 billion that private utility companies owe for their own mistaken decisions to build the existing nuclear power plants. Some states, like California, have already agreed to this.

- **Mixed Oxide Fuel (MOX).** The powerholders are trying to have the production of MOX fuel accepted as government policy. MOX is a means to recover plutonium from nuclear weapon warheads and from spent reactor fuel and to reprocess it as new fuel for nuclear reactors. Advocates argue that producing MOX would help resolve the question of what to do with nuclear warheads and spent reactor fuel and would reduce the cost of running nuclear plants.

- **Sell nuclear reactors overseas.** The U.S. nuclear industry has always tried to sell reactors overseas, especially in Third World nations, but sales have been drastically reduced there, too. Consequently, the U.S. powerholders have been trying to include the sale of nuclear reactors as part of economic assistance programs, especially to former Communist nations, such as North Korea and the states that used to make up the Soviet Union.

- **Buying off environmental organizations.** A final utilities strategy has been to "buy off" thousands of non-profit groups, especially those professional opposition organizations that deal with energy issues, by giving them philanthropic donations (these were as high as $110 million in 1996 & 1997[8]).

The anti-nuclear energy movement has a range of strategies and constituencies fighting these powerholder moves, and a wide variety of environmental, alternative energy, and community organizations, as well as local and state governments and utilities are promoting a paradigm shift to the alternative of a soft energy path. Energy conservation and solar and wind energy generation would not only replace the need for nuclear energy, but would also reduce the demand for electricity produced by oil, coal, and gas fossil fuel plants. Finally, the movement needs to achieve the goal of publicly owned and state-regulated electrical power so that people can better promote conservation and alternative energy sources and control their electricity generation, distribution, and finances.

8

The Gay and Lesbian Movement in the United States

Nancy Gregory[1]

ALTHOUGH THE 1969 Stonewall riot is annually commemorated as marking the beginning of the gay and lesbian movement in the United States, the movement's origin actually dates back to 1924, when the Society for Human Rights was founded by an itinerant preacher in Chicago. Since then, through the Homophile Movement, the turmoil of lesbian separatism, and the crisis of the AIDS epidemic, the Gay and Lesbian Movement has made significant progress. Whether it has achieved success in terms of its legal goals is arguable. If, however, as Dennis Altman contends, "the gay movement is as much aimed at overcoming the internalized self-hatreds and doubts of homosexuals as it is at ending legal and social restrictions,"[2] it can be deemed successful. Although many gay men and lesbians remain closeted, the predominant internalized homophobia of the past has given way to self-acceptance for the majority of gay people.

Stage One: Normal Times (1945–1960)

Many commentators cite the social upheavals brought about by World War II as the genesis of a "gay awakening" in the U.S. In both sex-segregated military units and female-dominated factories, gay people found new opportunities to meet each other.[3] In addition, the 1948 publication of the Kinsey report on male sexual behavior described a significantly greater incidence of homosexual activity than had previously been assumed. In the post-war U.S., the prevalence of homosexuality — though widely considered to be a perversion — entered the consciousness of both gay and straight Americans.

The post-war U.S. also saw the rise of McCarthyism, which branded homo-sexuals as "sex offenders" and "security risks" and included them in the so-called anti-Communist purges of the period. Many gay people were rejected for federal employment and expelled from the military between 1947 and 1950. In 1953, President Eisenhower issued an executive order that explicitly barred homosexu-als from federal employment. Repression by the powerholders was not confined to employment, either; bar raids and police entrapment of homosexuals occurred regularly, with scores of people being arrested at a time. Given the widespread homophobia during this period, the powerholders needed to exert virtually no effort to convince the public that this discriminatory treatment was legitimate and necessary. In this climate, the majority of gay people gathered furtively in clubs and bars to fulfill their personal social needs

It was not until the founding of the Mattachine Society in 1951 that an organized opposition to the discrimination could be identified. Based in Los Angeles, chapters of the Mattachine Society opened in several large U.S. cities through the 1950s, with the aim of bringing homosexuals together, educating both homosexuals and heterosexuals about the issues that confronted gay people, and seeking civil rights for gay people as other minorities had done.[4] In 1955 a comparable organization for women, the Daughters of Bilitis (DOB), was founded in San Francisco.[5] The DOB's mission was more modest than that of the original Mattachine Society and focused primarily on public education. During the 1950s, DOB was also successful in establishing chapters throughout the United States. Though small in membership and limited in scope, Mattachine and DOB were vitally important to the movement as they provided the first sig-nificant opposition to the status quo.

Two additional events during this period marked opposition to the major-ity's view of homosexuality. In 1951, Edward Sagarin (whose pseudonym was Donald Webster Cory) published *The Homosexual in America,* which argued for tolerance of homosexuals and presented gay life from the perspective of a gay writer. In 1953, several Mattachine members published *One,* the first publicly dis-tributed homophile magazine in the U.S. When the U.S. Post Office banned the distribution of *One* in 1954, its publishers filed suit, claiming an infringement of their First Amendment right to free speech. In a rare early victory for the move-ment, the U.S. Supreme Court ruled in favor of *One* in 1958.

Stage Two: Prove the Failure of Official Institutions (1961–1964)

With gay men and lesbians gathering together in small groups in many of the major U.S. cities, the Homophile Movement (as the pre-Stonewall movement was known) had emerged by 1961. Consistent with Bill Moyer's assertion that a movement's source of power lies in the strongly held beliefs and values of the people, "gay men and lesbians joined with other minorities in the 1950s in pressing for liberal democratic societies to live up to their self-professed ideals of 'liberty, equality, and the pursuit of happiness' for all."[6] Given the extreme hostility its members faced, however, the early Homophile Movement cautiously — even apologetically — sought tolerance from society. Beginning in 1961, the movement experienced the first rumblings of a more activist approach, primarily from Frank Kameny, founder of the Washington, D.C., Mattachine Society. Kameny and other leaders of the opposition had to "prove the failure of official institutions" to their fellow gay people as much as to the public at large.

Kameny's personal awakening came in 1957, when he was fired from his position with the U.S. Army Map Service because of his homosexuality. Rather than accept this discriminatory treatment, Kameny appealed all the way to the Supreme Court. In March 1961, the Court refused to hear the case, letting the lower court rulings against Kameny stand and ending his legal battle. In November 1961, Kameny founded the D.C. chapter of Mattachine, taking a self-described "activist militant" approach. Kameny was considered militant at the time because he refused to accept the powerholders' view of homosexuals as "sick," "sinners," or "perverts." Rather than defer to so-called experts theorizing about the "problem" of homosexuality, he insisted that the experts could not know more about homosexuals than homosexuals themselves.[7] In 1962, Washington Mattachine drafted a statement of purpose calling for full equality between homosexuals and heterosexuals, and sent copies to the president, vice-president, the entire Supreme Court, and every member of Congress. In addition, the group published a quarterly newsletter, which it sent to selected members of the federal government, including J. Edgar Hoover, director of the FBI, who had the Washington Mattachine under surveillance.

Kameny's opposition extended to the current leadership and attitude of the movement as well, and he took his "anti-sickness" message to the Mattachine Society New York (MSNY) in 1964. By asserting that "Gay is Good" (echoing Stokely Carmichael's slogan "Black is Beautiful") and that gay people should take pride in their homosexuality, Kameny was successful in motivating the MSNY to elect a new leadership and embrace an activist strategy.

The anti-sickness campaign was also waged by the DOB. Barbara Gittings, who founded the New York DOB in 1958, became the editor of the group's publication, *The Ladder*, in 1962. She immediately sought to move the journal toward a gay-positive, mass-movement position. Fearful of this new militancy, however, the DOB leadership stripped Gittings of her post in 1965.[8]

Given the timidity within the movement and the hostility without, the powerholders continued to be able to operate in a discriminatory and repressive manner with virtually no opposition. Having accepted the sickness label themselves, most gay people were completely ready to defer to the pronouncements of the medical establishment and the restrictions of governmental authority. Thus the primary task of the movement at this stage was to convince gay people that the problem was not in themselves, but in the social and legal institutions that oppressed them.

Stage Three: Ripening Conditions (1965–1968)

On the first day of 1965, a public confrontation with San Francisco authorities marked the beginning of a new stage in the movement. The previous year, a group of liberal clergy — seeing the connection between the Homophile and civil rights movements — had founded the Council on Religion and the Homosexual to reach out to the gay community. On New Year's Day they staged a costume ball to raise funds for the new organization. The San Francisco police were intent on disrupting this first widely publicized event produced for the city's gay community. They photographed and filmed guests as they arrived at the ball and "inspected" the premises nine times during the course of the evening. Three people, including a heterosexual ally, were arrested and charged with obstructing a police officer in the performance of his duties; eventually, all three were acquitted on a technicality. The ball and the trial garnered significant media attention and roused the anger of many gay San Franciscans. As they personalized the issue, some, for the first time, began to perceive themselves as members of an oppressed minority group.[9]

The social upheavals of the 1960s, and particularly the civil rights movement, had a significant impact on the development of ripening conditions. In May 1965 a small group of homophile activists took their protests public with demonstrations at the White House, Pentagon, Civil Service Commission, and State Department, and on July 4 a group picketed Independence Hall in Philadelphia. These actions received an unprecedented amount of national media coverage, and even ran on the major wire services. A coalition group, ECHO (East Coast Homophile Organizations), continued to stage public demonstrations through 1965 and 1966, and in 1967 the Homophile Action League was founded in Philadelphia. League chapters soon appeared in other major cities.

A combination of rising expectations and a personalization of the problem produced a critical mass of discontent in the Homophile Movement during Stage Three. Though many gay leaders continued to promote an assimilationist approach, more and more activists embraced the notion of gay pride and equality. These movement forces gained support in 1968 when the North American Conference of Homophile Organizations (NACHO) resolved that homosexuality was as valid as heterosexuality.[10] This coalition of 26 organizations from around the country endorsed Frank Kameny's slogan "Gay is Good" and adopted a Homosexual Bill of Rights, which outlined the movement's immediate goals:

1. Private consensual acts between persons over the age of consent shall not be an offense
2. Solicitation for any sexual act shall not be an offense except upon the filing of a complaint by the aggrieved party, not a police officer or agent
3. A person's sexual orientation or practice shall not be a factor in the granting or receiving of federal security clearances, visas, and the granting of citizenship
4. Service in and discharge from the armed forces and eligibility for veteran's benefits shall be without reference to homosexuality
5. A person's sexual orientation or practice shall not affect his eligibility for employment with federal, state, or local governments, or private employers.[11]

By the end of Stage Three, the time was right for the emergence of a new social movement. Within a year of the NACHO conference, the Homophile Movement would be supplanted by what eventually became known as the Gay and Lesbian Movement.

Stage Four: Take-Off (1969–1972)

> On the Friday night of 27-28 June 1969, New York police raid-ed a Greenwich Village gay bar called the Stonewall. Bar raids were an American institution ... and in the preceding three weeks, five New York gay bars had already been raided. What made the Stonewall a symbol of a new era of gay politics was the reaction of [those] ... who confronted the police first with jeers and high camp and then with a hail of coins, paving stones, and parking meters. By the end of the weekend, the Stonewall bar had been burned out, but a new form of collective resistance was afoot: gay liberation.[12]

The Stonewall riot was the trigger event of the gay and lesbian movement in the U.S. Writer and activist Margaret Cruikshank describes Stonewall as "a symbolic end to victim status,"[13] and a gay journalist writing in 1969 called it "the hairpin drop heard 'round the world."[14] Though the mainstream media coverage was negative, the riot provided the catalyst for which younger, more militant gay men and lesbians were waiting.

One month after Stonewall, the Gay Liberation Front (GLF) was founded in New York City. In December 1969 the Gay Activist Alliance (GAA) was formed there as well. The two groups pursued different strategies: the GLF stressed coalition building with other oppressed groups to fight for the dismantling of repressive economic and social structures, while the GAA focused solely on gay liberation and emphasized the need to focus on rights guaranteed by the Constitution.[15] Though they took different approaches, however, both the GLF and GAA focused on organizing the grassroots for confrontations with the powerholders. With chapters in large and small cities around the country, both groups liberally employed "zaps" — such as gay kiss-ins, sit-ins, and disruptions of meetings — as well as more traditional pickets and marches to dramatize the oppression of gay people and to demand sexual freedom and equal rights. Civil disobedience was used for the first time in the movement during this period, as a small number of activists chained themselves to furniture and fixtures in powerholder strongholds, such as the New York City Council chamber, the offices of New York City mayor John Lindsay, and the offices of Democratic presidential nominee George McGovern.

While some of its members continued to apply pressure outside the system, the GAA also worked for change within it. Embarking on a course of legislative advocacy, the GAA lobbied unsuccessfully in 1970 for a gay rights ordinance in New York City. In 1971 the GAA called on New York State to implement civil rights legislation as 3,000 gay men and lesbians marched on the capitol building in Albany. Other large demonstrations were held in 1970 in New York City, Los Angeles, San Francisco, and Chicago to commemorate the Stonewall riots. In 1971, what later became known as Gay Pride Day was celebrated by people in Philadelphia, Detroit, and Washington, D.C. The breadth of the new movement was demonstrated in that year and the next: 65 gay and lesbian activists in Missouri attended the first-ever gay liberation meeting in that state; 200 Connecticut gay people marched on police headquarters in Bridgeport to protest official harassment; and gay activists in Ohio and Hawaii were successful in their efforts to repeal sodomy statutes.

Media powerholders, including the *Los Angeles Times, Harper's* magazine, and the Academy of Motion Picture Arts and Sciences, were targets of GLF/GAA zaps during Stage Four. One protester was even able to get onto the set of the *CBS Evening News* with Walter Cronkite, holding up a sign proclaiming "Gays Protest CBS Prejudice" during a live broadcast.[16] The opposition's demonstrations paid off in 1970, when two GAA activists were guests on the *Dick Cavett Show*, and in 1972, when *The New Republic* acknowledged the increasing political power of gay men and lesbians in an article entitled "The Gay Vote." Also in 1972, gay men received unprecedented mainstream media attention with the airing of an ABC television movie, That Certain Summer. The gay press acclaimed the movie for its positive, non-stereotypical portrayal of a gay couple.[17]

In Stage Four, the general public certainly became aware of the gay and lesbian movement, if not supportive of it. As GAA activist Arnie Kantrowitz wrote: "Nineteen seventy-one was the year we grew loud enough to be heard, and like us or not, America could no longer deny that we were there."[18] Neither could the powerholders. By 1972, they could no longer refer to gay people as "sex murderers," as they had done in 1949, but the "sin" and "sickness" labels still stuck, preventing the opposition from effectively characterizing gay men and lesbians as members of an oppressed minority group deserving of equal rights. According to Kantrowitz, "[In 1971] we truly believed that once we had presented our case to the nation, our rights would be granted immediately. It took a lot of battering before we realized we were in for the long haul."[19]

Stage Five: Perception of Failure (1973–1989)

Though the gay and lesbian movement in 1973 didn't enjoy the level of public support that usually indicates a movement has successfully taken off, it had achieved that level within the gay and lesbian community. In fact, for many gay people the movement had been so successful at liberating their personal lives that they concluded the struggle was over. In addition, the increasing professionalization of the movement (the National Gay Task Force and the Lambda Legal Defense and Education Fund were both incorporated in 1973) allowed the gay rank and file to participate by writing checks instead of protesting, a trend that alienated the activists of the previous stage. According to one, "gay respectability" was the "anti-activist gay theology" of the POOs, which focused on mainstream lobbying and civil litigation efforts.[20] Paradoxically, while gay and lesbian visibility had never been greater, fewer and fewer people attended Gay Pride marches and rallies.

The detrimental consequences of this move to a solely insider strategy were demonstrated at the 1976 Democratic National Convention in New York City. Without the influence of ultra-liberal George McGovern, Democratic Party powerholders retrenched and retreated on gay rights, prohibiting any discussion of gay and lesbian concerns at the convention. Gay activists called for a 10,000-strong rally to protest this exclusion, but only 600 demonstrators showed up.[21]

A second factor that sapped the movement's strength in 1973 was the rise of lesbian separatism. Greatly influenced by the women's movement (though lesbians had to fight for visibility and acceptance there), many lesbian feminists rejected the gay rights movement as irredeemably misogynist and sexist. "Lesbians are feminists, not homosexuals," Jill Johnston wrote in 1975.[22] Because lesbian separatists also denounced gay women as people who "relate genitally to women, [but] give their allegiance to men," deep divisions were created between lesbians, as well as with gay men.[23] The gap continued to widen over the next 12 or more years as women and men created separate social and cultural communities. Occasionally an especially threatening action by the powerholders — such as California's Briggs Initiative in 1978, which aimed to drive gay and lesbian teachers from public schools — brought the two camps together in opposition, but it wasn't until the AIDS crisis produced a tremendous anti-gay backlash in the mid-1980s that gay men and lesbians were truly reunited.[24]

No one can deny the enormous toll the AIDS epidemic has taken on the gay community and the movement. In addition to the decimation of the community by illness and death, ignorance produced bitter splits within the movement in the early days of the epidemic, as some leaders supported powerholder efforts to close gay bathhouses and others denounced them as yet another example of "pushing morality under the guise of medical expertise."[25]

While gay men and lesbians responded to this community emergency with increased skill and expertise, the energy required for basic crisis management meant that little was left for other demands. However, by the late 1980s the extreme anti-gay backlash engendered by the AIDS epidemic — evangelical minister Jerry Falwell had described AIDS as "God's punishment upon homosexuals" — galvanized the movement for a new round of activism.[26]

Stage Six: Majority Public Opinion (1973–1982)

In Stage Six, Moyer says, "the movement's chief goal ... is to nurture, support, and empower grassroots activists and groups." By 1973, the infrastructure of the gay and lesbian community was in place to pursue this goal as over 1,000 local organizations had sprung up around the country. In addition to providing services and support to gay men and lesbians, many groups sponsored programs to educate heterosexuals about gay people and the discrimination they faced.[27] This outreach to the straight community was especially important in religious institutions, as charges of immorality continued to hinder the movement's efforts to convince a majority of the general public that gay people comprised a legitimate minority group in need of protection from discrimination. In 1973, several mainline Protestant denominations launched the National Task Force on Gay People in the Church to seek reforms in the National Council of Churches.

It was at the local level that activists enjoyed the most political and legislative success. Between 1973 and 1977, local organizations were able to secure anti-discrimination legislation in dozens of municipalities. Gay and lesbian Democratic clubs were formed in cities around the country, and openly gay politicians ran for public office. On the national level, in 1973–74 the movement celebrated a major defection from the powerholders' camp when the American Psychiatric Association (APA) voted to remove homosexuality from its list of mental disorders. Without the backing of the APA, the "sickness" label began to lose its potency with the general public. Also during this period, the American Bar Association adopted a resolution calling for the repeal of all sodomy laws (1973), the National Teachers Association added sexual orientation to its anti-discrimination policy (1974), and the U.S. Civil Service Commission removed its ban on hiring gay people for civilian federal government jobs (1975).[28]

Despite these cracks in the armor, the powerholders — led by the emerging religious right — unleashed a forceful backlash against the movement in 1977. Demonizing gay people as "child molesters" and a "threat to the family," the so-called Save Our Children campaign was launched in Dade County, Florida, by pop singer Anita Bryant. It was an attempt to overturn gay civil rights legislation that had been enacted only six months before.[29] Encouraged by a larger than 2 to 1 victory in Florida, and with the strong support of Jerry Falwell and others in the religious right, Bryant took her show on the road and led anti-gay referendum campaigns throughout the country. In 1978, gay rights legislation was repealed in St. Paul, Minnesota; Witchita, Kansas; and Eugene, Oregon.[30] Inspired by Bryant's success, California State senator John Briggs launched a voter initiative in 1978 that would have expelled all gay and lesbian teachers from the public school system, along with any straight teachers who "presented homosexuality positively."[31]

Fortunately, the Briggs Initiative proved to be a re-trigger event for the movement. Only 3,000 gay San Franciscans had protested the Dade County repeal in 1977; in 1978, a record 250,000 turned out for the city's Gay Pride Day. In addition, when the Briggs Initiative made the ballot in California, 30 organizations, using an array of tactics, were formed around the state to block it. Indicative of the level of public support the movement had achieved by this stage, the gay and lesbian opposition was able to garner anti-Briggs endorsements from several large labor unions and from African-American and Chicano leaders, including Cesar Chavez.

In November 1978 the movement celebrated two great victories and suffered one devastating loss. The tide of anti-gay referendum success was stopped when California voters rejected the Briggs Initiative by 58 to 42 percent, and when Seattle voters chose to retain their city's gay rights ordinance, 63 to 37 percent.[32] Only three weeks later, however, San Francisco's newly elected city supervisor and beloved gay activist Harvey Milk was assassinated. On May 21, 1979, when Milk's assassin was convicted only of manslaughter, thousands of people rioted in the city. The maturity and discipline of the movement was evident the following night when 10,000 demonstrators — monitored by 400 lesbian and gay peacekeepers — gathered nonviolently in the Castro district to celebrate what would have been Milk's 49th birthday. That fall, in reaction to the growing anti-gay backlash, the first-ever national gay rights march drew 100,000 protesters to Washington, D.C.

The AIDS epidemic provided the movement's next rallying point — for both the powerholders and the opposition. Though the disease had been identified in 1981, and the number of afflicted gay men grew exponentially thereafter, it wasn't until Rock Hudson's death in 1985 that AIDS received much public attention. Then, as Sarah Schulman writes, "as soon as the dominant culture noticed AIDS, they started to distort its meaning and use this visibility to isolate and punish people who were infected. In other words, 1985 proved that heterosexual awareness equaled AIDS hysteria."[33] Ignorance and fear were potent tools the powerholders used to maintain the public's support; to the religious right's "immoral" label, they added "diseased."

This strategy worked well in the mid-1980s, when legislation was introduced in jurisdictions around the country to limit patient rights in the name of public health. It also made it easy for the U.S. Supreme Court to halt judicial progress on the right to privacy in its 1986 Bowers v. Hardwick decision, which upheld the constitutionality of Georgia's sodomy statute. What made the Bowers decision particularly oppressive was the fact that the justices specified they were ruling in regard to the legality of homosexual sodomy, not heterosexual sodomy.[34] Lesbians were caught up in the AIDS backlash as well, and anti-gay violence against both men and women increased while the powerholders stalled on providing sufficient resources to fight the disease.

Having achieved the maturity of Stage Six, the movement was able to respond to the AIDS epidemic and the resulting anti-gay backlash through a variety of channels. Professional opposition organizations such as the National Gay and Lesbian Task Force and the Human Rights Campaign Fund documented the incidence of anti-gay hate crimes and lobbied the powerholders for legal protections and increased funding for AIDS. A principled dissent group, ACT UP (AIDS Coalition to Unleash Power), formed chapters throughout the U.S. to stage dramatic direct actions, including civil disobedience, to protest powerholder indifference to the AIDS crisis. Finally, hundreds of grassroots groups around the country provided services to people with HIV/AIDS; fought local battles, such as those to ensure HIV-positive children were allowed to attend public schools; and continued to press for gay visibility and equal rights.[35]

In October 1987, gay and lesbian activists mobilized a second round of national protests in Washington, D.C., drawing 500,000 demonstrators for a march to the Capitol and 600 protesters for civil disobedience actions at the Supreme Court. The breadth of the gay and lesbian movement was demonstrated at these events, not only by the diversity of the participants, but also by the array of their demands. In addition to attention to HIV/AIDS issues, the movement's other goals — civil rights protections, unobstructed military service, and domestic partnership and custody rights — were all extensively addressed.[36]

Stage Seven and Stage Eight: Success and Continuing the Struggle (1990 to the future)

Through a process of attrition, the powerholders have yielded on several important issues since 1990. In recognition of the equal status of people with HIV and AIDS, the 1990 Americans with Disabilities Act included HIV/AIDS in its anti-discrimination provisions. Also in 1990, the first federal pro-gay legislation was enacted when the Hate Crimes Statistics Act became law. The Act requires the Justice Department to collect data on hate-motivated violence, whether the hate is based on religion, race, ethnicity, or sexual orientation. Passage of the Hate Crimes Act was significant because it represented the first time the federal government acknowledged the minority status of gay people on an equal basis with other recognized groups.

After stalling at two, several more states have passed anti-discrimination legislation since 1991. Presently 12 states — California, Connecticut, Hawaii, Maryland, Massachusetts, Minnesota, New Jersey, Nevada, New Hampshire, Rhode Island, Vermont, and Wisconsin — and over 100 localities have civil rights laws on the books according to the Human Rights Campaign website in January 2000. In 1992, a voter initiative in Oregon to prohibit anti-discrimination legislation was rejected. Though a similar amendment passed in Colorado that year, in 1994 the Colorado Supreme Court ruled it unconstitutional, and in 1996 the U.S. Supreme Court upheld that ruling by a six to three decision.[37]

According to Urvashi Vaid, former executive director of the National Gay and Lesbian Task Force:

> Gay, lesbian, and AIDS activists made 1992 a pivotal year for two reasons. First, because we mounted the most effective national political effort of our movement's history and helped to defeat a President; and second, because the straight media and candidates took notice.[38]

It may have been "the economy, stupid," but the fact that Democratic presidential nominee Bill Clinton could endorse federal gay civil rights legislation, call for an end to the ban on openly gay and lesbian soldiers in the military, actively court the gay and lesbian vote, and win the presidency, was a significant victory for the movement. The movement's political strength was further demonstrated at the April 30, 2000, Millennium March on Washington for Equality when President Clinton addressed hundreds of thousands of demonstrators via videotape to tout his administration as "the most inclusive in history."[39] The 2000 march marked the first time in four national demonstrations that the country's highest-ranking political office-holder addressed the crowd. While Clinton's record in office has been disappointing, his acknowledgment — as a central powerholder — of the opposition is definitely a sign of movement success.

Another significant indication of movement success was the April 2000 passage in Vermont of the Act Relating to Civil Unions. The Vermont law allows same-sex couples to join in legally recognized civil unions and thus become entitled to over 300 benefits — including child custody and visitation, medical decisions and family leave, estate inheritances, and tax breaks — available under state law to married couples. Since the 1996 federal Defense of Marriage Act (DOMA) defines marriage as an institution reserved exclusively for heterosexuals, the impact of the Vermont victory could be even more critical if, as expected, the Civil Unions statute is used to challenge the constitutionality of the DOMA under the U.S. Constitution's "full faith and credit" clause, which requires states to recognize marriages performed in other states.[40]

While it has been difficult to achieve legal recognition of same-sex couples — only two other states, California and Hawaii, and 48 localities currently have domestic partnership laws on the books — more and more employers have acknowledged the partners of their gay and lesbian employees. In June 2000, the "Big 3" U.S. automakers — Ford, General Motors, and Daimler Chrysler — with the backing of the United Auto Workers union, agreed to extend health care benefits to the domestic partners of employees. The new policy "marked the first time that virtually an entire sector of American commerce, along with its leading union, decided collectively to provide domestic partner benefits." When Coca-Cola announced, also in June 2000, that it would provide health care coverage to the same-sex partners of employees, it joined over 3,400 employers nationwide, including 99 Fortune 500 companies, to extend such benefits.[41]

Despite these movement victories, the 1998 murder of Matthew Shepard, a gay University of Wyoming student, and the ongoing, though much less publicized, harassment and violence faced by gay people, prove that "continuing the struggle" is more important than ever. Further evidence that the fight goes on came in June 2000 when the U.S. Supreme Court ruled, by a five to four decision in the case of Boy Scouts of America v. Dale, that the Boy Scouts could continue to ban gay males from the organization. The Court's decision was viewed as especially threatening because of the fear that it will be used in the future by other large, open membership groups to circumvent hard-won state and local anti-discrimination laws.

In its final stage, according to the Movement Action Plan, a social movement must both follow up, ensuring that its success is maintained, and carry on, striving for the achievement of its other goals. The gay and lesbian movement is clearly institutionalized, and gay and straight people alike support it through professional opposition organizations, direct action groups, and grassroots associations. It has much more to accomplish now that its issues are on the public agenda. As the slogan of the direct action group Queer Nation says, "We're here. We're queer. Get used to it."

9

The Breast Cancer Social Movement[1]

Mary Lou Finley

IN THE 1990s, a new women's health movement with a focus on breast cancer emerged in the U.S. political arena. The movement gained national visibility with the 1991 organizing of the National Breast Cancer Coalition, an advocacy group set up to lobby federal politicians in Washington, D.C. This coalition now has more than 300 member groups, which provide education, support, and advocacy for women with breast cancer throughout the country.

The breast cancer movement aims to increase women's participation in decisions concerning breast cancer, both at the individual and societal levels. Local groups focusing on both support and advocacy have joined together at the national level to lobby for public policy changes that will strengthen efforts to —

- treat and seek a cure for breast cancer;
- provide increased access to health care and other protections for women with breast cancer; and
- prevent breast cancer.

There has been a powerful interaction between other components of the women's movement, the overall women's health movement, and the breast cancer movement, and victories in the larger women's movement have played a critical role in the unfolding of the breast cancer movement. In MAP terms, the breast cancer movement can be seen as a sub-movement of the women's health movement, operating in many respects independently, but also clearly part of a larger impetus toward change in the status of women.

Background: The Women's Movement and the Women's Health Movement

The contemporary wave of the women's liberation movement (as it was then called) began in 1969–70, with the formation of a number of women's consciousness raising groups and action groups, and the publication of several influential books that presented an analysis of women's oppression to a wider public. (Particularly noteworthy were Betty Friedan's *The Feminine Mystique* (1963), Robin Morgan's edited anthology *Sisterhood is Powerful* (1970), and a series of booklets called *Notes from the First Year, Notes from the Second Year,* and *Notes from the Third Year,* published in 1969, 1970, and 1971, and later reprinted in *Radical Feminism* (1973), edited by Anne Koedt, Ellen Levine, and Anita Rapone).

The women's liberation movement challenged male control over women's lives, male-dominated institutions, and the widespread discounting of issues of importance to women such as child care and housework. The impetus for the movement came from two directions:

- From women who had been active in the civil rights movement and other late 1960s movements and who saw the relevance of analyses they learned about in those movements to their own situation.
- From a more mainstream effort of professional women, originally coalesced at a conference called by President John F. Kennedy in 1963.[2]

From the beginning, the women's health movement was an important sub-movement, applying a feminist analysis to women's health issues, particularly reproductive issues. The women's health movement sought to place more information about health matters into women's hands through publications such as *Our Bodies, Our Selves,* first self-published as a newsprint booklet by the Boston Women's Health Book Collective and sold for 30 cents in 1970.[3] With this new information, women began to question their doctors — at that time over 92 percent male[4] — as a part of the larger effort to gain control over their own lives. Women challenged obstetrician-gynecologists about many aspects of childbirth and reproductive health care, and other women began a movement to return to midwifery and home births. Some groups fought in the courts and through the government for women's right to have a legal abortion. Under the banner of reproductive rights, women also fought to end forced sterilizations foisted upon poor women.[5]

The larger women's movement focused on a wide range of issues including equal access to everything from school sports to medical schools, equal pay and equal treatment on the job, and more representation in the political arena. This last effort was particularly important for the breast cancer movement. The National Women's Political Caucus encouraged the election of more women from both parties. By the 1990s, when breast cancer issues began to come before Congress, there were over 40 women in the House of Representatives and 6 women in the Senate, which was an important factor in the early successes of the breast cancer movement.

While the breast cancer movement did not gain national visibility until the early 1990s, these earlier activities laid the groundwork for the movement. They happened during a time of growth and change in the overall women's movement, when women were gaining more access and more rights in many arenas. For example, in the early 1990s a woman headed the National Institutes of Health (NIH) for the first time. Women were gradually gaining more and more seats in medical schools until, in 2000, nearly half of medical students in the U.S. were women.[6] Those victories in the larger movement provided the context for the changes that were relevant to the breast cancer movement.

Much of the work of this movement has come from local groups, which spearheaded many of the early efforts and which provided — and still provide — a source of support and education for women with breast cancer as well as a vehicle for advocacy and activism. However, for the sake of brevity I will focus chiefly on the activities of the national movement.

Stage One: Normal Times (1950s–1960s)

The breast cancer movement, like the rest of the women's health movement, was in Stage One up to approximately 1970. Breast cancer was largely a private experience, with women patients expected to trust their physicians — who were almost invariably male — to make decisions for them regarding treatment for cancer. Breast cancer was spoken of in whispered tones even among women; in the 1950s, one could scarcely say the word "breast" in polite company.

However, in the early 1950s an organization called Reach to Recovery began to provide woman-to-woman support for breast cancer patients during hospitalization. This group could be seen as an early precursor of later movement support groups. Women who had survived breast cancer offered support to women undergoing treatment. The group functioned within the framework of traditional women's roles, with members offering women advice on, for example, how to feel feminine and keep a husband happy after the loss of a breast.

Stage Two: Prove the Failure of Existing Institutions (1973–1986)

This stage began about 1973, somewhat later than other sub-movements in the women's health movement, such as those focused on reproductive rights. A sense that the medical establishment was failing women with breast cancer began to develop during this time. The standard treatment since the 1890s, radical mastectomy — an extensive surgery that involved removal of the entire breast and some underlying muscles — had serious side effects and was often not effective, as many women still died within a few years of the surgery.[7] Few doctors would entertain the possibility of other, less drastic surgeries because of the American medical establishment's practice of observing the current "standard of care." Any physician who provided anything else put himself at professional risk. Meanwhile, breast cancer incidence continued to increase, affecting 1 out of 14 women in the U.S.

This situation began to shift in the mid-1970s, as European research began to show that less drastic surgeries might be equally effective. Controversies over types of surgery arose within the medical establishment. Physician George Crile's *What Women Should Know About the Breast Cancer Controversy* — a work that was considered "radical fringe" for its time — revealed these debates to women themselves.

Popular books and articles began to appear, providing public education about breast cancer and encouraging patients to be involved in decisions about treatment, particularly the type of surgery they underwent. In 1974, Betty Ford and Happy Rockefeller, wives of President Gerald Ford and New York Governor Nelson Rockefeller, publicly discussed their breast cancers and called attention to the need for breast cancer detection, thus helping to bring breast cancer "out of the closet" and into the public eye and breaking the hold of the privatization of the breast cancer experience.

In 1975, Rose Kushner, a Washington, D.C.-based journalist, who was in many respects a one-woman breast cancer movement in those days, wrote about her breast cancer experience in *Breast Cancer: A Personal History and Investigative Report*.[8] She also opened the Breast Cancer Advisory Center in Rockville, Maryland, to provide information to women facing a breast cancer diagnosis. Kushner began organizing local support and education groups called Y-ME for women with breast cancer. (The groups were named for her book, retitled *Why Me?* in its 1977 reprinting.)

While these activities began to bring the issue into public view, the medical establishment continued to resist suggested changes and no cure was in sight. Women began to feel more and more that the health care system, which they relied upon, did not work for them regarding breast cancer, fulfilling the goal of MAP's Stage Two.

Stage Three: Ripening Conditions (1986–1991)

Stage Three is the period when the groundwork is laid for change: vehicles for change are identified, networks developed, and early victories are won on some sub-issues. For the breast cancer movement, this stage began in the 1980s.

First, local activist groups formed, focusing on both support for women with cancer and activist agendas. In 1986, Jackie Winnow founded an Oakland group. Winnow had been active in providing support for AIDS patients in San Francisco prior to her breast cancer diagnosis, and she took her cues from the strong AIDS activist movement. In 1989, Susan Shapiro, a young woman active in the feminist community, who had been diagnosed with breast cancer, launched a group in Cambridge, Massachusetts. She wrote an article entitled "Cancer as a Feminist Issue" for a local feminist paper and called for the formation of a group that would combine political action, direct service, and education.[9] Dr. Susan Love, who would play a significant role in Stage Four (see below), was a member of this group. Also in 1989, several groups of women with breast cancer formed the Long Island Breast Cancer Coalition and, after learning that Long Island had a particularly high rate of breast cancer, called for a scientific investigation of possible environmental causes.[10] Other groups were founded focusing on the needs of women of color and lesbians.

Another set of activist groups formed to lobby for informed consent laws at the state level. These laws would require doctors, who at that time made the decisions about what treatment their breast cancer patients received, to provide women with a choice of type of surgery and between surgery and other treatments for breast cancer. The medical establishment strongly opposed these laws, seeing them as intrusions into the domain of physician expertise. However, determined groups of women activists, primarily breast cancer survivors and their friends and relatives, launched intensive lobbying campaigns.[11] Informed consent laws regarding choice of breast cancer surgery were passed in 17 states.

In MAP terms, we could say that this sub-issue (and the sub-movement surrounding it) gained widespread support because the customary treatment of women by their doctors (which sometimes involved performing biopsy and mastectomy as a part of one surgery, so that the woman entered the operating room not knowing if she had cancer and awoke having lost a breast) violated widely held values about personal choice, which were increasingly being applied in the health arena. Though the larger movement was only in Stage Three, these locally based groups formed a sub-movement that was able to push through to Stage Seven, Success, on the issue of informed consent.

Another small but significant early victory came when Rose Kushner was appointed to the National Cancer Advisory Board as a consumer representative, the first such representative in the Board's history. The National Association of Breast Cancer Organizations, a group of mainstream medical providers and researchers, was formed in 1986.

Women continued to write about their breast cancer experiences, sometimes as a conscious part of the feminist movement's emphasis on telling our stories and developing a collective analysis out of those stories. Particularly important was Audre Lorde's *Cancer Journals*, published in 1980. Lorde was a well-known African American feminist poet when she was diagnosed with breast cancer; in her own inimitable way she visualized an "army of one breasted women" demanding more funding for breast cancer research and treatment. Lorde brought an important literary voice to this issue until she died in 1992 from breast cancer.

In the mid 1980s a massive, expensive research project on breast cancer prevention was set in motion when funding for the Women's Health Initiative, as it was then called, was finally approved. The Initiative included research on the prevention of both breast cancer and heart disease. The ten-year fight for this research funding was spearheaded by Dr. Maureen Henderson, a high-powered medical academic at the Fred Hutchinson Cancer Research Center in Seattle, who was one of the few women physicians from the pre-1970 era, and who used the status she had gained professionally to fight for breast cancer prevention research. The movement's efforts to obtain funding through normal channels in the NIH were not successful, so Henderson took the fight to Congress, where she gained crucial allies in the Women's Congressional Caucus. This was perhaps the first mobilization of women in Congress on behalf of women's health issues, and it laid the groundwork for later requests to Congress from the breast cancer movement.

About 1990 the National Institutes of Health established the Office for Women's Health Research and began to require research proposals to more fully address women's health research. As one of the first initiatives in women's health research, the Center for Disease Control established a program to provide free breast and cervical cancer screening for poor women without health insurance.

Stage Four: Take-Off (1991–1992)

These events paved the way for movement groups to succeed in gaining major public visibility for the issue of breast cancer. The spark that triggered the take-off was subtle, but powerful. In 1991, Dr. Susan Love, a breast cancer surgeon (and an early activist in the Cambridge feminist cancer group), published a book entitled *Dr. Susan Love's Breast Book* and went on a speaking tour to promote it. At her readings and presentations she was struck by the strong responses she received from women who clamored for more political action about breast cancer. She concluded that the time was ripe for a national movement. Dr. Love and Fran Visco, a Philadelphia attorney and breast cancer survivor, together with other breast cancer activists founded the National Breast Cancer Coalition (NBCC), with over 200 local groups as members.

The NBCC was instrumental in reframing the issue so that it had a sharper focus — breast cancer rather than cancer in general; a clear constituency — women, particularly younger women in their 30s and 40s; and a new set of demands — a focus on the causes of the disease and on a cure. The Coalition clearly defined its constituency as breast cancer survivors and their families and friends. And it demanded that a cure be found, dropping the medical establishment's focus on detection and screening. The group's slogan, printed on posters, pins, and T-shirts, was: "Breast Cancer. Say it. Fight it. Cure it. Damn it!"

For the NBCC's first action in the fall of 1991, members organized a massive letter-writing campaign. Within six weeks they gathered 600,000 letters, far more than the 175,000 they had attempted to collect, and presented them to Congress and the president. President Bush did not acknowledge this request, but Congress increased the 1992 breast cancer research budget from $102 million to $142 million.

Though this movement did not use civil disobedience as many other movements do in Stage Four, it had its own brand of feistiness. Women in their 30s, 40s, and 50s, mothers and grandmothers, stepped outside their traditional roles to become demanding and strong. The life-threatening conditions they faced gave them strength and a kind of moral power, which commanded attention as they shifted their role from patients to political actors.

The NBCC also supported the Long Island Breast Cancer Coalition's call for an investigation into possible environmental causes of breast cancer, though it was not a major focus in 1991–92.

Stage Five: Perception of Failure

The movement did not show signs of the feeling of failure and sense of powerlessness that afflict many movements after their initial take-off. It had some strong, obvious successes early on (see the description of Stage Seven, below), as well as a central movement group that clearly recognized these successes, which may have played a role in the avoidance of this pitfall. Also, this movement appeared to have fewer negative rebels at its take-off stage. This is the group that has the most difficult time after take-off and is most prone to declines in morale and feelings of powerlessness. The negative rebel role is most often associated with young, rebellious men, and may be little in evidence in a movement of mothers and grandmothers.

Stage Six and Stage Seven: Majority Public Opinion and Success (1993–2000)

The breast cancer movement received massive public support during and shortly after the take-off stage and won significant victories very quickly; hence I am combining the discussions of Stages Six and Seven.

With this large base of public support it has been possible for the movement to work through mainstream institutions and pass relevant legislation. The National Breast Cancer Coalition had an important victory in its first year of existence: activists demanded more funding for breast cancer research, and Congress doubled the amount! Particularly remarkable was Congress's decision, in 1992, to allocate $210 million from the Department of Defense budget for breast cancer research, establishing the Department of Defense Breast Cancer Research Program. Congress took this extraordinary step because it was convinced of the necessity for such funding, but found itself locked into a budget allocation procedure that did not permit further domestic spending. There was room for further defense spending, however, in an amount that was approximately equivalent to the National Cancer Institute's budget for breast cancer research, thus effectively doubling research funding in one year. This was a major victory, which heartened activists and strengthened the movement.

The 1993 success of a major campaign demonstrates the massive early support for the movement. That year the NBCC collected 2.6 million signatures on a petition calling for a National Breast Cancer Action Plan and delivered them to President Bill Clinton, leading to the adoption of the action plan with NBCC president Fran Visco as co-chair.

Other early victories included a Congressional decision to order a study of environmental links to breast cancer on Long Island (in response to the concerns of the Long Island Breast Cancer Coalition and others), and more survivor-consumer participation in key decision-making roles. Patient/consumer representatives have been included on:

- Panels considering funding decisions after peer review in the Department of Defense Breast Cancer Research Program
- National Cancer Advisory Board
- National Cancer Institute Director Search Committee
- National Breast Cancer Action Plan co-chair

In November 1999, in preparation for further lobbying of Congress and those running for congressional offices, the NBCC commissioned a public opinion poll, which found that:

- approximately 90 percent of the respondents agreed that breast cancer research should be a national priority; and
- more than half of respondents indicated that they would be more willing to vote for a political candidate if he or she made finding a cure for breast cancer a top priority.[12]

This poll showed very clearly that breast cancer research has gained overwhelming public support. Further evidence of this success came in the fall of 2000 when news reports indicated that Democratic presidential candidate Al Gore made his support for breast cancer issues the focus of an important campaign speech.

Stage Eight: Continuing the Struggle (1990s to the future)

The National Breast Cancer Coalition has continued massive lobbying efforts each year to maintain the gains in research funding won in 1992. In spite of many budget cuts, and even after the Republicans took over Congress, funding has been more or less maintained.

It has been a tougher challenge to retain the Department of Defense Breast Cancer Program funding, but this is a favorite of the movement because it is a newer program, which means there is more survivor/consumer input into the decisions about which research is to be funded. The program was funded for $175 million in 2000, and there is a strong lobbying effort to maintain it at that level for 2001.

The NBCC has become increasingly sophisticated in its lobbying efforts. For example, it provides a website (www.stopbreastcancer.org) where members and supporters can easily access information on the positions members of Congress have taken on these issues. The website also lists contact information, so breast cancer movement activists can let their representatives know where they stand.

As it continues the struggle, the breast cancer movement has raised new issues and focused attention on long-term concerns about access to health care, which have been slower to reach success. Many of these sub-issues are at Stages Two and Three at this point, but continue to gather additional support. For example the NBCC's legislative priorities for 2000 included:

- Increasing access to breast cancer treatment for uninsured low-income women who are screened and diagnosed with breast or cervical cancer in the existing program operated by the federal Center for Disease Control.
- Strengthening protection from future insurance and employment discrimination in the wake of the discovery of the breast cancer gene.
- Increasing Medicare coverage for breast cancer patients participating in research clinical trials.
- Passing a strong and enforceable patient's bill of rights for patients in managed care health plans.[13]

In October 2000 President Clinton signed into law a bill fulfilling the first priority regarding the provision of access to breast cancer treatment for uninsured, low-income women.

There is also a major new focus on the environmental links to breast cancer. The incidence of breast cancer is higher in the U.S. than in many other countries, and, significantly, when women migrate to the U.S. from other countries, their breast cancer rates soon approximate those of women born in the United States. This strongly suggests that there is something in the environment — food supply, water, or air — that plays a major role in breast cancer. Given this evidence, there has been strikingly little research on the causes of breast cancer, particularly potential environmental causes. Research on the impact of pesticides on breast tissue has suggested that pesticides may be a factor, as such chemicals have been shown to accumulate in breast tissue and to be present at higher levels in women with breast cancer than those without it. Some have argued that there are massive numbers of chemicals used in plastics, food wraps, etc., that mimic hormones, particularly estrogen, and that these chemicals may be implicated in breast cancer, which has long been known to be affected by estrogen.

Breast Cancer Action, a group in Berkeley, California, has been tracking potential environmental links for over a decade. The national movement has been somewhat slow to pick up this issue, though it is now a major focus; new research funding for the National Institute of Environmental Health is a major NBCC priority this year.

NBCC is also doing its own investigations regarding environmental links to breast cancer, developing a position paper, identifying gaps in research, and reviewing the outcome of research currently underway. As the movement becomes more sophisticated in its understanding of the issues, its advocacy work can only be strengthened.

This focus on the *causes* of breast cancer represents a major paradigm shift for the breast cancer movement. This paradigm shift, with its emphasis on the environmental links to cancer and the corporate links to environmental problems, suggests that the breast cancer movement may soon be ready to join with other movements in efforts to fight those forces of modern culture that are destroying Earth's life-support systems, as Bill Moyer discusses in the Conclusion of this book.[14]

Conclusions

What is remarkable about this movement is that it succeeded, a very short time after take-off, in obtaining Congressional approval for one of its major goals: dramatic increases in funding for breast cancer research. In addition, it won victories on some of its minor goals: patient/survivor participation in decision-making, and an early environmental study. This victory also highlights earlier victories in the larger women's movement and women's health movement, which paved the way for the breast cancer movement's success. For example, efforts to end discrimination against women in high positions had resulted in the appointment of a woman director of the National Institutes of Health. Efforts to elect women to political office resulted in a rapid expansion of the number of women in Congress, who were there to give support on these issues. Dr. Susan Love's work as a breast cancer surgeon was pivotal in the launching of the national movement; her success in the formerly male bastion of surgery was a result of earlier battles to open spaces for women in medical schools and to overcome women's traditional socialization, which discouraged them from attending medical school and choosing "male" specialties.

Early successes were also no doubt assisted by the specific focus on breast cancer and by the nature of the disease itself. Breast cancer is widely viewed as a particular tragedy for women because it is the leading cause of death for women in their 40s. Though the rate of breast cancer is higher in older women, breast cancer's visibility among younger women in the midst of career and motherhood has had a galvanizing effect, and those women have been particularly strong, ener-getic, and powerful advocates. Further, breast cancer is an "equal opportunity" issue, afflicting rich and poor, powerful and powerless, liberal and conservative alike. Strong support in Congress came from liberal Democratic senator Tom Harkin, who in the early 1990s headed the Senate Committee on Health and Human Services and who had lost two sisters to breast cancer, as well as from Republican Congresswoman Barbara Vucanovich of Nevada, who was herself a breast cancer survivor. The movement's decision to focus public attention on women with breast cancer (a shift away from the medical establishment's focus on physicians and researchers) was powerfully effective. In this way, this movement reinforced the goals of the larger women's movement: women were actively taking charge of their lives and becoming public, political actors on behalf of their own needs and issues.

However, it has been more difficult to achieve progress in the search for environmental links to breast cancer and in demands for increased access to care. These will continue to require a strong movement. There are vested interests in the chemical industry that are likely to discourage research on the potential rela-tionship of environmental toxins to breast cancer. (For example, Berkeley's Breast Cancer Action found that AstraZeneca, the company that created Breast Cancer Awareness Month in 1985, also produces a variety of pesticides and chemicals (some of which are known to be carcinogenic), as well as tamoxifen, which is used in treatment for breast cancer patients.[15] Success in this work may require alliances with other groups working on environmental issues, particularly toxics in the community.

The problem of access to health care for the poor and uninsured is a major national dilemma with many vested interests. This problem will not be easily resolved for women with breast cancer, and it too may require alliances with other groups fighting for general access to health care for the poor and uninsured.

The breast cancer movement has provided a much-needed wake-up call during this era of rising breast cancer incidence. Women survivors, families, and friends have banded together to call attention to this critical health problem and have been able to bring more resources into the fight against the disease and to provide support and assistance for women who have been stricken. This move-ment remains vigorous, and seems certain to continue as a potent political force in the future.

10

The Globalization Movement

Juliette Beck[1]

MAP IS A USEFUL MODEL for analyzing contemporary social movements. In this chapter, I apply the MAP stages and roles to the current globalization movement. The many sub-movements such as those against the World Trade Organization (WTO), debt cancellation, genetic engineering, sweatshops, and those for ecological economics, fair trade, and indigenous people's rights are still discovering that they are part of one global movement challenging an unjust global economy that is dominated by a handful of multinational corporations. This chapter will focus on the key legislative challenges to the "corporate power grab" agreements of the 1990s (specifically NAFTA, GATT/WTO and Fast Track) and the mass protest in Seattle to show the progression of this historic social movement against corporate rule and for an ecologically sustainable and socially just global society in the United States.

Multinational corporations control almost every aspect of modern life, from the food we eat to the news we learn from to the government we live under. In the last few decades, multinational corporations have grown so huge that 51 of the 100 largest economies in the world are corporations. The role of governments has been relegated to implementing policies that help corporations increase their profits, even when these policies are detrimental to workers, the environment, community well being and future generations. Countries in the global south are forced to participate in the global economy according to the rules set by corporate-dominated institutions like the World Bank, International Monetary Fund (IMF) and the WTO. The U.S. movement is joining the decades, if not centuries old, global resistance to this unjust system that can also be described as neoliberalism or neocolonialism.

Under corporate globalization, progress is defined by expanded economic growth (GDP), as measured by profit generating activity. This growth, the corporations argue, is best achieved by allowing corporations unrestricted access to cheap labor, natural resources and consumer markets. To achieve this, governments have now created both a sophisticated legal framework that gives unprecedented new rights to private investors and institutions that have the power to enforce these rules, even when they conflict with popular will. Also, corporations' insatiable appetite for growth, and the consumerism created to feed this system, have created an environmental crisis of epic proportions that may soon prevent 80 percent of humanity from being able to meet its most basic human needs.

An alternative, "people's globalization" worldview encompasses a shared commitment to building a peaceful, environmentally sustainable and socially just global society. Progress would instead be measured by ecological health, the advancement of human rights, and community-defined quality of life. This vision celebrates diversity and will most likely be made up of self sustaining, regional and local economies. Trade in goods and services would be done in a way that raises living standards when workers and farmers are fairly compensated. As this movement history shows, grassroots globalization and fair trade have already begun to promote the cooperation and compassion needed to create an ecologically sane society in which everyone has dignified work, housing, education, healthcare, nutritious food and a healthy community.

Stage 1 - Normal Times - Free Trade is the Rising Tide that Lifts All Boats

Free trade has been billed by economists and opinion makers as key to advancing global economic growth, peace, and stability. Thus, Congress has historically approved trade agreements with little debate. Since 1974, Congress has readily transferred the authority to negotiate trade agreements to the executive branch through a legislative vehicle called "Fast Track." This mechanism prevents Congress from amending trade agreements negotiated by the White House and limits Congressional debate. Both NAFTA (the North American Free Trade Agreement) and the Uruguay Round of GATT (General Agreement on Tariffs and Trade) that established the WTO were undemocratically negotiated, mainly by the Bush Administration, and passed under Fast Track with the Clinton Administration publicly touting the benefits as the "rising tide that lifts all boats."

Historically, trade agreements dealt only with tariffs, duties and quotas between countries. Yet the agreements of the 90s were quantum leaps in corporate power. In addition to opening up markets, these "corporate managed trade" agreements contained provisions that limit governments' ability to regulate corporate activity and foreign investment occurring within their countries. The agreements expanded the reach of the corporations into more subjective areas of domestic policy such as food safety, taxation and government procurement. NAFTA and WTO were more about ushering in an era of corporate rule than promoting trade in goods and services. Congress passed NAFTA and GATT in

1993 and 1994 respectively in spite of activists best efforts to show how these corporate globalization initiatives would negatively effect wages, jobs, the environment, development, highway and food safety, and democracy itself.

Stage 2— The Failed Experimentt

In June of 1997, Public Citizen's Global Trade Watch, a Washington based public interest organization founded by Ralph Nader that continues to play a key "reformer role", released a report called "The Failed Experiment, NAFTA at Three Years." This report was one of many well-researched documents that critics used to prove that NAFTA had failed to live up to its promises and in fact was causing more harm than good in all three NAFTA countries — Canada, the U.S. and Mexico. The report challenged the myth that "trade equals prosperity for all" with hard statistics showing that NAFTA had resulted in decreased wages, worsening of the border environment, as well as increased layoffs, threats to food and highway safety, and drug trafficking. The toothless NAFTA side agreements that had been set up to protect labor rights and the environment, created a new bureaucracy to air complaints, but did nothing to help workers settle disputes against renegade corporations nor did they help communities clean up industrial contamination.

Organized labor was instrumental in building the case against NAFTA-style trade agreements. In 1997, the 13 million member strong AFL–CIO passed a resolution against Fast Track, reinforcing their position that all trade agreements should contain enforceable labor and environmental protections. The Teamsters, playing the role of "reformer," stepped up their campaign against the still unimplemented NAFTA cross border trucking agreement that was to allow sub-standard Mexican trucks and ununionized, underpaid drivers to transport goods all over the U.S. by 1995.

In Spring of 1997, the NAFTA Accountability Act was introduced in Congress. This legislation would have required NAFTA to be renegotiated if government assessments found that the impacts of NAFTA had caused more harm than good. Grassroots groups around the country such as the volunteer run group "Bay Area 50 Years is Enough" organized letter writing campaigns and fair trade coalition meetings with members of Congress to gain support for the legislation. Although the measure was never brought up for a vote, these efforts helped build public awareness of the failure of NAFTA and proved critical to the success of the next major trade battle in Congress against Fast Track.

Stage 3 – Ripening Conditions- More Free Trade Failures and the Birth of Creative, High Tech Resistance

The battle to defeat "Fast Track" trade negotiating authority is a successful sub movement that is now in the seventh stage. The Citizens' Trade Campaign, a key

change agent network, set strategy and coordinated district meetings with representatives of organized labor, Sierra Club, National Family Farm Coalition and
other grassroots groups and their members of Congress during the 1997 August
congressional recess. Armed with job loss data and real life stories of WTO and
NAFTA failures, teams of citizen lobbyists convinced a majority of congress
members that NAFTA had failed workers and the environment and should not
be expanded vis a vis Fast Track. Around the same time, the WTO's tribunals were
ruling against protections for clean air, dolphins, and endangered sea turtles –
proving environmentalists' worst nightmares true. Groups that had previously
thought the WTO "reformable" reversed their position and joined the "WTO has
got to go" chorus.

Fair trade activists followed up the Congressional visits with letter writing
campaigns, phone banks, public debates and creative actions, such as, staging a
funeral with tombstones depicting the factories that laid off workers and moved
factories to Mexico under NAFTA. Carefully crafted "fair trade not free trade"
messages were delivered to the general public. The Teamsters, for example, passed
out peanuts at a San Francisco Giants baseball game with a "Nuts to NAFTA"
flyer attached. All of the tactics used during the Fast Track battle were critical to
publicly demonstrating the "victims" of NAFTA and developing a majority public
opinion against "free" trade in favor of "fair" trade.

On September 25, 1997 the Clinton Administration withdrew the Fast Track
bill because it lacked enough votes to pass Congress. This was a historic victory that
shook the corporate elites to the core. Unfortunately, the defeat of Fast Track only
strengthened the resolve of business groups to advance their agenda in other
venues, such as the Multilateral Agreement on Investment (MAI) and the WTO.

The MAI was a "bill of rights" for multinational corporations that had been
negotiated in secret until Public Citizen obtained a copy of the text and posted it
on the internet, sparking a successful year long international campaign. Because
the MAI sought to limit the authority of local governments to regulate foreign
investment, the issues of democracy and local sovereignty enabled fair trade
activists to garner the support of local governments, a key "reformer" constituency.
In November 1998, for example, the San Francisco Board of Supervisors passed a
resolution opposing the MAI. By next fall, the twenty-nine wealthy countries that
had been negotiating the MAI ended the talks. While the MAI battle may appear
to have gone through all the MAP stages, it is actually in stage six. The MAI
agenda is spreading into other corporate globalization venues, such as the Free
Trade Area of the Americas. Opponents have not yet implemented new laws to
make corporations accountable to the communities they operate in.

In order to galvanize support for international trade, President Clinton
invited the WTO to meet in the U.S. in the fall of 1999 and launch a

"Millennium Round" of global trade talks. Clinton's hubris could not have backfired in a more dramatic way than the events that shook Seattle November 30-December 4, 1999. The Geneva-based institution's lack of transparency and democracy made it a sitting duck for media savvy fair trade organizers. The WTO functions like a global government because it has the power to both create and enforce rules for the global economy. In its four year history, the WTO's secret tribunals consistently ruled in favor of corporate interests in a variety of areas such as public health, against the European ban of bovine growth hormone fed beef, and family farms, against a European pact with poor Caribbean banana farmers.

By the time the WTO came to Seattle for its annual meeting, it had a clear track record of violating key values of how a public institution, particularly one that functioned like a global government, should operate. Most people agreed that the rules for the global economy should be written in a forum that is open, fair, and democratic. This message helped build even more support for fair trade. A late 1999 poll by the University of Maryland found that 78 percent of Americans thought the WTO should pay more attention to environmental and labor concerns.

In London in the late 90s, a submovement called "Reclaim the Streets" was emerging that inspired artists and activists to reclaim public spaces and transform financial centers into "festivals of resistance" using art and culture, such as giant puppets and rave music. On June 18, 1999, a coalition of groups held a "global carnival against capitalism" to coincide with the G-8 (eight wealthiest countries) meetings in Cologne, Germany. All around the world, parties and protests were held in financial districts and outside stock exchanges, banks and multinational corporations. In San Francisco on June 18, Art and Revolution, a local anarchist-artists collective helped mobilize over 2,000 people to take over the downtown financial district and stage a big street party without any permits. One of the banners blocking an intersection read, "globalize liberation, not corporate power." This creative action was a warm up for the WTO protest and helped launched the road to Seattle.

The newly formed Direct Action Network (DAN) and other movement building groups used to playing a "rebel role", such as Rainforest Action Network, Global Exchange and the Ruckus Society, put out a call for a "mass nonviolent direct action to shut down the WTO on the morning of November 30." DAN organized a road show designed to teach people mass action skills, such as nonviolence, affinity group formation, and consensus decision making. Activists also learned how street theater and giant puppets could be used to demonstrate the real life impacts of seemingly abstract economic policies and deescalate police violence. The roadshow was an important part of creating a new culture of resistance and helped inspire entire communities of activists, many from the northwest environmental movement that was experienced in the art of nonviolent civil disobedience, to put their bodies on the line to stop the WTO.

Stage 4 TAKE OFF – "The Battle of Seattle"

The Seattle WTO protests were clearly the trigger event that launched the anti-global corporatization movement into the fourth MAP stage in a dramatic and victorious way. Then President Clinton had completely underestimated the power of grassroots activism in the age of the internet. Over 50,000 people took to the streets in a festival of resistance on November 30, including many thousands from organized labor. The global elites were caught off guard despite the widely publicized plan to shut down the opening meeting by physically blocking the entrances to the convention center. The successful action immediately triggered a violent crack down by the police. Images of tear gas and storm trooper-like cops ricocheted around the world. No more than a couple dozen black clad, self-described anarchists took to destroying windows of mainly multinational corporations like Starbucks and Nike, yet the televised media in particular blew both the property destruction and the images of the few people carrying out the "ineffective rebel" role out of proportion.

Movement activists were immediately consumed in a debate over property destruction. Although the nonviolence guidelines had asked participants in the mass action not to destroy property, there was a conscious effort not to judge each other's tactics or marginalize people who supported property destruction. Others noted that property destruction effectively alienated mainstream people and advocated instead for strictly nonviolent "mass movement building" tactics that would more readily attract people who were not yet part of "the movement." People who believed that it was important to fight capitalism by physically destroying private property were playing out the negative rebel role. This fed the police strategy of depicting the protesters as "violent" in order to justify the excessive use and display of force.

Before the tear gas had even cleared in Seattle, the call went out for "A16" to be the next mass action, this time aiming to shut down the spring meetings of the World Bank and the IMF on April 16 and 17, 2000 in Washington, DC. Over 20,000 people participated in A16, including members of the AFLCIO, whose last minute endorsement ensured a repeat showing of the famous Seattle coalition – an important labor and environmental alliance that was symbolized by the uniting of "Teamsters and turtles". The World Bank/IMF delegates were bused in at 5am before protesters had time set up to blockades, but the capital city itself was shutdown for two days, as police had advised people not to come to work in the downtown area.

While most people recognized that A16 had successfully raised awareness of how corporate globalization was exacerbating global poverty and environmental destruction, many emails and discussions echoed the concern that "mass action" might not be sustainable and inclusive enough to attract other people to participate in the burgeoning movement. Many also questioned the movement's commitment to anti-racist organizing in the communities of color that are bearing the brunt of corporate globalization in the U.S. Mass actions that did little to further local organizing efforts were harshly criticized. Yet calls went out for Seattle style mass-actions at the Republican and Democratic National Conventions (RNC and DNC respectively) and other meetings of the global financial elite including the World Economic Forum in Melbourne, Australia and World Bank/IMF fall meetings in Prague.

The numbers of participants at the RNC and DNC was smaller than at A16 and the Seattle WTO protests. The civil disobedience actions, scuttled by the police, were ineffective at garnering media attention or disrupting the convention activities. Just as they had done in Washington, DC during A16, the police used devious tactics to mischaracterize activists as "violent, Moltov cocktail-making, 'negative rebel' anarchists." The police raided the convergence center where thousands had gathered for workshops, meals, art making and planning meetings. They also held bogus press conferences aimed at criminalizing activism in the eyes of the public. In Philadelphia, rumors were leaked that the protesters threw acid filled eggs at the police. A number of people were arrested on completely trumped up charges and held on $1 million bail. A sense of "movement failure," as predicted in MAP stage five, was emerging.

Despite well organized actions that linked corporate globalization with local economic rights efforts, such as a the Kensington Welfare Rights Union march in Philadelphia, and the sweatshop workers' and immigrant rights march in Los Angeles, the political impact of the convention protests was marginal at best. The movement's demands to curtail the global reach of corporations were unaddressed. The Democratic Party leadership wouldn't even entertain a debate to change the trade plank in the party platform that called for supporting the previously rejected Fast Track trade negotiating mechanism. Both parties unabashedly hobnobbed with corporate elites at ritzy parties sponsored by the likes of tobacco giant Philip Morris, Washington lobbyist firm Patton Boggs, and the nuclear industry association.

Both existing and newly formed movement groups helped put globalization on the social agenda in new and creative ways. On September 26, 2000, the date of the World Bank/IMF meetings in Prague, over 60 grassroots coalitions — spearheaded by the national labor activist network called Jobs with Justice — organized actions to support local efforts aimed at curbing corporate power, such as union organizing campaigns. This was an important step in spreading the global justice movement to community groups while engaging internationally focused activists in local economic justice struggles.

Stage 5 – Perception of Failure

To date the best examples of Stage 5 burnout and depression have occurred among people who thought the goal of the protests at the RNC and DNC should have been to shut down the conventions. Many of the activists in Prague had also hoped to shut down the World Bank and IMF meetings as well, yet the protesters there barely succeeded in getting past the police barricades to the building where the meetings were taking place. At the DNC, the role of direct action was actually downplayed by many local organizers who questioned the merit of exposing activists of color and local communities to more police violence. Activists that had come to Los Angeles looking for the "next Seattle" instead found mainly mass marches on issues ranging from "human need not corporate greed" to police brutality.

The focus on violence – both against the protesters and the police – was nearly the only news being reported by the mainstream media. Consequently, many organizers frequently dismissed the mainstream media (and thus the public) as irrelevant. The Independent Media Centers (www.indymedia.org), however, provided activist-created news to millions online around the world.

The Direct Action Network (DAN) is experiencing some MAP stage five patterns of dropout and confusion. While DAN is expanding in some cities, in other places, like San Francisco, meeting attendance has declined and the group is struggling to define its work.

Meanwhile, the global elites are reacting to the movement's success by promoting new societal myths of "compassionate globalization" or "globalization with a human face". This is essentially a deceptive public relations strategy in which they acknowledge the legitimacy of some of the movement's demands— such as debt cancellation for the world's poorest countries — but do nothing to change the economic policies that are making corporations wealthy at the expense of the majority. Their actual policies could be seen in Washington, D.C. right after the WTO protests in Seattle. Congress passed two corporate managed trade bills – the deceitfully named "African Growth and Opportunity Act" and a trade pact with China. Some fair trade activists were devastated, believing that these defeats indicated that the movement has failed, or worse yet, they said that it doesn't even exist.

Stage 6 – Majority Public Opinion:
Time to reclaim our power, rebuild communities and restore the Earth.

The global corporatization movement is now entering into the sixth MAP stage. Polls show that a majority of the U.S. public supports the concerns being raised by the movement. A poll reported in the September 11, 2000 Business Week cover story revealed that 74 percent of the public believe that corporations have too much power. 95 percent of those polled agreed with the statement: "U.S. corporations should have more than one purpose. They also owe something to their workers and the communities in which they operate, and they should sometimes sacrifice some profit for the sake of making things better for their workers and communities." A number of sub-movements are adopting strategies to translate this popular sentiment into systemic change.

Fair trade groups are using a number of strategies to put globalization on the political agenda of federal, state and local legislators. Over 700 groups from 80 different countries have signed on to an international campaign to demand that governments "sink or shrink" the WTO. In California, the senate has established a committee to explore the state's role in global trade policy, specifically the way that NAFTA and the WTO have trumped local sovereignty. For example, a Canadian chemical corporation, Methanex, is now using NAFTA's corporate court to seek $970 million in compensation for profits lost when the state phases out MTBE, a toxic groundwater pollutant partially produced by Methanex.

Groups are also putting forth solution-oriented proposals. Public Citizen is working on an alternative to Fast Track that will ensure that trade policies are developed in a democratic, balanced way. Civil society organizations and trade unions united under the umbrella of the Hemispheric Social Alliance have drafted a "people's globalization" initiative called the Alternatives of the Americas. This document contains specific policy recommendations on issues ranging from food security to immigration. It will be used to educate various sectors of society including the media and decision makers about a positive alternative to the Free Trade Area of the Americas, a corporate globalization pact that is currently being negotiated in secret by all the governments in the western hemisphere except Cuba.

Human centered economic alternatives to the corporate controlled global economy, such as community supported agriculture, fair trade, community banking and local currencies, are being successfully implemented in piecemeal fashion by groups working within the alternatives sub-movement. These ecologically sane and socially just alternatives should be coalesced and expanded as part of a clearly defined stage 6 strategy. Fair trade certified coffee is one such alternative that is now being sold in cafes and supermarkets throughout the country thanks to the work of change agent groups like Equal Exchange, Transfair USA and Global Exchange. Fair trade coffee is certified by an international, non-profit agency that ensures farmers in the global south receive credit and a fair price for their coffee ($1.26 per pound). The fair trade seal also guarantees consumers that the coffee was grown under humane and environmentally sustainable conditions. Fair trade helps people in the global north recognize that they play an important role in advancing human rights and sustainability in this interconnected global economy.

Movement activists and organizations now need to clearly define and articulate a vision for an environmentally sustainable, peaceful and socially just society. Some have described this paradigm shift as "deglobalization" or "localization"— the process of returning power and control over the economy to local communities. Democratic control over investment decisions will help ensure that private enterprises serve the needs of local communities, not the other way around. Unaccountable and irresponsible multinational corporations and institutions should be eliminated. The World Bank, IMF and WTO will need to be replaced with democratic entities that can facilitate the transformation to a socially just and ecologically sustainable era. Activists should be careful not to resuscitate the flawed and failed global institutions that are trying to recover from their legitimacy crises by offering some changes and benefits, such as debt cancellation, to impoverished communities.

The movement towards a new global era that esteems the life cycle, not the money cycle, will be community driven and will take many forms. Movement activists can now help accelerate this values transformation by engaging all sectors of society – farmers, workers, parents, teachers, etc. – in a visioning process to illuminate how to live in a democratic, sustainable and equitable way. Activists can catalyze grassroots globalization by sharing examples from communities, such as indigenous peoples, that are living sustainably. With every major ecosystem in rapid decline from overconsumption, progress and personal growth will have to quickly take on new meanings. Society is at a critical crossroads – either resources get allocated according to those who can afford to buy them, or social activism creates a new system where every child born has access to food, education, healthcare, meaningful work in the future and a nurturing community. This change starts with each of us learning to love and respect all life everywhere, not money and material wealth.

Conclusion

Toward the Future

IN MARCH 1959, I was voted out of the Presbyterian Church because I invited a Catholic and a Jew to talk to the youth group. This incident led me to the Quakers, which in turn prompted my early "retirement" as a management systems engineer for an international corporation, just three years after graduating from Pennsylvania State University. I knew that I wanted to do something more meaningful with my life. I had no idea that it was the start of "the sixties" and never suspected that I was beginning my new profession as a full-time activist.

It is from this vantage point, as a lifelong activist, that I look back at the evolution of contemporary social movements in the United States. I participated in many of the important social movements of the last 40 years, and it has been my privilege to work with and train thousands of activists in these and other movements, nationally and internationally.

In the 1960s, the civil rights movement launched the modern era of social activism in America. Larger numbers of people began participating as social movements addressed an ever widening array of society's problems and conditions. In each succeeding decade the number of people and of movements has increased, and more complex tools of analysis and organizing methods have been developed. My own analysis, the Movement Action Plan, grew into a detailed framework for strategically understanding and conducting social movements as I worked to create change and help increase the effectiveness of others.

The following review of the contributions and the limitations of modern social movements is based on my experience and attempts to refine my own thinking by studying the theories of analysts in other fields. In reflecting on these, I believe that 21st-century social movements must take on the even broader agenda of personal and social transformation, and I propose several new strategic directions for activists to consider.

Modern Era Social Movements

The civil rights, anti-Vietnam War, and anti-nuclear war movements of the 1960s were all "issue oriented" and were energized by the emergence of socially conscious youth and by the new student and counterculture movements. Participants in this new era of citizen activism used the nonviolent principles and methods developed by Gandhi and King, which have been adopted by many succeeding movements in the United States and around the world.

In the 1970s, influenced by the women's movement, some activists began to consider the importance of individual change in the process of social change. Feminism, especially, turned the spotlight on the destructive impact patriarchy had on personal and social relationships. Influenced also by Quakers and the human potential movement, activism was increasingly characterized by new models and methods for democratic group dynamics and organizational forms, such as collectives and consensus decision making. These were integrated into the anti-nuclear energy movement that took off in 1977 with the Seabrook nuclear power plant occupation and arrests.

The focus of social activism expanded during this decade to include a wide range of disenfranchised groups — women, gays and lesbians, students, working-class people, native Americans, and people of color. By putting the issues of these groups on the public agenda, social movements fostered an awareness of the shadow side of American life in the modern era. The primary goal of these movements was to give marginalized populations their rights and bring them into full participation in mainstream society.

Understanding and describing the way in which American society violated the rights of these oppressed groups and its own deeply held cultural values was facilitated by an analytical approach known as "deconstructionism." Deconstructionists focused on revealing what was wrong with an oppressive, patriarchal, capitalist society. The "multiculturalism" movement emerged and advocated that marginalized and oppressed people should not only reclaim their heritage and cultures, but should also be widely acknowledged and honored.

In order to honor and support all the different oppressed groups, with their values and politics that sometimes conflicted with other oppressed groups, multiculturalism adopted the principle of "pluralistic relativism." This was a new egalitarian worldview that advocated every group's right to its own culturally based reality and version of "truth," which was to be considered as valid as any other. Consequently, any claims to universal values or truths (such as the importance of nonviolence or environmental sustainability) that challenged the truths of any marginalized individual or group were often resisted as being hierarchical and oppressive, just as the dominant society was oppressive.

The belief in "radical freedom" was simultaneously adopted by a wide range of political and cultural groups, including the youth-based counterculture, anarchists, political Yippies, multiculturalists, and liberation movements on the left. Ironically, it was also an ideology long held by libertarians and free-market capitalists on the right. Its impact was heightened by the counterculture of the 1970s, whose "me generation" proclaimed the view that all people and groups should be free to "do their own thing." Ironically, this fit in nicely with modern society's fundamental principle that everyone should seek his or her own self-interest in the cut-throat, competitive marketplace, whether in the realms of economics, politics, or the dynamics of activism.

While recognizing the important and revolutionary contribution that the application of pluralistic relativism has made on behalf of marginalized groups, social analysts Ken Wilber and Robert Kegan, among others, have also challenged the unhealthy and reactionary versions of personal politics.[1] They point out the dangers of extreme individualism, which gives unquestioning support to individual freedom without a corresponding responsibility, especially when it is based on egocentric narcissism, epitomized by the attitude "Do your own thing." They charge that such extreme individualism undermines the higher goal of achieving a more evolved society that is based on cooperation and unity among individuals, and relationships among diverse groups based not only on their differences but also on their commonalties and mutual concerns.

These critics also see the importance of placing social activism in the larger framework of human developmental stages. They identify many of the problems that concern activists as typical of the particular stage an individual or society has reached. A critical role of social activism, therefore, is to help individuals and societies progress from one developmental level to the next in a healthy way. I believe these larger developmental theories are important tools for social activism and have been incorporating them into my own thinking and training, Many activists, however, might reject these and all other developmental theories as being hierarchical and oppressive, stifling individual freedom.

Social activism continued to grow in the 1980s, and politically engaged citizens took on bigger global issues. Two new mass social movements emerged — the anti-nuclear energy and the anti-nuclear weapons campaigns — and two others took off — one against the U.S. intervention in Central America and the other against apartheid in South Africa, both of which included the inspired participation of faith-based institutions and individual activists. These movements received worldwide attention and advanced international activism.

All of these issues required an extensive analysis of military, political, and economic policies and systems at home and internationally. Mass-based organizing, nonviolent actions, and sustained campaigns characterized each of these movements, many of which had sub-movements that progressed through MAP's eight stages and used all four roles of activism — citizen, rebel, change agent, and reformer.

While virtually all of the issues and social movements of the previous three decades remained in the last decade of the 20th century, the 1990s was also a time of international social activism. After the collapse of communism in the Soviet Union and Eastern Europe, activists challenged the expansion of the power of global corporate-market capitalism. Many groups actively opposed the North American Free Trade Agreement (NAFTA), the Multilateral Agreement on Investment (MAI), and the World Trade Organization (WTO). The anti-WTO demonstration in Seattle at the end of 1999 signaled the take-off stage of a world-wide movement against corporate capitalism's expanding control over the political economies and social policies of nations throughout the world.

This movement has expanded beyond the specific issues addressed by movements in previous decades to confront the corporation-controlled global political-economic system itself. It turns the spotlight on the undemocratic and oppressive nature of global corporate control, especially with regard to people in the Third World, but also as it is destructive to workers, the society, and the environment in the U.S. and other industrialized nations. Consequently, the movement against corporate domination includes groups addressing such varied issues as homelessness, poverty, social services, food safety, labor, health care, civil rights, the environment, democracy, and Third World debt.

The activism of the 1990s increased cooperation among social movements around the world, including those in Third World countries, and connected labor and environmental issues with international and domestic concerns. The anti-corporate globalization movement is also the first social movement to take full advantage of Internet technology to gather data and mobilize diverse groups into action across great distances.

Modern era social movements — pluses and minuses

Many of the movements from the 1960s through the 1990s were successful in achieving at least a portion of their goals and objectives. They have developed sophisticated tools of analysis and organization and adapted and popularized the use of the nonviolent direct action methods of Gandhi and Martin Luther King. In addition, during this period social activism made three other critical contributions to social change: deconstructionist analysis, multiculturalism, and pluralistic relativism, all of which we will have to address differently in the 21st century.

- **Deconstructionist analysis.** During a period when the powerholders are trumpeting the wonders and success of the modern era of economic growth and prosperity through the "free" market, privatization, and globalization, social activists have developed devastating critiques of what is wrong with every facet of present-day society. They have painted a vivid picture of how social systems and institutions are failing to live up to the moral and ethical principles of democratic nations. These movements are grounded in well-documented rational analysis of the problems and how they are caused by society's power-holders, social systems, and institutions.

- **Multiculturalism.** While the powerholders and media laud the unprecedented success of the modern era, social movements include large populations that were marginalized, disenfranchised, or oppressed. The goals of liberation movements arising from these marginalized populations include overcoming oppression and prejudice; building the pride and strength of their own communities; and gaining rights, privileges, and a place in society on an equal basis with everyone else. An increasing sensitivity to diversity issues has made social activism a far more inclusive and powerful force for social change.

- **Pluralistic relativism.** A critical aspect of diversity is to honor the experience, culture, and perspectives of every group in society, especially the oppressed and disenfranchised. Normally these voices either go unheard or are dismissed in favor of the views of the powerholders and the dominant paradigm, culture, or group. Pluralistic relativism sees truth as being relative to the experience and culture of each diverse group and, therefore, tends to be fiercely anti-hierarchical.

Activism of the last 40 years has also been characterized by some critical strategic limitations that must be overcome if social movements are to be successful in the new millennium.

- Most citizen activism has been based on an underlying belief in the viability and unlimited continuation of the modern era's mantra of ever-increasing economic growth and prosperity.

- Efforts to change society's oppressive and unjust social systems and institutions have been carried out without a parallel effort to change the consciousness of individuals, including those in social movements, or to change the culture of activism itself.

- The ideologies of deconstruction and cultural relativism, which have underpinned the sensitivity to individualism and diversity, were often raised to the level of "political correctness," resulting in movements violating their own values and principles. For example, the politically correct line that "everyone can do their own thing" gave the green light for relatively few people to act out their anger and rage and advocate physical skirmishes with the police and property damage, such as in the anti-corporate globalization demonstrations in Seattle and throughout 2000. This behavior, however, violated the wishes of the organizers of those events, who called for total nonviolence. The minority who wanted violence were able to do their own thing, but the demonstration organizers and great majority of participants were not able to do *their* own thing, which was to have a totally nonviolent demonstration.

- There was another critical problem that limited social movement effectiveness in the new era of social activism: it had few strategic models, such as MAP, to guide it. Because 21st-century activists also lack adequate theories and direction for the new task of social transformation, I will introduce some in the next section.

Five Strategic Guidelines for Social Activism in the 21st Century

We are in a time of crisis and opportunity. It is a time of crisis because the present social system is making critical problems worse and is not sustainable; it is destroying the environmental life-support systems, depleting critical resources, and threatening human life on the planet. At the same time, we have the opportunity to achieve a momentous leap forward to a new era and a new way of being human as part of our historical, evolutionary developmental process.

In the 21st century, social activism has a critical role to play in assisting a transition from the present modern era to a new ecological era of human equality and environmental sustainability. To meet the challenge of the new century, social activists need to consider adopting the following five strategies.

1. **Continue to expand local, national, and international efforts to alleviate the world's immediate problems and crises**
   The world's immediate social problems and crises are ongoing, and the modern era continuously creates new problems and bigger crises. Some activists have become discouraged because social problems continue to snowball despite their gallant efforts, and some of today's crises seem too big to tackle. But imagine just how much worse off we would be without the social activism of the last 40 years — or the past 200 years. The crises we now face can only be successfully challenged by social movements that engage people at the local, regional, and international levels to connect their issues to changes in the larger social systems. Only such interconnected worldwide activism can bring about the necessary paradigm shifts discussed below.

2. **Recognize that the world's critical social and environmental problems cannot be solved within the present modern era of maximum material growth and prosperity**
   We live in a brief period of history that glorifies the modern industrial philosophy of material economic growth and prosperity. Led by the United States government and mammoth conglomerate international corporations, virtually all the world's nations, leaders, and institutions proclaim their allegiance. Even China, Russia, Poland, and other former Communist states are participating through the corporate-led globalization system's institutions, such as the World Bank and the World Trade Organization. Activists must be aware of two of the

most commonly used societal myths supporting this philosophy, and the societal secrets that discredit them.

The first *societal myth* is that the international system of growth and prosperity will end poverty, hunger, and disease and create political democracies around the world. The powerholders trumpet that the modern era has brought unprecedented levels of economic growth and prosperity that will continue indefinitely into the future. They rightly point out that hundreds of millions of people have achieved levels of consumption, affluence, health, and longevity undreamed of, even by royalty, a century ago. There are approximately 23 economically "developed" nations and all the rest are told that they are "developing" countries.[2]

The first *societal secret* of the modern era is that while it is creating growth and prosperity for some, it is creating poverty, hunger, disease, and reduced quality of life for the great majority. Despite its obvious success, the modern era of economic growth and prosperity has a colossal downside: it creates astounding economic, social, and environmental problems. Instead of being helped by the modern era's corporate globalized system, the majority of people in Third World countries experience increasing poverty, hunger, disruption of traditional culture, loss of land, unemployment, oppressive or dictatorial governments, and warfare. While these problems affect well over 50 percent of the people in the "developing" countries, even 10 to 15 percent of the people in the United States experience various degrees of poverty, slum housing or homelessness, unemployment, incarceration, or inadequate medical care.[3] This downside of the modern era is totally excluded from the accounting system that is used to guide corporate and governmental decisions.

Moreover, the powerholders' primary strategies to solve the world's problems stemming from the modern era — economic growth and direct aid programs — not only fail to help, but usually make the problems worse. The chief strategy is to promote more economic growth on the theory that a "rising tide lifts all boats." But while decades of record-setting worldwide economic growth has created tens of millions more middle- and upper-class consumers, it has produced even more poor people. The capitalist market system inherently continues to distribute most of the **benefits** of growth to the affluent minority and most of its **costs** to the poor majority. Consequently, the growth of the market economy has produced a widening gap between rich and poor, both within nations and between the already rich and poor nations, as well as creating additional environmental devastation.[4]

Additionally, the foreign aid programs that purported to help the poor in the "developing" nations have created mountainous debt and dependency relationships, and enable the imposition of "structural adjustments" that benefit international corporations and investors. Both of these have also forced the curtailment of social services and other benefits to the poor, thereby increasing the poverty and suffering of the majority. This strategy does not work for the poor even in the United States, the world's leader in economic growth and prosperity, where the top 1 percent of the population owns as much wealth as the bottom 95 percent, and where 10 to 15 percent of the population still lives in poverty.[5]

Finally, while there is increasing pressure on Third World nations to adopt the facade of democracy through national elections, the democratic rights of all countries are being supplanted by the autocratic power of corporation-dominated international institutions such as multinational corporations, the World Bank, and the World Trade Organization.

The second *societal myth* of the modern era of growth and prosperity is that everyone can eventually live at Western levels of consumption. "Economics is the science of growth," was the injunction of university economic textbooks when I attended classes in the 1950s, and growth remains the centerpiece of western economics. Today, as they gather under the banner of globalization, virtually all the world's powerholders pledge themselves to joining the bandwagon of globalized economic growth. The presumption is that their populations can be become full partners in the era of material consumption. The advocates of worldwide globalization raise up the ultimate vision of a future time when the rising tide of continuous economic growth and prosperity will have lifted all "developing" boats. As President Clinton, the leader of world globalization for the past eight years, said, "All of us now have to build a global economy that leaves no-one behind."[6]

The second *societal secret* is that not only is it impossible to achieve the promised growth and prosperity for the world's poor, but it is even impossible to sustain the current level of growth and prosperity because it is destroying our environmental life-support systems, depleting natural resources, and leading to ecological disasters and economic collapse. For three decades there has been mounting indisputable evidence that unfettered growth and consumption are destroying environmental life-support systems and depleting key natural resources. Many scientists fear that this environmental devastation will result in catastrophes and threaten human existence on the planet, at least as we now know it.[7] Most activists are familiar with this litany of problems, which includes the melting of the polar ice that threatens to flood the world's coastal cities; depletion of the protective ozone layer; global warming that will change the world's weather patterns and threaten agriculture production; and pollution or depletion of critical resources such as water, air, arable land, and oil.

These problems exist today, just when the nations with the majority of the world's people — China, India, the former Soviet states, and many Third World nations — have adopted concerted policies to start participating fully in the era of economic growth and prosperity and achieve the goal of becoming developed.

This is a flawed dream. A research project that measured the effect of humanity's "ecological footprint" reports that it would take from five to six Earths to bring everyone up to the level of today's U.S. economy. The researchers conclude that the process of developing more nations will simply speed up the current race to ecocide.[8] Moreover, most of today's programs that are supposed to alleviate environmental and resource problems of growth and prosperity will merely delay the inevitable collapse and thereby increase its impact when it eventually occurs.

3. **Realize that the goals of most social movement programs are based on false expectations about the success of the modern era of economic growth and prosperity**
    Almost all social movements — including those that advocate peace, ending poverty and hunger, developing the Third World nations, or helping economically disenfranchised groups — are based on the goal of providing everyone with their just and full benefits of economic growth and prosperity. While these are important and laudable efforts, social activists need to investigate fully whether this goal is attainable and sustainable based on the limits of the natural world.

    Even much of the current anti-corporate globalization movement is hindered by a belief that the global system of growth and prosperity can work for everyone. This ignores the reality of limited resources and the degradation of the environment caused by modern industrialism and the consumer society. It would be irresponsible for social activists to promote programs that help the oppressed and poor to participate in the modern era's worldwide economic system if it either structurally cannot include them or will collapse even sooner if it does. It is incumbent on social activists, therefore, to develop a strategy of transformation to a new just and sustainable era that will consider everyone equally.

4. **Organize strategically for transformation from the modern era of economic growth and prosperity to a new era of ecology, justice, and sustainability**
    To achieve this transformation to a new paradigm, activists need to became familiar with the developmental nature of individuals and societies. Just as we as individuals develop through stages from birth to death, societies may be seen as passing through developmental stages. With this in mind, today's social and environmental problems can be viewed as resulting from the present developmental stage, which I have called "the modern era of economic growth and prosperity." Solutions to the world's problems ultimately require a developmental transformation to a new human era. Consequently, social activists need to consciously develop analyses, visions, strategies, and programs within the larger context of creating a momentous paradigmatic leap to a new era.
    Replace the growth and consumption paradigm with an ecological and well-being paradigm
        While the modern era of economic growth and prosperity has many positive characteristics, including a high production of goods and service, technological

advancement, democratic forms of government, ideological values of civil and human rights, and a stable and established social order and authority, it has a massive downside. This downside includes economic growth and prosperity accruing only to the economic elite, whether individuals or corporations; enormous social, political, and economic stratification, with an ever-widening gap between the minority of haves and majority have-nots; scarcity amid plenty; an ideology of adversarialism and competition; the destruction of the environment and depletion of natural resources; an emphasis on the private market over community benefit and control; and the promotion of individualistic psychological qualities of egocentrism, narcissism, insecurity, low self-esteem, and dependency. In fact, these problems are so built into the modern era of civilization that anthropologist Richard Heinberg has concluded that the characteristics are fundamental aspects of each of the 21 recorded civilizations over the past 5,000 years.[9]

There are many descriptions of and different names given to the alternative era of ecology-justice-sustainability. Some of its features would include improved quality of life for all instead of materialistic quantity and affluence for some; an end to the insecurity of scarcity by guaranteeing everyone on earth that their physical needs — the basic necessities of life — would be met; a low maximum limit on material affluence; an emphasis on cooperation, caring, and sharing; development of non-material aspects of human potential; economic principles, based on the limits of Planet Earth, that would maintain ecological and resource preservation and a steady state economy; maximum political and economic decentralization; participatory democracy; universal values, such as identified in the United Nation's Declaration of Human Rights; democratic global structures of integration, coordination and, where necessary, enforcement; and, finally, individual transformation from an egocentric to a universal caring psyche.[10] The most important thing now is not so much a completed vision, but to engage people from every country in the process of creating and achieving such a vision of the new era.

Create an analysis, vision, and action strategy for transformation

First, as part of the process of engaging people in creating a paradigm shift, activists need to develop an analysis that shows that the problems we are addressing are caused by the modern era itself and can only be ultimately solved by a new era that includes the next developmental step for humanity. Second, we need to identify and describe a preliminary vision of a new human era that can solve the problem. Finally, the movement needs to conduct strategic actions that are part of the transformation from the present to the envisioned next era. This could include a wide variety of actions, including educating activists and the public regarding the need for a paradigm shift and creating building blocks toward the new society in whatever ways are possible.

Use existing developmental theories of societal transformation

Fortunately there are theories of societal transformation, such as those of Don Beck, Ken Wilber, and Robert Kegan, that activists can use to help them develop analyses, visions, strategies, and actions for personal and social change.[11] For example, Spiral Dynamics, promoted by Don Beck and Chris Cowan, is a theoretical framework that describes eight stages of human development that can be applied to individuals, societies, or the human species as a whole.[12] This model can help activists create strategies for social transformation and also help them analyze how the reactionary shadow side of social activism itself now works against the transformation process.

Ken Wilber describes the positive role that social activism plays in the process of social transformation, as well as its shadow side, including ways that distortions of activism are inadvertently a barrier to achieving positive social change.[13] Robert Kegan describes five levels of individual psychological and relationship development through which people need to progress to function in a truly peaceful society.

Overcome activists' resistance to social transformation

Many activists have long recognized the need to include strategies for social transformation in their social movements, and some have already begun to use these and other theoretical models. There are, however, a number of reasons why many activists are bound to be resistant. First, they are too busy on the front lines and have no time for anything else, or they are afraid that any new effort will take the focus from current programs that are addressing immediate serious social issues.

Other activists will oppose transformation because it requires new personal qualities and new organizational values. Individual activists will need to learn the skills of cooperation and caring, and social movement organizations will need to value unity and develop respect for the deeply held values, myths, and beliefs of all cultures, including those of their opponents. While this will be difficult to accomplish out in the world, it will also be difficult for some activists to make the necessary changes within themselves.

In addition, Beck, Wilber, Kegan, and others point out that the process of social transformation will require adding reconstruction to deconstruction analysis, unity to diversity, and universal integralism to pluralistic relativism. Many deconstructionists, however, have been so focused on criticism and what's wrong that they have also criticized all different progressive ideas and cannot support positive holistic visions for the future. Many of those promoting diversity, differences, and separateness have difficulty thinking in terms of commonalties, alliances, cooperation, unity among all groups, and building bridges between the oppressed and the dominant groups. Finally, "ideological" multiculturalists, who promote pluralistic relativism and difference among groups as their end goal, have trouble with social transformation efforts that include universal values and truths and global systems and structures because, as Ken Wilber points out, they see all developmental theories as hierarchical, all universal truths as elitist, and all hierarchical structures as oppressive.[14]

5. **Include personal and cultural transformation as a central strategy for creating a peaceful world — starting with activists ourselves and our organizations**
Social movements have primarily focused on changing social systems and institutions to achieve their goals of a more peaceful, democratic, just, and sustainable world. However, there are many reasons why these goals cannot be achieved without equal attention to creating personal and cultural transformation — starting with activists ourselves.

Ken Wilber and others point out that human society is made up of three interconnected and interdependent parts: individuals, culture, and social systems and institutions, the "I", "we," and "it."[15] They are different aspects of the same whole; consequently, one can't be transformed for long without the requisite changes in the other two. Therefore, even if a society's social systems and institutions were transformed to the peaceful paradigm, the change would not last without a parallel transformation of that society's individuals and culture. Similarly, the good society is unlikely to develop without individual change because, outside of dictatorships, social system and institutional change usually *follows* personal and cultural change on the part of at least some of the population. Finally, to achieve personal and cultural change in society, social activists have to lead by example, demonstrating the desired alternative we seek.

The transformation from the modern society of individuals striving to achieve personal gain and prosperity in a competitive marketplace to a new cooperative, ecological, just, and sustainable society involves a paradigm shift. This shift has been described by social critic Riane Eisler as moving from a "dominator" to a "partnership" model of human relationships.[16]

At the individual level, this involves a developmental leap from an egocentric, competitive, and self-serving personality. Many theorists have identified three general stages of individual moral development. Ken Wilber labels them as preconventional, conventional, and post-conventional.[17] Feminist psychologist Carol Gilligan identifies four developmental stages: selfish, caring, universal caring, and integrative.[18]

For a large number of individuals, making this transition would be quite a psychological leap. As Paul Shepard suggests in *Nature and Madness*, the modern era of civilization requires a "psychological juvenilization" and a "selfish immaturity."[19] People who are selfish, arrogant, prideful, overly logical, controlling, and fiercely competitive are considered normal in modern culture because these personality traits are necessary and appropriate in a dominator and consumer society.

If humanity is to survive the 21st century, however it must switch to a new peaceful era that requires a new human consciousness. To paraphrase Einstein, we cannot create a new partnership society with the same mentality that created the present dominator society. If we do not change ourselves, we cannot change the world.

The need for a spiritual perspective

Linda Stout, founder of Spirit In Action, reports that in her national survey, grassroots activists across America said that spirituality was one of the most critical things missing in activism.[20] Although this is not a term that has been much accepted in social movement culture, it is understandable why it is so strongly missed. Spirit refers to the strong inner urge for meaning in our lives, an urge that involves a deep, positive connection with each other, the planet, and an evolving universe. Compassion, kindness, love, equality, support, and caring, therefore, are qualities of spirit. They bring us back in touch with our true nature. When we experience these qualities we tend to feel more fulfilled, joyful, energized, and happy. These are also the qualities of the peaceful model that we seek.

Social movements and their organizations, however, are often characterized by just the opposite traits, such as competitiveness, self-righteousness, and arrogance. When we act towards others in angry, selfish, controlling, greedy, competitive, and hostile ways, we tend to feel separate, unfulfilled, and unhappy, and our bodies then react in ways that are physically unhealthy. These are qualities that separate us from our true nature and are characteristic of the dominator paradigm of our present society.[21]

Social activism that is engaged in the work of transforming ourselves and our society from the dominator to a peaceful partnership model of human relationships, therefore, can be experienced as spiritual work. Spirit is found in the process itself, as we are involved in the politics of meaning that connect us to our human nature.

Social movement activism would be more effective if it included this kind of personal transformation. Movement activists and their organizations need to "walk their talk" by modeling the new way of being in the peaceful era that is required to ultimately resolve the problems that concern them. Remember Gandhi's dictum, "the means are the ends in the making." In addition, more people would join social movement organizations, and fewer would drop out, if the movement offered a friendly, safe, trusting, fulfilling, fun, supportive, and loving environment.

Next Steps

To address the important issues of the 21st century, social activists not only need to continue what we are doing, but must also overcome some of the traditional limitations of activism, as well as adopt new approaches to address the larger issues facing humanity. In order to be catalysts to convert our current planetary crises into opportunities for human transformation, activists must change ourselves and our activism. Some might form study-action groups to apply MAP to current social movements and begin new activities that are part of the long-term process of the transition to a peaceful paradigm, both in our personal lives and in our social movement activities and organizations.

There is reason to believe that we can make this transformation and assist the global society in making a paradigmatic leap. Social transformation theories tell us that the universe is in a constant state of change and that even big transformations happen much more quickly and more often than we think. And sociologist Paul Ray and Sherry Ruth Anderson have found that 50 million Americans, who he calls "cultural creatives," are already in favor of the social transformation described above.[23]

My hope is that this book enables the MAP models and methods to reach a broad audience of social activists, concerned citizens, students, and teachers, and increases their understanding and effectiveness in bringing about social change. I believe that facing up to the impending resource wars and environmental crash, although initially a depressing thought, could motivate tens of millions of people to support the need for a fundamental shift to a peaceful era. Finally, I hope that my reflections in this chapter will encourage social activists to place the transformation from the modern dominator era of growth and consumerism to a new peaceful era of ecology, justice, and sustainability at the center of their own efforts.

GLOSSARY

Actual policies and practices. These are the policies and practices that the powerholders are really implementing, which are deliberately kept hidden from the public because they violate widely held values, beliefs, traditions, laws, and expectations. They are the opposite of the *official* policies and practices.

Affinity group. A method of organizing, used in many nonviolent direct actions, that gathers activists into small groups that make decisions by consensus. For example, instead of arriving at demonstrations as an unorganized collection of individuals and friends, potential participants are urged to form into groups ahead of time. When all participants are in affinity groups, even large demonstrations are organized.

Agent provocateur. A person hired by the powerholders to infiltrate a social movement to gather intelligence or to disrupt, disable, de-legitimize, or destroy a social movement, organization, or individual activist. Many of the behaviors of *agents provocateurs* and negative rebels are indistinguishable.

Bureaucratic management. The powerholders' first level of strategy, which is to prevent a social problem from becoming a public issue.

Campaign. A prolonged social movement activity composed of a series of demonstrations and different events focused on a particular issue, goal, and powerholder target, which could last for a period of weeks, months, or years, such as a strike, boycott, or series of sit-ins at a particular restaurant or group of restaurants in a particular town.

Change agent role. The social movement function performed by activists to educate, organize, and mobilize grassroots citizenry on a social problem. It is especially predominant in MAP's Stage Six.

Citizen role. The function performed by activists, which represents the universal values, beliefs, and behaviors (e.g., justice, democracy, and freedom) that are widely accepted and deeply believed by the general population.)

Civil disobedience. A demonstration or activity in which the participants deliberately violate a law in order to raise a larger social value. Nonviolent demonstrators typically notify the authorities ahead of time and cooperate with them. They are willing to accept the consequences of violating the law, which might include going through legal procedures, including time in jail.

COINTELPRO (Counterintelligence Program). The counterintelligence program that the White House and FBI set up in the 1960s to disrupt and neutralize the anti-Vietnam war movement; it eventually was used against many other people and movements.

Construction. Construction is a political, philosophical, sociological or psychological perspective that says people or social systems construct their own reality.

Crisis management. The powerholders' second level of strategy, which is to prevent a social problem that has suddenly become a public issue from becoming a *political* issue that is seriously debated in the halls of government.

Deconstructive analysis. In *Doing Democracy*, the term "deconstructive analysis" is used to describe the way in which social movement activists and multiculturalists, especially since the 1960s, critically claim that much of political, economic, social and psychological life has been defined and created by the powerholders and the social systems and institutions to the benefit of the powerholders and disbenefit of everyone else, especially marginalized groups.

Demonstration. A social movement event or action that usually lasts one or more days, such as a march, picket, or rally, which may or may not include civil disobedience.

Dialectic. A debate between conflicting points of view; a process of change that involves an interplay between opposite tendencies, leading to a new perspective; to proceed in a process of logical argumentation.

Dilemma demonstration. A nonviolent action demonstration that is strategically designed to put the powerholders in a lose-lose dilemma: their position is eroded whether they arrest/attack the demonstrators or let the demonstration continue.

Endgame. The final part of MAP's Stage Seven, in which the social movement finally succeeds in achieving its goal.

Endgame strategy. The strategy by which a social movement or a sub-movement can most likely achieve its goal or a sub-goal and complete the seventh stage of MAP.

Four roles of activism. The four archetypical functions of activists in a social movement (citizen, rebel, change agent, and reformer) that, according to MAP theory, need to be effectively fulfilled by participants if a social movement is to succeed.

Grand strategy. The ultimate strategy of social movements, which is to promote participatory democracy so that the people have control over the political, economic, and environmental sectors of their lives.

Grassroots. People, activists and organizations that are based and grounded at the local level.

Growth and prosperity. The powerholders of the industrialized nations, led by the United States and joined by the powerholders of most countries, tout "growth and prosperity" as the guiding mantra, goal, and purpose of the modern industrial era. They proclaim success by pointing to record-breaking levels of economic material growth, affluence, and consumption that are achieved through the worldwide market, dominated by international conglomerate corporations, and increasingly mediated by supra-organizations like the World Trade Organization.

Holarchal development. The perspective that the evolutionary development of individuals, cultures, nations, and the universe takes place by each succeeding level or stage differentiating itself from the previous stage, then including it and all the other previous stages. Consequently, each succeeding stage is more complex and is both a whole in itself and a part of the next stage. This contrasts with pathological hierarchic development in which each stage replaces all of the previous stages. The MAP eight stage model is an example of holarchal development.

Initiative. Some states allow citizens to put propositions on the ballot during an election for voters to support or defeat. Some of these "initiatives" are legally binding decisions, while others are mere opinion polls.

Lunch counter "sit-in" movement. The 1960 social movement in which black and white students sat in the seats of lunch counters and restaurants that refused service to African Americans until they were arrested or eventually served. The sit-in movement launched the 1960s civil rights movement.

MAP (Movement Action Plan). A set of strategic theories and models that explains the process of success for social movements. It is used by theorists and activists to understand, analyze, and conduct social movements.

Model. A model is a standard for imitation or comparison. It can be a simplified representation of a system or phenomenon, with any hypotheses required to describe the system or explain the phenomenon.

Negative rebel. Activists who ineffectively perform the rebel role of social movement activism.

NIMBY (Not-in-my-back-yard). Those who oppose nuclear reactors and other environmental hazards in their own locality.

Official policies and practices. The policies and practices that powerholders publicly proclaim, as opposed to their actual policies and practices, which they hide from public view.

Paradigm. A model or conceptual framework that gives "a unified perspective over a range of experiences." It can "explain and help us understand why events occur as they do," which in turn guides our choice of beliefs and actions. Paradigms can be used to get populations to support or reject political, economic, social, and environmental perspectives of reality. Example: Planet Earth is flat and the universe revolves around it.[1]

Paradigm shift. The move from one paradigm to another, such as the shift from believing the world is flat to believing it is round.

People Power Model. A theory that political, economic, or social power and control ultimately resides in the ordinary citizens.

Pluralistic relativism. Acknowledgment of the existence, experience, culture, and perspectives of every sub-group in society or the world, especially minorities, the oppressed, non-dominant, and the disenfranchised. Truth is seen as being local and relative to each group. This perspective tends to challenge all efforts at universal truths (except the claimed universal truth of pluralistic relativism that there is no universal truth) as being hierarchic and oppressive.

POO (Professional opposition organization). Social movement organizations that primarily carry out the reformer role. They often have a traditional organizational structure with a strong executive director and a board of directors, and are located in national and state capitals.

Power. The ability to get what one wants. Political power is having the means, influence, and pressures, including authority, rewards, and sanctions, to achieve your objectives. Power can be held by the state and private institutions and by the people opposing them.[2]

Power elite. That small minority that uses social systems and institutional structures to wield an inordinate amount of political, economic, and social control, primarily to the benefit of themselves and others of their choosing and to the disbenefit of the majority population and the general welfare.

Power elite model. A theory of power that says political-economic power is primarily held by the power elite, who have control over the general population.

Powerholders. Those institutions, corporations, and individuals that hold a preponderance of political and economic power through socio-political-economic structures and relationships, rather than mere personal attributes.

Rebel role. The function performed by activists that involves protest activities, such as demonstrations, rallies, marches, and blockades, to resist powerholder policies and programs that violate universal values. It is especially predominant in MAP Stage Four.

Reform. A change in laws, policies, procedures, programs, etc., that is generally considered to be progressive. However, many acts purported to be reforms are reactionary and regressive, such as many so-called tax or welfare reforms.

Reformer role. The function performed by activists that primarily uses parliamentary, judicial, legislative, administrative, electoral, and other normal official institutional channels to achieve social change.

Re-trigger events. Trigger events that happen in Map Stages Six, Seven, and Eight that precipitate a brief period of nonviolent social actions and conditions that are similar to those that occur at the beginning MAP's Stage Four, "Movement Take-off."

Satyagraha **(Gandhi's view of power).** The powerholders' power is based on the consent of the people; to function, it requires their cooperation, submission, and obedience. The power of social movements, therefore, is based on the ability to mobilize the populace in a moral struggle in which the people withdraw their consent, using methods such as noncooperation, defiance, disobedience, refusing benefits, and creating alternatives. This moral struggle requires total nonviolence in attitude and actions towards people and property.

Social movement. A collective action in which the populace is alerted, educated, and mobilized, over years and decades, to challenge the powerholders and the whole society to redress social problems and restore critical social values.

Societal myths. The widely held, socially acceptable beliefs, values, ideologies, and slogans that are used by the powerholders to justify social conditions and the powerholders' policies and programs. They are the opposite of societal secrets.

Societal secrets. The social conditions and powerholder policies, programs, opinions, and other behaviors that grossly violate society's widely held values, beliefs, laws, and traditions, but are deliberately hidden from the public by the powerholders and are the opposite of the societal myths.

Sociodrama action campaign. A dramatic nonviolent direct action demonstration that publicly reveals the societal secrets and how the powerholders' actual policies and programs violate widely held and cherished values and beliefs. The action can be carried out over a period of time, making it a campaign; actions are often repeated in many different places at once, such as the civil rights movement's lunch counter sit-ins.

Strategy. The plans, tactics, methods, utilization of people and resources, maneuvers, timing, etc., that are carefully crafted to best achieve a social movement's short- and long-term goals. At a less lofty level, strategy sometimes merely refers to the best option at the time.

Sub-movement. Social movements usually have many sub-issues or goals, each with its own social movement, called a sub-movement. Sub-movements go through the MAP eight stages at their own pace, separate from each other and the larger movement. For example, the restaurant sit-in movement successfully went through the eight MAP stages in 1960, but the larger civil rights movement was still in Stage Four, Take-off.

Tactics. Any of the many plans and activities to achieve smaller goals within a specific strategy.

"Take-off" stage. The fourth MAP stage in which a social movement, sparked by a trigger event, bursts into the public spotlight and rapidly spreads around the region, nation, or beyond.

Theory. A theory is a set of general statements that provide an explanation for some phenomenon in the world. The goal of theory is to both explain and predict what happens under particular circumstances. Theories help researchers (and the general public) identify important questions to ask and identify what information must be collected to attempt to make sense out of a given situation.

Trigger event. An event that dramatizes a social problem and puts it into the public spotlight. At the start of MAP Stage Four, it puts the problem into the public spotlight for the first time and launches the rebel stage of the movement. When it happens in later stages, this process is repeated for a shorter period of time. Trigger events occurring before Stage Four usually go unnoticed.

NOTES

Introduction

1. Robert A. Goldberg, *Grassroots Resistance: Social Movements in Twentieth Century America* (Belmont, CA: Wadsworth, 1991), p. 4.

2. John D. McCarthy and Mayer Zald, "Resource Mobilization and Social Movements: A Partial Theory," *American Journal of Sociology* 82, no. 6 (1977): 1212-1241.

3. Bill Moyer, *Doing Democracy* (Gabriola Island, BC: New Society Press, 2001), p. 1.

4. Gene Sharp, *The Politics of Nonviolent Action*, 3 vols. (Boston, MA: Porter Sargent, 1973).

5. For this history of the origins of social movements we are indebted to Sidney Tarrow, *Power in Movement: Social Movements, Collective Action, and Politics*, 2nd ed. (Cambridge, UK: Cambridge University Press, 1994). Especially see Part I, "The Birth of the Modern Social Movement," pp. 29-70.

6. See William A. Gamson, *The Strategy of Social Protest* (Chicago, IL: Dorsey Press, 1990) for an exception to this.

7. Sociologists Michael Bassis, Richard Gelles, and Ann Levine, in defining theory, say that "a theory is a set of relatively abstract statements that explains some aspect of the world. The ultimate goal of scientific theory is to explain and predict phenomena, and ... (more immediately) to lead researchers to ask good questions, to formulate interesting problems, and to pose intelligent hypotheses" (*Sociology: An Introduction*). Feminist thinkers such as Dale Spender have defined feminist theory in an "expansive way," noting that it "reaches out to movements for political change on one hand and reaches within to the inner reality of women's lives on the other," and that "it often takes a less abstract form than other theory"

(*Feminist Theorists: Three Centuries of Key Women Thinkers*). Patricia Hill Collins, in her discussion of the traditions of black women intellectuals, notes that "very different kinds of ... 'theories' emerge when thought is joined with pragmatic action" (*Black Feminist Thought: Knowledge, Consciousness, and the Politics of Empowerment*). These scholars have been useful to us in our consideration of the nature of theory.

8. Every time a new social movement takes off with big demonstrations and civil disobedience, the powerholders and media are quick to frame it as being "just like the 1960s," to project the idea that big social movements were something that happened in the 1960s, not now. This is a deliberate strategy to discourage people from recognizing the reality that they are creating a new social movement right now. (And yes, it *is* like the 1960s.)

9. See M. Edelstein, *Contaminated Communities: The Social and Psychological Impacts of Residential Toxic Exposure* (Boulder, CO: Westview Press, 1988), and A. Levine, *Love Canal: Science, Politics and People* (Lexington, MA: Lexington, 1985).

Part I: The Movement Action Plan

Chapter 1

1. Alaine Touraine, *The Voice and the Eye: An Analysis of Social Movements* (Cambridge, UK: Cambridge University Press, 1981).

2. I first came across this term in a talk by Richard Gregg, and then in his book *The Power of Nonviolence* (London, UK: James Clark, 1960), Chapter 2.

3. See Arnold Toynbee, *The History of Civilization* abridged, 6 vols. (London, UK: Oxford University Press, 1987).

4. See Murray Dobbin, *The Myth of the Good*

204

Corporate Citizen: Democracy Under the Rule of Big Business (Toronto, ON: Stoddart Publishing, 1998); Michael Parenti, *Power and the Powerless* (New York, NY: St. Martin's Press, 1978); Robert Alford and Roger Friedland, *Power of Theory* (Cambridge, UK: Cambridge University Press, 1985); G. William Domhoff, *Who Rules America Now?* (Englewood Cliffs, NJ: Prentice Hall, 1983).

5. Gene Sharp, *Social Power and Political Freedom.* (Boston, MA: Porter Sargent, 1980), p. 27.

6. See Parenti, *Power and the Powerless*, and Domhoff, *Who Rules?*.

7. See Gene Sharp, *Social Power*, especially Chapter 2.

8. Chuck Collins and Felice Yeskel, *Economic Apartheid in America* (New York, NY: The New Press, 2000), p. 105.

Chapter 2

1. Joanna Macy, *World As Lover, World As Self* (Berkeley, CA: Parallax Press, 1991), p. 35.

2. Richard Gilber, "The Dynamics of Inactions," *American Psychologist* (November 1988).

3. Ward Churchill, et.al., *The Cointelpro Papers: Documents from the FBI's Secret Wars Against Domestic Dissent* (Boston, MA: South End Press, 1993).

4. Leigh Barker, "Violence, Infiltration and Sabotage," *Animals Agenda* (July/August 1989).

Chapter 3

1. A movement's progression through the eight stages is holarchical not hierarchical. While each succeeding stage has its own distinct characteristics, it also includes all of the previous stages. A movement in Stage Six, for example, can have aspects of the previous five stages.

2. Hannah Arendt, *On Revolution* (New York, NY: Viking Press, 1963).

3. Roger W. Cobb and Charles D. Elder, *Participation in American Politics: The Dynamics of Agenda-Building* (Boston, MA: Allyn & Bacon, 1972).

Chapter 4

1. Except in most dictatorships and police states.

2. Roger W. Cobb and Charles D. Elder, *Participation in American Politics.*

3. An exception is the first six months of the take-off stage, when activists are excited about their social movement.

Part II: Social Movement Theory and MAP

Chapter 5

1. Mary Jo Deegan, *Jane Addams and the Men of the Chicago School, 1890-1918* (New Brunswick, NJ: Transaction Press, 1988).

2. Barney Glaser and Anselm Strauss, *The Discovery of Grounded Theory* (Chicago, IL: Aldine, 1967).

3. Allen Rubin and Earl R. Babbie, *Research Methods for Social Work*, 2nd ed. (Pacific Grove, CA: Brooks/Cole Publishers, 1993), pp. 43-44.

4. James M. Jasper, *The Art of Moral Protest* (Chicago, IL: University of Chicago Press, 1997), p. 20.

5. Ibid.

6. Ibid., p. 21.

7. William Kornhauser, *The Politics of Mass Society* (Glencoe, IL: Free Press, 1959).

8. Neil Smelser, *Theory of Collective Behavior* (New York, NY: Free Press, 1962), pp. 15

9. Mancur Olson, *The Logic of Collective Action* (New York, NY: Schocken, 1965).

10. M. Lipsky, "Protest as a political resource" *American Political Science Review* 62, pp. 1144-1158.

11. Doug McAdam, "Conceptual origins, current problems, future directions," in *Comparative Perspectives on Social Movements*, edited by Doug McAdam, John D. McCarthy, and Mayer Zald (Cambridge, UK: Cambridge University Press, 1996), pp. 23-40.

12. P.K. Eisinger, "The Conditions of Protest Behavior in American Cities," *American Political Science Review* 67 (1973) 11-28, cited in McAdam, "Conceptual origins." p. 23

13. McAdam, "Conceptual origins." p. 23

14. See Enrique Larana, Hank Johnston, and Joseph Gusfield, *New Social Movements: From Ideology to Identity*, (Philadelphia, PA: Temple University Press, 1994).

15. Scott A. Hunt, Robert Bedford, and David A. Snow, "Identity Fields: Framing Processes and the Social Construction of Movement Identities," in *New Social Movements: From Ideology to Identity.*

16. Gene Sharp, *The Politics of Nonviolent Action*,

3 vols. (Boston, MA: Porter Sargent, 1973). There is a rich literature on nonviolence, which we do not have the space to review thoroughly here. See the bibliography for further references.

17. See Doug McAdam, John D. McCarthy, and Mayer Zald, eds., *Comparative Perspectives on Social Movements* (Cambridge, UK: Cambridge University Press, 1996), p. 2.

18. Bronislaw Misztal and J. Craig Jenkins, "Starting from Scratch is Not Always the Same: The Politics of Protest and the Postcommunist Transitions in Poland and Hungary," in *The Politics of Social Protest: Comparative Perspectives on States and Social Movements*, edited by J. Craig Jenkins and Bert Klandermans (Minneapolis, MN: University of Minnesota Press, 1995), pp. 324-340.

19. Sidney Tarrow, *Power in Movement: Social Movements, Collective Action, and Politics*, 2nd ed. (Cambridge, UK: Cambridge University Press, 1998), pp. 199-200. In the first edition of his book (1994), Tarrow used the term "cycles of protest," which has been cited by other researchers since then. However, in the second edition of his book (1998) he noted that he preferred the broader term "cycles of contention."

20. Jo Freeman, *The Politics of Women's Liberation* (New York, NY: David McKay, 1975).

21. Edward J. Walsh and Rex Warland, "Social Movement Involvement in the Wake of a Nuclear Accident: Activists and Free Riders in the TMI Area," in *Social Movements: Readings on Their Emergence, Mobilization, and Dynamics*, edited by Doug McAdam and David Snow (Los Angeles, CA: Roxbury Publishing Co., 1997).

22. Aldon Morris, *The Origins of the Civil Rights Movement: Black Communities Organizing for Change* (New York, NY: Free Press, 1984), pp. 139-173. See also Myles Horton with Judith Kohl and Herbert Kohl, *The Long Haul: An Autobiography* (New York, NY: Doubleday, 1990), the life story of the founder and long-time director of the Highlander Research and Education Center (earlier called the Highlander Folk School) Also see the video *You Got to Move*, directed by Lucy Phenix (1985) for an excellent video history.

23. Pamela Oliver, "If You Don't Do It, Nobody Else Will: Active and Token Contributors to Local Collective Action," in McAdam and Snow's *Social Movements*. (See discussion of Snow, Zurcher, and Ekland-Olson's work on recruitment to a Buddhist movement in America.)

24. See James Downton and Paul Wehr, *The Persistent Activist: How Peace Commitment Develops and Survives* (Boulder, CO: Westview Press, 1997) for an exception.

25. David A. Snow and Robert D. Benford. "Ideology, Frame Resonance, and Participant Mobilization," in *From Structure to Action: Social Movement Participation Across Cultures*, edited by Bert Klandermans, Hanspeter Kriesi, and Sidney Tarrow (Greenwich CT: JAI Press, 1988), pp .197-217, cited in McAdam, "The framing function of movement tactics: Strategic dramaturgy in the American civil rights movement" in McAdam et al, *Comparative Perspectives*, p. 338.

26. McAdam, "Framing function," *see above* p 347.

27. Tarrow, *Power in Movement*.

28. McAdam, "Framing function," p. 340.

29. Ibid.; Paul Burstein, Rachel Einwohner, and Jocelyn Hollander, "The Success of Social Movements: A Bargaining Perspective," in Jenkins and Klandermans' *The Politics of Social Protest*, also notes the lack of research on movement outcomes.

30. McAdam, "Framing function," p. 339.

31. Noel Sturgeon, "Theorizing Movements: Direct Action and Direct Theory," in *Cultural Politics and Social Movements*, edited by Marcy Darnovsky, Barbara Epstein, and Richard Flacks (Philadelphia, PA: Temple University Press, 1995), p. 36.

32. McAdam, "Framing function," p. 354.

33. Tarrow, *Power in Movement*, p. 202.

34. Burstein et al., "Success of Social Movements," p. 277; see also Gamson *Strategy of Social Protest*.

35. Tarrow, *Power in Movement*, (1st ed.) (1994) p. 154.

36. Ronald Libby, *Eco-Wars: Political Campaigns and Social Movements* (New York, NY: Columbia University Press, 1998) p. 23. (See pp. 17-23 for fuller discussion).

37. Tarrow, *Power in Movement*, p. 202.

38. McAdam, "Framing function", p. 339.

39. Downton and Wehr, *The Persistent Activist*, see especially p. 6 and pp. 67-68; see also John Lofland, "The Soar and Slump of Polite Protest: Interactive Spirals and the Eighties Peace Surge," *Peace and Change* 17 (1992), pp. 34-59.

40. Alberto Melucci, "The Global Planet and the Internal Planet: New Frontiers for Collective Action and Individual Transformation," in Darnovsky, et al's *Cultural Politics*.

Part III: Case Studies

Chapter 6

1. Thanks to Ellen A. Johnson for her research contribution to this case study.

2. For how baseball began the desegregation battles see William Marshall, *Baseball's Pivotal Era, 1945-52* (Louisville, KY: University Press of Kentucky, 1999), and Bruce Adelson, *Brushing Back Jim Crow: The integration of minor-league baseball in the American South* (Charlottesville, VA: University Press of Virginia, 1999).

3. See Aldon D. Morris, *The Origins of the Civil Rights Movement: Black Communities Organizing for Change* (Boston, MA: The Free Press, 1984), pp. 26-30.

4. The Montgomery Bus Boycott story is widely told. See, for example, Martin Luther King, *Stride Toward Freedom: The Montgomery Story—Birth of Successful Nonviolent Resistance* (New York, NY: Harper & Row, 1958); Taylor Branch, *Parting the Waters: America in the King Years 1954-63* (New York, NY: Simon & Schuster, 1988), pp. 143-205; David J. Garrow, *Bearing the Cross: Martin Luther King, Jr., and the Southern Christian Leadership Conference* (New York, NY: Morrow, 1986), pp. 11-82.

5. See Morris, *Origins*, pp. 12-16, 26-39.

6. Other lesser-known mass-based integration campaigns occurred in Baton Rouge, Tallahassee, and Birmingham and also served not only to inspire, but also to provide the methodology, experience, and leadership that helped the emergence of the new mass movements across the South.

7. See Morris, *Origins*, pp. 40, 73.

8. Ibid., pp. 197-215 for a description of the early months of the sit-in movement.

9. Madeleine Adamson and Seth Borgos, *This Mighty Dream* (London, UK: Routledge & Kegan Paul, 1985), pp .84-86.

10. Stephen B. Oates, *Let the Trumpet Sound: The Life of Martin Luther King* (Scarborough, ON: Signet, 1982), p. 400. Black Power had been used for years by such African American leaders as Paul Robeson and Adam Clayton Powell

11. Though near the end of his life it was widely reported that Malcolm X was coming closer to Dr. King's view.

12. Martin Luther King, *Where Do We Go From Here: Chaos or Community?* (New York, NY: Bantam, 1967), pp. 31 and 70-71.

13. Ibid., pp. 110-112.

14. Martin Luther King, *Why We Can't Wait* (New York, NY: New American Library, 1964), p. 118.

15. Inge Powell Bell, *CORE and the Strategy of Nonviolence* (New York, NY: Random House, 1968), p. 11.

16. King, *Why We Can't Wait*, p. 112.

17. Ibid., p. 121.

18. Ibid., p. 117.

19. The Student Nonviolent Coordinating Committee (SNCC), the Congress of Racial Equality (CORE), the Southern Christian Leadership Conference (SCLC), and the National Association for the Advancement of Colored People (NAACP).

20. Doug McAdam, *Freedom Summer* (Oxford, UK: Oxford University Press, 1988).

21. Oates, *Let the Trumpet Sound*, p. 413. A fuller description of the Chicago open housing campaign can be found on pp. 411- 416.

22. Bell Gale Chevigny, "The Fruits of Freedom Summer," *The Nation* (August 8/15, 1994), p. 154.

23. Adamson and Borgos, *This Mighty Dream*, p. 97.

24. Oates, *Let the Trumpet Sound*, p. 444.

25. Garrow, *Bearing the Cross*, p. 539.

26. Martin Luther King, *Where Do We Go From Here*, pp. 8 and 157.

27. King, *Why We Can't Wait*, pp. 136-137, and Oates, *Let the Trumpet Sound*, p. 460.

Chapter 7

1. This speech was subsequently published as "De-Developing the United States Through Nonviolence" in several progressive publications. Throughout the rest of the decade I

distributed over 50,000 reprints of the article as I traveled across Western Europe and the United States giving talks and helping new anti-nuclear energy groups form. At first I often received hostile responses from activists who either supported nuclear energy or did not want the focus turned away from the anti-Vietnam War effort. Copies are available for three dollars. See the author contact information in the appendix.

2. My own Philadelphia Life Center's affinity group had 30-minute daily interviews from jail on National Public Radio. Instantaneously, nuclear power became a hotly debated public issue.

3. For example, after two weeks in jail in the Manchester, New Hampshire, armory, I drove directly to Kansas to attend the founding meeting of the Sunflower Alliance, composed of dozens of new local action groups from around that state.

4. See "Pulling the Nuclear Plug," in *Time Magazine* (February 13, 1984), p. 12.

5. See "States Rights and Shoreham's Future," in the *New York Times* (February 21, 1987), p. 3. Also see "Pulling the Nuclear Plug," in *Time Magazine* (February 13, 1984), p. 12, and "Something rotten in Suffolk?" in *Forbes Magazine* (February 11, 1985).

6. "Seabrook protest — 74 arrested," in *San Francisco Sunday Examiner & Chronicle* (May 25, 1986), p. A-8.

7. See Harvey Wasserman, "Bush's Pro-Nuke Energy Strategy," in *The Nation* (May 20, 1991); Theodore M. Besmann (of the government's Oak Ridge National Laboratory), "A Brave New Era For Nuclear Power," in the *San Francisco Chronicle* (July 14, 1990); Jim Weiss, "Nuclear Power — the next generation," in *In These Times* (February 22, 1993).

8. See, "Prevent the death of democracy," in the *San Francisco Bay Guardian* (December 9, 1998), p. 11.

Chapter 8

1. Nancy Gregory lives in Baltimore, Maryland. This is a revised version of a paper she wrote in 1995 while a student in Steven Soifer's Social Work and Social Action class.

2. Dennis Altman, *The Homosexualization of America.* (Boston, MA: Beacon Press, 1982), 120.

3. E. Marcus, *Making History* (New York, NY: Harper Collins, 1992).

4. W.J. Blumenfeld and D. Raymond, *Looking at Gay and Lesbian Life* (New York, NY: Philosophical Library, 1988).

5. E. Marcus writes, "According to historian John D'Emilio, the name Mattachine was taken from mysterious masked medieval figures, who, one of the organization's founders speculated, might have been homosexuals." Later in *Making History*, Marcus explains that the name Daughters of Bilitis "was inspired by the heroine of the fictional *Songs of Bilitis*, which was written by the late-nineteenth-century author Pierre Louys, who portrayed Bilitis as a sometime lesbian and contemporary of Sappho."

6. B.D. Adam, *The Rise of a Gay and Lesbian Movement* (Boston, MA: Twayne Publishers, 1987).

7. Marcus, *Making History.*

8. Adam, *Rise of a Movement.*

9. Marcus, *Making History.*

10. Adam, *Rise of a Movement.*

11. Marcus, *Making History*, 92.

12. Adam, *Rise of a Movement*, p. 75.

13. Margaret Cruikshank, *The Gay and Lesbian Liberation Movement* (New York, NY: Routledge, 1992), p. 69.

14. Cited in M. Thompson, *Long Road to Freedom: The Advocate History of the Gay and Lesbian Movement* (New York, NY: St. Martin's Press, 1994), p. 19.

15. Blumenfeld and Raymond, Looking; T. Marotta, *The Politics of Homosexuality* (Boston, MA: Houghton Mifflin,1981).

16. Marcus, *Making History.*

17. Thompson, *Long Road.*

18. Ibid., p. 49.

19. Cited in Thompson, *Long Road*, p. 50.

20. Marcus, *Making History.*

21. Thompson, *Long Road.*

22. Cited in Adam, *Rise of a Movement*, p. 94.

23. Mary Daly, *Gyn/Ecology* (Boston, MA: Beacon Press, 1978). Cited in Adam, *Rise of a Movement*, p. 94.

24. Sarah Schulman, *My American History* (New York, NY: Routledge, 1994); Thompson, *Long Road.*

25. Thompson, *Long Road*.

26. Cited in Adam, *Rise of a Movement*.

27. Blumenfeld and Raymond, *Looking*.

28. Thompson, *Long Road*.

29. Adam, *Rise of a Movement*.

30. Ibid.; Marcus, *Making History*.

31. Adam, *Rise of a Movement*.

32. Ibid.; Marcus, *Making History*.

33. Schulman, *My American History*.

34. N.D. Hunter, S.E. Michaelson, and T.B. Stoddard, *The Rights of Lesbians and Gay Men: The Basic ACLU Guide to a Gay Person's Rights*, 3rd ed. (Carbondale, IL: Southern Illinois University Press, 1992).

35. Marcus, *Making History*; Thompson, *Long Road*.

36. Thompson, *Long Road*.

37. Report of the Lambda Legal Defense and Education Fund, 2000 (www.lldef.org).

38. Thompson, *Long Road*, p. 391.

39. "Hundreds of Thousands March on Capitol to Support Gay Rights," in the *Baltimore Sun* (May 1, 2000), p. 3A.

40. Report of the Human Rights Campaign, 2000 (www.hrcusa.org) and LLDEF, 2000

41. HRC, 2000, LLDEF, 2000.

Chapter 9

1. An earlier draft of this paper was presented at the Association for Health Services Research meetings in Chicago in June 1995.

2. For early histories of the feminist movement see Jo Freeman, *The Politics of Women's Liberation* (New York, NY: David McKay, 1975); and Sara Evans, *Personal Politics: The Roots of Women's Liberation in the Civil Rights Movement and the New Left* New York, NY: Random House, 1979).

3. The current edition is *Our Bodies, Our Selves for the 21st Century*, still written by the Boston Women's Health Book Collective (New York, NY: Simon & Schuster, 1998). This book has sold over 4 million copies and been translated into many languages.

4. John Eason, "Women in White," *University of Chicago Magazine* 93 (October 2000), p. 20.

5. For a history of the early years of the women's health movement see Sheryl Burt Ruzek, *The Women's Health Movement: Feminist Alternatives to Medical Control* (New York,

NY: Prager, 1978).

6. Eason, "Women in White."

7. Michael Baum, "Breast Cancer — Lessons from the Past," *Clinics on Oncology* 1, no. 3 (November 1982), pp. 649-660.

8. Rose Kushner, *Breast Cancer: A Personal History and Investigative Report* (New York, NY: Harcourt Brace Jovanovich, 1975). In 1977 this book was revised and reprinted under a new title, *Why Me? What Every Woman Should Know About Breast Cancer to Save Her Life* (New York, NY: New American Library, 1977). In the introduction, Rose Kushner indicated that she had learned that "we aren't ready for a book boldly titled Breast Cancer." The denial is too great.

9. The stories of both Winnow and Shapiro are covered in Alisa Solomon, "The Politics of Breast Cancer," *Village Voice* 36, no. 20 (May 14, 1991), p. 22.

10. Ibid., and Tatiana Schreiber, "Environmentalists and Breast Cancer Activists Tell New York Commission: Act Now!" *Resist* 2, no. 4 (April 1993), p. 1.

11. See Theresa Montini, "Gender and Emotion in the Advocacy for Breast Cancer Informed Consent Legislation," *Gender and Society* 10, no. 1 (February 1996), p. 9.

12. "Campaign Vote Breast Cancer," *Call to Action* 6 (March 2000), p. 6.

13. "NBCC Legislative Update," *Call to Action* 6 (March 2000), pp. 4–5.

14. For a review of recent literature on environmental links to breast cancer see Sandra Steingraber, "The Environmental Link to Breast Cancer," in *Breast Cancer: Society Shapes an Epidemic*, edited by Anne Kaspar and Susan Ferguson (New York, NY: St Martin's Press, 2000), pp. 271-299.

15. For further information on chemical companies and breast cancer see: Peter Phillips and Project Censored, "#2 Censored: Chemical Corporations Profit off Breast Cancer," in *Censored 1999* (New York, NY: Seven Stories Press, 1999); Barbara Brenner, "Seeing Our Interests Clearly" and "Follow the Money II," *Breast Cancer Action* (1998), available at www.bcaction/news/9902.02.html; and Sharon Batt and Liza Gross, "Cancer, Inc.," *Sierra* (September-October 1999). All of the above are cited in Paul Ray and Sherry Ruth Anderson, *The Cultural Creatives: How 50*

Million People Are Changing the World (New York, NY: Harmony Books, 2000).

Chapter 10

1. Juliette Beck is the coordinator of the Global Democracy Project for Global Exchange where she focuses especially on the international movement against corporate globalization of the political economic system.

Conclusion

1. See the works of Ken Wilber and Robert Kegan cited below.

2. I call them the over-industrialized and never-to-be-developed nations.

3. Chuck Collins and Felice Yeskel, *Economic Apartheid in America* (New York, NY: The New Press, 2000).

4. Between 1960 and 1990, the greatest economic growth era in human history, the gap between the richest and poorest nations doubled according to a UNESCO report (see David Suzuki and Holly Dressel, *Naked Ape to Superspecies* [Toronto, ON: Stoddard Publishing, 1999]). While the elites in the world's industrialized nations proclaim that increased economic growth will create prosperity for everyone in what they call the "developing" nations, the U.S. Space Command doesn't think so. In its Year 2000 document called *Vision for 2020*, the Pentagon states that because of corporate "globalization of the world economy" there will be a widening gap between the "haves and have-nots." And space superiority will be needed to protect challenges to corporate control around the world.

5. Collins and Yeskel, *Economic Apartheid.*

6. *Sydney Morning Herald* (December 16, 2000), p. 13.

7. There have been many dire warnings of impending environmental and resource disaster, including the World Commission on the Environment and Development (1987); the Warning to Humanity signed by 1,600 scientists, including half of the living Nobel Laureates (1992); and the 2000 report of the prestigious U.N. Intergovernmental Panel on Climate Change, made up of hundreds of the world's leading scientists, which concluded that global warming was far more serious than the panel had thought. The Earth's temperature could increase by 2.7 to 11 degrees this century without major corrective environmental efforts. (*San Francisco Chronicle*, October 26, 2000, p. 3).

8. Mathis Wackernagel and William Rees, *Our Ecological Footprint: Reducing Human Impact on the Earth* (Gabriola Island, BC: New Society Publishers, 1996).

9. Richard Heinberg, *A New Covenant with Nature* (Wheaton, IL: Theosophical Publishing House, 1996).

10. Some of these concepts and ideas can be found in Richard Heinberg, *New Covenant;* Charlene Spretnak, *Resurgence of the Real* (London, UK: Routledge, 1999); Donella Meadows, et al., *Beyond the Limits: Confronting Global Collapse, Envisioning a Sustainable Future* (New York, NY: American Forum, 1992); James Baines, *The Peace Paradigm* (East Orange, NJ: Global Education Associates, 1970); Joe Dominguez and Vicki Robin, *Your Money or Your Life* (Seattle, WA: New Road Map Foundation, 1985); and many others.

11. See Ken Wilber, *Boomeritis* (Boston, MA: Shambala Press, 2001), *Integral Psychology* (Boston, MA: Shambala Press, 2000), *The Integral Vision* (Boston, MA: Shambala Press, 1999), and the introductions to volumes seven and eight of *The Collected Works of Ken Wilber* (Boston, MA: Shambala Press, 1999). Also see Chapter 10 of Robert Kegan, *In Over our Heads* (Cambridge, MA: Harvard University Press, 1994), which describes how heroic efforts to help disenfranchised groups fully enter into modern society are "not about the limits of modernism" itself, but that everyone should be brought equally into it.

12. Don Beck and Christopher Cowan, *Spiral Dynamics* (Malden, MA: Blackwell, 1996).

13. See, for example, Ken Wilber's books *Boomeritis* and *The Integral Vision*, and the introduction to volume seven of *The Collected Works of Ken Wilber.*

14. See Wilber, *Collected Works*, vol. 3, pp. 413-421, 620-626. Jeremy Bernstein coined the term "ideological multiculturalism" in his book *The Dictatorship of Virtue.*

15. This is a fundamental theory on which Wilber's philosophy is based and runs throughout all of his work. It's called the big three and is a contraction of the four quadrants framework.

16. Riane Eisler, *The Chalice and the Blade* (San Francisco, CA: Harper & Row, 1987).

17. Wilber, *Collected Works*, vol. 4, p. 190.

18. Ibid., pp. 329-330, 368.

19. As quoted in Heinberg, *New Covenant*, p. 56.

20. Linda Stout, "Barriers to Movement Building," unpublished report, 2000. See Spirit in Action's web site (www.spiritinaction.net). Linda is also helping to set up local "circles of change" groups around the country.

21. Medical scientists now report that our bodies respond with a stronger immune system and other signs of physical health when we exhibit these positive qualities and likewise exhibit unhealthy symptoms, such as high blood pressure and a weakened immune system, when we are under stress or angry, depressed, or unhappy.

22. Paul H. Ray and Sherry Ruth Anderson, *The Cultural Creatives* (New York, NY: Harmony Books, 2000).

Glossary

1. See Mark B. Woodhouse, *Paradigm Wars* (Berkeley, CA: Frog Ltd. Books, 1995).

2. Gene Sharp, *Social Power & Political Freedom* (Boston, MA: Porter Sargent, 1980), page 27.

BIBLIOGRAPHY

Part I: The Movement Action Plan

Alford, Robert & Roger Friedland. *Power of Theory*. Cambridge, UK: Cambridge University Press, 1985.

Arendt, Hannah. *On Revolution*. New York, NY: Viking Press, 1963.

Baines, James. *The Peace Paradigm*. Vol. 1, no.1 of The Whole Earth Papers. East Orange, NJ: Global Education Associates, 1970.

Barker, Leigh. "Violence, Infiltration and Sabotage." *Animals Agenda* (July/August 1989).

Bassis, Michael, Richard Gelles, and Ann Levine. *Sociology: An Introduction*. 2nd ed. New York, NY: Random House, 1984.

Beck, Don and Christopher Cowan. *Spiral Dynamics*. Malden, MA: Blackwell, 1996.

Burns, James MacGregor and Stewart Burns. *The Pursuit of Rights in America*. New York, NY: Knopf, 1991.

Churchill, Ward, et. al. *The Cointelpro Papers: Documents from the FBI's Secret Wars Against Domestic Dissent*. Boston, MA: South End Press, 1993.

Cobb, Roger W. and Charles D. Elder. *Participation in American Politics: The Dynamics of Agenda-Building*. Boston, MA: Allyn & Bacon, 1972.

Collins, Chuck and Felice Yeskel. *Economic Apartheid in America*. New York, NY: The New Press, 2000.

Collins, Patricia Hill. *Black Feminist Thought: Knowledge, Consciousness, and the Politics of Empowerment*. 2nd ed. New York, NY: Routledge, 2000.

Dobbin, Murray. *The Myth of the Good Corporate Citizen: Democracy Under the Rule of Big Business*. Toronto, ON: Stoddart Publishing, 1998.

Domhoff, G. William. *Who Rules America Now?* Englewood Cliffs, NJ: Prentice-Hall, 1983.

Dominguez, Joe and Vicki Robin. *Your Money or Your Life*. Seattle, WA: New Road Map Foundation, 1985.

Downton, James and Paul Wehr. *The Persistent Activist: How Peace Commitment Develops and Survives*. Boulder, CO: Westview Press, 1997.

Edelstein, M. *Contaminated Communities: The Social and Psychological Impacts of Residential Toxic Exposure*. Boulder, CO: Westview Press, 1988.

Eisler, Riane. *The Chalice and the Blade*. San Francisco, CA: Harper & Row, 1987.

Gamson, William A. *The Strategy of Social Protest*. Chicago, IL: Dorsey Press, 1990.

Gilber, Richard. "The Dynamics of Inactions." *American Psychologist* (November 1988).

Goldberg, Robert A. *Grassroots Resistance: Social Movements in Twentieth Century America*. Belmont, CA: Wadsworth, 1991.

Gregg, Richard. *The Power of Nonviolence*. London, UK: James Clark, 1960.

Heinberg, Richard. *A New Covenant with Nature*. Wheaton, IL: Theosophical Publishing House, 1996.

Kegan, Robert. *In Over our Heads*. Cambridge, MA: Harvard University Press, 1994.

Lauer, Robert H. and Jeanette C. Lauer. *Sociology: Contours of Society*. Los Angeles, CA: Roxbury, 1998.

Levine, A. *Love Canal: Science, Politics and People*. Lexington, MA: Lexington, 1985.

Macy, Joanna. *World As Lover, World As Self*. Berkeley, CA: Parallax Press, 1991.

McCarthy, John D. and Mayer Zald. "Resource Mobilization and Social Movements: A Partial

Theory." *American Journal of Sociology* 82, no. 6 (1977),1212-1241.

Meadows, Donella, et.al. *Beyond the Limits: Confronting Global Collapse, Envisioning a Sustainable Future.* New York, NY: American Forum, 1992.

Parenti, Michael. *Democracy for the Few.* New York, NY: St. Martin's Press, 1985.

———. *Power and the Powerless.* New York, NY: St. Martin's Press, 1978.

Ray, Paul H. and Sherry Ruth Anderson. *The Cultural Creatives.* New York, NY: Harmony Books, 2000.

Sharp, Gene. *Social Power and Political Freedom.* Boston, MA: Porter Sargent, 1980.

———. *The Politics of Nonviolent Action.* Three volumes. Boston, MA: Porter Sargent, 1973.

Spender, Dale. *Feminist Theorists: Three Centuries of Key Women Thinkers.* New York, NY: Pantheon, 1983.

Spretnak, Charlene. *Resurgence of the Real.* London, UK: Routledge, 1999.

Stout, Linda. "Barriers to Movement Building." Unpublished report, 2000. See Spirit in Action's web site, www.spiritinaction.net.

Suzuki, David and Holy Dressel. *Naked Ape to Superspecies: A Personal Perspective on Humanity and the Global Ecocrisis.* Toronto, ON: Stoddart Publishing, 1999.

Tarrow, Sidney. *Power in Movement: Social Movements, Collective Action, and Politics.* Second edition. Cambridge, UK: Cambridge University Press, 1994.

Touraine, Alaine. *The Voice and the Eye: An Analysis of Social Movements.* Cambridge, UK: Cambridge University Press, 1981.

Toynbee, Arnold Joseph. *The History of Civilization.* Volumes I-VI, abridged. London, UK: Oxford University Press, 1987.

U.S. Space Command. *Vision for 2020.* Available at www.spacecom.af.mil/usspace.

Wackernagel, Mathis and William Rees. *Our Ecological Footprint: Reducing Human Impact on the Earth.* Gabriola Island, BC: New Society Publishers, 1996.

Wilber, Ken. *Boomeritis.* Boston, MA: Shambala Press, 2001.

———. *Integral Psychology.* Boston, MA: Shambala Press, 2000.

———. *The Integral Vision.* Boston, MA: Shambala Press, 1999.

———. *The Collected Works of Ken Wilber.* Boston, MA: Shambala Press, 1999.

Wilhelm, Richard and Cary F. Baynes. *The I Ching.* Princeton, NJ: Princeton University Press, 1977.

Woodhouse, Mark B. *Paradigm Wars.* Berkeley, CA: Frog Ltd. Books, 1995.

Young, Alfred F. "The Framers of the Constitution and the Genius of the People." *In These Times* (September 9-15, 1987).

Part II. Social Movement Theories and MAP

Bondurant, Joan V. *Conquest of Violence: The Gandhian Philosophy of Conflict.* Revised edition. Berkeley, CA: University of California Press, 1965.

Burstein, Paul, Rachel Einwohner, and Jocelyn Hollander. "The Success of Social Movements: A Bargaining Perspective." In *The Politics of Social Protest: Comparative Perspectives on States and Social Movements.* Volume 3 of the Social Movements, Protest and Contention Series, edited by J. Craig Jenkins and Bert Klandermans. Minneapolis, MN: University of Minnesota Press, 1995.

Cooney, Robert and Helen Michalowski. *The Power of the People: Active Nonviolence in the United States.* Philadelphia, PA and Gabriola Island, BC: New Society Publishers, 1987.

Deegan, Mary Jo. *Jane Addams and the Men of the Chicago School*, 1890-1918. New Brunswick, N.J.: Transaction Press, 1988.

Dellinger, David. *Revolutionary Nonviolence.* New York, NY and Indianapolis, IN: Bobbs-Merrill, 1970.

Downton, James and Paul Wehr. *The Persistent Activist: How Peace Commitment Develops and Survives.* Boulder, CO: Westview Press, 1997.

Duncan, Ronald (ed.). *Selected Writings of Mahatma Gandhi.* London, UK: Fontana/Collins, (1951) 1971.

Easwaran, Eknath. *Gandhi the Man: The Story of His Transformation.* Tomales, CA: Nilgiri Press, 1997.

Eisinger, Peter K. "The Conditions of Protest Behavior in American Cities." *American Political Science Review* 67 (1973), 11-28. As cited in Doug McAdam, "Conceptual origins, current problems, future directions," in

Comparative Perspectives on Social Movements, edited by Doug McAdam, John D. McCarthy, and Mayer Zald, pp. 23-40. Cambridge, UK: Cambridge University Press, 1996.

Eppsteiner, Fred. *The Path of Compassion: Writings on Socially Engaged Buddhism.* Berkeley, CA: Parallax Press, 1988.

Freeman, Jo. *The Politics of Women's Liberation.* New York, NY: David McKay, 1975.

Freire, Paulo. *Pedagogy of the Oppressed.* New York, NY: Herder and Herder, 1970

Gamson, William A. *The Strategy of Social Protest.* Chicago, IL: Dorsey Press, 1990.

Gandhi, M.K. *Non-Violent Resistance* (Satyagraha). New York, NY: Schocken Books, 1951.

Gandhi, M.K. *An Autobiography or The story of my Experiments with Truth.* Translated from the Gujarati original by Mahadev Desai. 2nd ed. Ahmedabad, India: Navajivan Publishing House, 1940.

Glaser, Barney and Anselm Strauss. *The Discovery of Grounded Theory.* Chicago, IL: Aldine, 1967.

Goffman, Erving. *Frame Analysis.* New York, NY: Harper Colophon, 1974.

Gregg, Richard. *The Power of Nonviolence.* New York, NY: Schocken, 1966.

Harding, Vincent. *Hope and History: Why We Must Share the Story of the Movement.* Maryknoll, NY: Orbis Books, 1990.

Horton, Myles with Judith Kohl and Herbert Kohl. *The Long Haul: An Autobiography.* New York, NY: Doubleday, 1990.

Hunt, Scott A., Robert Benford, and David A. Snow. "Identity Fields: Framing Processes and the Social Construction of Movement Identities." In *New Social Movements: From Ideology to Identity,* edited by Enrique Larana, Hank Johnston, and Joseph Gusfield. Philadelphia, PA: Temple University Press, 1994.

Ingram, Catherine. *In the Footsteps of Gandhi: Conversations with Spiritual Social Activists.* Berkeley CA: Parallax Press, 1990.

Jasper, James M. *The Art of Moral Protest: Culture, Creativity, and Biography in Social Movements.* Chicago, IL: University of Chicago Press, 1997.

Jenkins, J. Craig and Charles Perrow. "Insurgency of the Powerless: Farmworker Movements (1946-1972)." *American Sociological Review* 42 (1977), pp. 249-68.

Johnston, Hank, Enrique Larana, and Joseph Gusfield. "Identities, Grievances, and New Social Movements." In *New Social Movements: From Ideology to Identity,* edited by Enrique Larana, Hank Johnston, and Joseph Gusfield. Philadelphia, PA: Temple University Press, 1994.

King, Jr., Martin Luther. *Autobiography of Martin Luther King, Jr.* Edited by Clayborne Carson. New York, NY: Warner Books, 1998.

Kornhauser, William. *The Politics of Mass Society.* Glencoe IL: Free Press, 1959.

Kruse, Corwin. "Mobilizing Impressions: Impression Management as a Selective Incentive for Participation in Social Movement Organizations." Presented at the meetings of the American Sociological Association, San Francisco, August 1998.

Lakey, George. *Powerful Peacemaking.* Philadelphia, PA and Gabriola Island, BC: New Society Publishers, 1987.

Le Bon, Gustave. *The Crowd: A Study in the Popular Mind.* New York, NY: Penguin (1895) 1977.

Libby, Ronald T. *Eco-Wars: Political Campaigns and Social Movements.* New York, NY: Columbia University Press, 1998.

Lipsky, M. "Protest as a political resource" *American Political Science Review* 62 (1968), pp. 1144-1158.

Lofland, John. "The Soar and Slump of Polite Protest: Interactive Spirals and the Eighties Peace Surge." *Peace and Change* 17 (1992), pp. 34-59.

Lyman, Stanford M. (ed.). *Social Movements: Critiques, Concepts, Case Studies.* New York, NY: New York University Press, 1992.

Lynd, Staughton. *Nonviolence in America: A Documentary History.* Indianapolis, IN: Bobbs-Merrill, 1965.

McAdam, Doug. *Political Process and the Development of Black Insurgency, 1930-1970.* Chicago, IL: University of Chicago Press, 1982.

———. "Conceptual origins, current problems, future directions." In *Comparative Perspectives on Social Movements,* edited by Doug McAdam, John D. McCarthy, Mayer Zald, pp. 23-40. Cambridge, UK: Cambridge

University Press, 1996.

McAdam, Doug, John D. McCarthy, and Mayer Zald (eds.). *Comparative Perspectives on Social Movements*. Cambridge, UK: Cambridge University Press, 1996.

———. "Introduction: Opportunities, mobilizing structures and framing processes — toward a synthetic, comparative perspective on social movements." In *Comparative Perspectives on Social Movements*, edited by Doug McAdam, John D. McCarthy, Mayer Zald, pp. 1-21. Cambridge, UK: Cambridge University Press, 1996.

McAdam, Doug and David Snow (eds.). *Social Movements: Readings on Their Emergence, Mobilization, and Dynamics*. Los Angeles, CA: Roxbury Publishing Company, 1997.

McAllister, Pam, ed. *Reweaving the Web of Life: Feminism and Nonviolence*. Philadelphia, PA and Gabriola Island, BC: New Society Publishers, 1982.

———. *You Can't Kill the Spirit*. First of the Barbara Deming Memorial Series: Stories of Women and Nonviolent Action. Philadelphia, PA and Gabriola Island, BC: New Society Publishers, 1988.

McCarthy, John D. and Mayer Zald. "Resource Mobilization and Social Movements: A Partial Theory." *American Journal of Sociology* 82, no. 6 (1977), pp. 1212-1241.

Melucci, Alberto. "The Global Planet and the Internal Planet: New Frontiers for Collective Action and Individual Transformation." In *Cultural Politics and Social Movements*, edited by Marcy Darnovsky, Barbara Epstein, and Richard Flacks. Philadelphia, PA: Temple University Press, 1995.

Misztal, Bronislaw and J. Craig Jenkins. "Starting from Scratch is Not always the Same: The Politics of Protest and the Postcommunist Transitions in Poland and Hungary." In *The Politics of Social Protest: Comparative Perspectives on States and Social Movements*. Volume 3 of the Social Movements, Protest and Contention Series, edited by J. Craig Jenkins and Bert Klandermans, pp. 324-340. Minneapolis, MN: University of Minnesota Press, 1995.

Morris, Aldon. *The Origins of the Civil Rights Movement: Black Communities Organizing for Change*. New York, NY: Free Press, 1984.

Oliver, Pamela. "'If You Don't Do It, Nobody Else Will': Active and Token Contributors to Local Collective Action." In *Social Movements: Readings on Their Emergence, Mobilization, and Dynamics*, edited by Doug McAdam and David Snow. Los Angeles, CA: Roxbury Publishing Company, (1984) 1997.

Olson, Mancur. *The Logic of Collective Action*. New York, NY: Schocken, 1965.

Rubin, Allen and Earl R. Babbie. *Research Methods for Social Work*. Second edition. Pacific Grove, CA: Brooks/Cole Publishers, 1993.

Sharp, Gene. *The Politics of Nonviolent Action*. Three volumes. Boston, MA: Porter Sargent, Publishers, 1973.

Sharp, Gene. *Exploring Noviolent Alternatives*. Boston, MA: Porter Sargent Publisher, 1970.

Shields, Katrina. *In the Tiger's Mouth: An Empowerment Guide for Social Action*. Gabriola Island, BC: New Society Publishers, 1994 (originally published in Australia in 1991 by Millenium Books, E.J. Dwyer Pty Ltd.).

Sibley, Mulford, ed. *The Quiet Battle: Writings on the Theory and Practice of Nonviolent Resistance*. Boston, MA: Beacon Press, 1969.

Sivaraksa, Sulak. *Seeds of Peace; A Buddhist Vision for Renewing Society*. (especially Chapter 9. "Buddhism and Nonviolence.") Berkeley, CA: Parallax Press, 1992.

Smelser, Neil. *Theory of Collective Behavior*. New York, NY: Free Press, 1962.

Snow, David A. and Robert D. Benford. "Ideology, Frame Resonance, and Participant Mobilization." In *From Structure to Action: Social Movement Participation Across Cultures*, edited by Bert Klandermans, Hanspeter Kriesi, and Sidney Tarrow, pp. 197-217. Greenwich, CT: JAI Press, 1988.

Snow, David A., Louis Zurcher, and Sheldon Ekland-Olson. "Social Networks and Social Movements: Microstructural Approach to Differential Recruitment." In *Social Movements: Readings on Their Emergence, Mobilization, and Dynamics*, edited by Doug McAdam and David Snow, pp.122-132. Los Angeles, CA: Roxbury Publishing Company, 1997.

Sturgeon, Noel. "Theorizing Movements: Direct Action and Direct Theory." In *Cultural Politics and Social Movements*, edited by Marcy Darnovsky, Barbara Epstein, and

Richard Flacks, pp. 35-51. Philadelphia, PA: Temple University Press, 1995.

Tarrow, Sidney. *Power in Movement: Social Movements, Collective Action, and Politics.* 2nd ed. Cambridge, UK: Cambridge University Press, 1998.

Thich Nhat Hanh. *Being Peace.* Berkeley, CA: Parallax Press, n.d.

Thoreau, Henry David. "Civil Disobedience." In *Walden and Other Writings of Henry David Thoreau,* edited by Brooks Atkinson, New York, NY: Random House, 1937 (originally published 1849).

Tilly, Charles. From *Mobilization to Revolution.* Reading, MA: Addison-Wesley, 1978.

Tolstoy, Leo. *The Kingdom of God is Within You.* New York, NY: Noonday Press, (1905) 1961.

Walsh, Edward J. and Rex Warland. "Social Movement Involvement in the Wake of a Nuclear Accident: Activists and Free Riders in the TMI Area." In *Social Movements: Readings on Their Emergence, Mobilization, and Dynamics,* edited by Doug McAdam and David Snow. Los Angeles, CA: Roxbury Publishing Company, 1997.

Wink, Walter, ed. *Peace is the Way: Writings on Nonviolence from the Fellowship of Reconciliation.* Maryknoll NY: Orbis Books, 2000.

Young, Andrew. *An Easy Burden: The Civil Rights Movement and the Transformation of America.* New York, NY: Harper Collins, 1996.

Part III. Case Studies

The U.S. Civil Rights Movement

Adamson, Madeleine and Seth Borgos. *This Mighty Dream.* London, UK: Routledge & Kegan Paul, 1985.

Adelson, Bruce. *Brushing Back Jim Crow: The integration of minor-league baseball in the American South.* Charlottesville, VA: University Press of Virginia, 1999.

Bell, Inge Powell. *CORE and the Strategy of Nonviolence.* New York, NY: Random House, 1968.

Branch, Taylor. *Parting the Waters: America in the King Years 1954-63.* New York, NY: Simon & Schuster, 1988.

Chevigny, Bell Gale. "The Fruits of Freedom Summer." *The Nation* (August 8/15, 1994), p. 154.

Garrow, David J. *Bearing the Cross: Martin Luther King, Jr., and The Southern Christian Leadership Conference.* New York, NY: Morrow, 1986.

Lewis, John. *Walking with the Wind: A Memoir of the Movement.* New York, NY: Simon & Schuster, 1998.

King, Martin Luther. *Stride Toward Freedom: The Montgomery story — Birth of successful nonviolent resistance.* New York, NY: Harper & Row, 1958.

———. *Why We Can't Wait.* New York, NY: New American Library, 1964.

———. *Where Do We Go From Here: Chaos or Community?* New York, NY: Bantam, 1967.

McAdam, Doug. *Freedom Summer.* Oxford, UK: Oxford University Press, 1988.

Marshall, William. *Baseball's Pivotal Era, 1945-52.* Louisville, KY: University Press of Kentucky, 1999.

Morris, Aldon D. *The Origins of the Civil Rights Movement: Black Communities Organizing for Change.* Boston, MA: The Free Press, 1984.

Oates, Stephen B. *Let the Trumpet Sound: The Life of Martin Luther King.* Scarborough, ON: Signet, 1982.

Ralph, James. *Northern Protest: Martin Luther King, Jr., Chicago and the Civil Rights Movement.* Cambridge: Harvard Univ. Press, 1993.

The Anti-Nuclear Energy Movement

Berman, Daniel and John O'Connor. *Who Owns the Sun: People, Politics and the Struggle for a Solar Economy.* White River Junction, VT: Chelsea Green Publishing, 1996.

Caldicott, Helen. *Nuclear Madness.* Brookline, MA: Autumn Press, 1978,

Faulkner, Peter, ed. *The Silent Bomb.* New York, NY: Random House, 1977.

Ford, Daniel, ed. *Melt Down: The Secret Papers of the Atomic Energy Commission.* (Originally published as *The Cult of the Atom*). New York, NY: Simon and Schuster, 1982.

Fuller, John G. *We Almost Lost Detroit.* New York, NY: Ballantine, 1976.

Gofman, John W. *Radiation and Human Health.* San Francisco, CA: Sierra Club Books, 1981.

Gofman, John W. and Arthur R. Tamplin. *Poisoned Power.* Emmaus, PA: Rodale Press, 1971.

Gyorgy, Anna and friends. *No Nukes: Everybody's guide to nuclear power*. Boston, MA; South End Press, 1979.

Olson, McKinley C. *Unacceptable Risk: The Nuclear Power Controversy*. New York, NY: Bantam Books, 1976.

Reynolds, W.C., ed. *The California Nuclear Initiative: Analysis and Discussion of the Issues*. Stanford, CA: Stanford University Institute for Energy Studies, 1976.

The Risks of Nuclear Power Reactors: A Review of the NRC Reactor Safety Study WASH-1400. Cambridge, MA: Union of Concerned Scientists, 1977.

Smeloff, Ed and Peter Asmus. *Reinventing Electric Utilities: Competition, Citizen Action and Clean Power*. Washington, DC: Island Press, 1997.

Wohl, Burton. *The China Syndrome*. New York, NY: Bantam Press, 1979.

The Gay and Lesbian Movement

Adam, B.D. *The Rise of a Gay and Lesbian Movement*. Boston, MA: Twayne Publishers, 1987.

Altman, Dennis. *The Homosexualization of America*. Boston, MA: Beacon Press, 1982.

Blumenfeld, W.J. and Raymond, D. *Looking at Gay and Lesbian Life*. New York, NY: Philosophical Library, 1988.

Cruikshank, Margaret. *The Gay and Lesbian Liberation Movement*. New York, NY: Routledge, 1992.

Human Rights Campaign. July 7, 2000. Available: www.hrcusa.org

"Hundreds of thousands march on Capitol to support gay rights." *Baltimore Sun* (May 1, 2000), p. 3A.

Hunter, N.D., S.E. Michaelson, and T.B. Stoddard. *The Rights of Lesbians and Gay Men: The Basic ACLU Guide to a Gay Person's Rights*. Third edition. Carbondale, IL: Southern Illinois University Press, 1992.

Lambda Legal Defense and Education Fund. July 7, 2000. Available: www.lldef.org

Marcus, E. *Making History*. New York, NY: HarperCollins, 1992.

Marotta, T. *The Politics of Homosexuality*. Boston, MA: Houghton Mifflin Company, 1981.

Moyer, Bill. *The Movement Action Plan*. Second edition. San Francisco, CA: Social Movement Empowerment Project, 1987.

Schulman, Sarah. *My American History*. New York, NY: Routledge, 1994.

Thompson, M. (ed.). *Long Road to Freedom: The Advocate History of the Gay and Lesbian Movement*. New York, NY: St. Martin's Press, 1994.

The Breast Cancer Social Movement

Altman, Roberta. *Waking Up, Fighting Back: The Politics of Breast Cancer*. Boston, MA: Little Brown, 1996.

Batt, Sharon. *Patient No More: The Politics of Breast Cancer*. Charlottetown, PEI: Gynergy Books, 1994.

Batt, Sharon and Liza Gross. "Cancer, Inc." *Sierra* (September-October 1999).

Baum, Michael. "Breast Cancer — Lessons from the Past." *Clinics on Oncology* 1, no. 3 (November 1982), pp. 649-660.

Beck, Melinda with Emily Yoffe, Ginny Carroll, Mary Hager, Debra Rosenberg, and Lucille Beachy. "The Politics of Breast Cancer." *Newsweek*, 66, no. 24 (December 10, 1990).

Boston Women's Health Book Collective. *Our Bodies, Our Selves for the 21st Century*. New York, NY: Simon & Schuster, 1998.

Brady, Judy (ed..). *1 in 3: Women with Cancer Confront an Epidemic*. Pittsburgh, PA/San Francisco, CA: Cleis Press, 1993.

Brenner, Barbara. "Seeing Our Interests Clearly." *Breast Cancer Action* (1998). Available at www.bcaction/news/9902.02.html.

———. "Follow the Money II." *Breast Cancer Action* (1998). Available at www.bcaction/news/9902.02.html.

Butler, Sandra and Barbara Rosenblum. *Cancer in Two Voices*. San Francisco, CA: Spinsters, 1991.

"Campaign Vote Breast Cancer," *Call to Action* 6 (March 2000), p. 6.

Clorfene-Casten, "The Environmental Link to Breast Cancer." *Ms.* 3, no. 6 (May/June 1993), p. 52.

———. "Inside the Cancer Establishment." *Ms.* 3, no.6 (May/June 1993), p. 57.

Crile, George Jr., M.D. *What Women Should Know About the Breast Cancer Controversy*. New York, NY: Macmillan, 1973.

Eason, John. "Women in White." *University of Chicago Magazine* 93 (October 2000), p. 20.

Evans, Sara. *Personal Politics: The Roots of Women's Liberation in the Civil Rights Movement and the New Left*. New York, NY: Random House, 1979.

Faulder, Carolyn. "The Nation with the Highest Death Rate Debates Prevention." *Ms.* 3, no. 6 (May/June 1993), p. 58.

Freeman, Jo. *The Politics of Women's Liberation*. New York, NY: David McKay, 1975.

Friedan, Betty. *The Feminine Mystique*. New York, NY: Dell Publishing, 1963.

Kaspar, Anne and Susan Ferguson (eds.). *Breast Cancer: Society Shapes an Epidemic*. New York, NY: St Martin's Press, 2000.

Koedt, Anne, Ellen Levine, and Anita Rapone. *Radical Feminism*. New York, NY: Quadrangle Books, 1973.

Kushner, Rose. *Why Me? What Every Woman Should Know About Breast Cancer to Save Her Life*. New York, NY,: New American Library, 1977. Originally published as *Breast Cancer: A Personal History and Investigative Report*. New York, NY: Harcourt Brace Jovanovich, 1975.

Lorde, Audre. *The Cancer Journals*. San Francisco, CA: Spinsters, 1980.

Love, Susan, M.D., with Karen Lindsey. *Dr. Susan Love's Breast Book*. Third edition. Cambridge, MA: Perseus Publishers, 2000. (First edition published in 1990.)

Montini, Theresa. "Gender and Emotion in the Advocacy for Breast Cancer Informed Consent Legislation." *Gender and Society* 10, no. 1 (February 1996), p. 9.

Morgan, Robin (ed.). *Sisterhood is Powerful: An Anthology of Writings from the Women's Liberation Movement*. New York, NY: Vintage Books, 1970.

"NBCC Legislative Update," *Call to Action* 6 (March 2000), pp. 4–5.

Phillips, Peter and Project Censored. "#2 Censored: Chemical Corporations Profit off Breast Cancer." In *Censored 1999*. New York, NY: Seven Stories Press, 1999.

Ray, Paul and Sherry Ruth Anderson. *The Cultural Creatives: How 50 Million People Are Changing the World*. New York, NY: Harmony Books, 2000.

Rennie, Susan. "Breast Cancer Prevention: Diet vs. Drugs." *Ms.* 3, no. 6 (May/June 1993), p. 38.

Ruzek, Sheryl Burt. *The Women's Health Movement: Feminist Alternatives to Medical Control*. New York, NY: Prager, 1978.

Schreiber, Tatiana. "Environmentalists and Breast Cancer Activists Tell New York Commission: Act Now!" *Resist* 2, no. 4 (April 1993), p. 1.

Soffa, Virginia. *The Journey Beyond Breast Cancer: From the Personal to the Political*. Rochester, VT: Healing Arts Press, 1994.

Solomon, Alisa. "The Politics of Breast Cancer." *Village Voice* 36, no. 20 (May 14, 1991), p. 22.

Steingraber, Sandra. "The Environmental Link to Breast Cancer." In *Breast Cancer: Society Shapes an Epidemic*, edited by Anne Kaspar and Susan Ferguson, pp. 271-299. New York, NY: St Martin's Press, 2000.

Stocker, Midge (ed.). *Cancer as a Women's Issue: Scratching the Surface*. Chicago, IL: Third Side Press, 1991.

The Globalization Movement

Anderson, Sarah and John Cavanaugh with Thea Lee. *Field Guide To The Global Economy*. New York, NY: The New Press.

Danahar, Kevin and Rober Burbach, eds. *Globalize This!: The Battle Against the World Trade Organization and Corporate Rule*. Monroe, ME: CommonCourage Press, 2000.

Dobbin, Murray. *The Myth Of The Good Corporate Citizen: Democracy Under the Rule of Big Business*. Toronto, ON: Stoddart, 1998.

Griswold, Dan. "The Future of the WTO." Special issue of *The Cato Journal: An Interdisciplinary Journal of Public Policy Analysis* 19, no. 3 (Winter 2000). (This is pro-WTO.)

Greider, William. *One World, Ready Or Not*. New York, NY: Touchstone, 1998.

Johnson, Chalmers. *Blowback: The Costs and Consequences of American Empire*. New York, NY: Owl, 2001.

Korten, David. *The Post-Corporate World: Life after Capitalism*. West Hartford, CT: Kumarian Press and San Francisco, CA: Berrett-Koehler Publishers Inc, 1999.

Landy, JoAnn, Ellen Frank, Martin Thomas, Saskia Sassen, and Robin Hahnel. "Symposium on Globalization: Hard Questions for the Left." *New Politics* 8, no. 1 (Summer 2000), pp. 12-42.

Mander, Jerry and Edward Goldsmith, eds. *The Case Against the Global Economy and for a turn toward the local.* San Francisco, CA: Sierra Club Books, 1996.

O'Meara, Patrick, Howard Mehlinger, and Matthew Krain. *Globalization and the Challenges of a New Century: A Reader.* Bloomington, IN: Indiana University Press, 2000. (A wide range of perspectives, from conservative Jeffrey Sachs to Tupac Amaru, Revolutionary Movement of Peru.)

Sassen, Saskia. *Globalization and its Discontents: Essays on the New Mobility of People and Money.* New York, NY: New Press, 1998.

Shrybman, Steven. *A Citizen's Guide to the World Trade Organization.* Ottawa, ON: Canadian Centre for Policy Alternatives and James Lorimer & Co., 1999.

Sweezy, Paul and Harry Magdoff. "After Seattle: A New Internationalism?" Special issue of *Monthly Review* 52, no. 3 (July/Aug, 2000).

Wallach, Lori and Michelle Sforza. *Whose Trade Organization? Corporate Globalization and the Erosion of Democracy.* Washington, DC: Public Citizen, 1999.

INDEX

ABOUT THE AUTHORS

Bill Moyer worked for many years as a trainer and consultant to social activist groups and social movements. He worked in the civil rights movement and for the American Friends Service Committee in the 1960s. In the 1970s he was a co-founder of the Philadelphia Life Center and the Movement for a New Society, and worked with others there to train activists from around the world. In the 1980s he was particularly active in the peace movement in Europe. From 1986 onward he lived in San Francisco and traveled extensively training activist groups in the theory and practical applications of the Movement Action Plan model, personal development for activists working to strengthen their own practices and their activist groups, and organizing for social transformation. Bill Moyer died of cancer in October, 2002, in San Francisco.

(1933-2002)

Readers wishing to contact those who are carrying on Bill's training work can consult the website www.doingdemocracy.com.

JoAnn McAllister is a researcher and program development consultant focusing on individual and community intervention and the process of change. She has been active in a variety of social movements and in developing community-based organizations for over 25 years. Currently she is an analyst for the San Francisco Superior Court focusing on domestic violence. For program development, evaluation, and research assistance based on social change strategies contact her at:

Context Consulting
P.O. Box 31937
San Francisco, CA 94131-0937
jmcallister@igc.org

Mary Lou Finley has been active in social movements since she worked on Martin Luther King's staff in Chicago in 1965-66 . She has a Ph.D. in sociology from the University of Chicago and is now on the faculty of the B.A. Completion Program at Antioch University in Seattle, where she teaches courses on social movements; homelessness; globalization; women's health; race, class, and gender; and other social issues.

Mary Lou Finley
Antioch University, Seattle
mlfinley@antiochsea.edu

Steven Soifer is an Associate Professor of Social Work at the University of Maryland, Baltimore, and received his Ph.D in social welfare policy from the Heller School at Brandeis Universiy. He teaches community organizing, social action, community development, and social planning/social change. He has been involved in many local, state-wide, national, and international movements, including the anti-intervention movement in Central America during the 1980s and the ongoing effort to bring peace to the Middle East.

Steven Soifer
University of Maryland
ssoifer@ssw.umaryland.edu

For information on teaching MAP in colleges and universities contact either Mary Lou or Steven.

Juliette Beck is the coordinator of the Global Democracy Project for Global Exchange where she focuses especially on the international movement against corporate globalization of the political economic system.

Nancy Gregory lives in Baltimore, Maryland, and has been an active member of the gay and lesbian movement for over 15 years.

If you have enjoyed *Doing Democracy*, you might also enjoy other

BOOKS TO BUILD A NEW SOCIETY

Our books provide positive solutions for people who want
to make a difference. We specialize in:

Progressive Leadership • Resistance and Community • Nonviolence
Environment and Justice • Conscientious Commerce
Sustainable Living • Ecological Design and Planning
Natural Building & Appropriate Technology • New Forestry
Educational and Parenting Resources

For a full list of NSP's titles, please call 1-800-567-6772 *or check out our web site at:*

www.newsociety.com

New Society Publishers

ENVIRONMENTAL BENEFITS STATEMENT

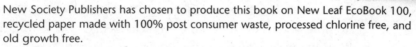

New Society Publishers has chosen to produce this book on New Leaf EcoBook 100,
recycled paper made with 100% post consumer waste, processed chlorine free, and
old growth free.

For every 5,000 books printed, New Society saves the following resources:[1]

31	Trees
2,826	Pounds of Solid Waste
3,110	Gallons of Water
4,056	Kilowatt Hours of Electricity
5,138	Pounds of Greenhouse Gases
22	Pounds of HAPs, VOCs, and AOX Combined
8	Cubic Yards of Landfill Space

---

[1]Environmental benefits are calculated based on research done by the Environmental Defense Fund and
other members of the Paper Task Force who study the environmental impacts of the paper industry.

For more information on this environmental benefits statement, or to inquire about environmentally
friendly papers, please contact New Leaf Paper – info@newleafpaper.com Tel: 888 • 989 • 5323.

NEW SOCIETY PUBLISHERS